THE DARK HEART OF HOLLYWOOD

Douglas Thompson is the author of more than 20 books. A biographer, broadcaster and international journalist, he is a regular contributor to major newspapers and magazines worldwide. His books, published in a dozen languages, include several bestselling biographies. He collaborated with Christine Keeler to tell the full story of the Profumo Affair in *Secrets and Lies* and in *The Beatles' Shadow*, with eminent psychotherapist Pauline Sutcliffe, told the poignant story of her brother Stuart, who named and helped found the Beatles with John Lennon. His book *The Hustlers*, about gangsters and gambling in 1960s London, is being developed as a major motion picture and was the subject of a Channel 4 documentary. His latest successes include *Shadowland*, about the American Mafia in London, and *Mafia Princess*, which are being adapted for film. Douglas Thompson divides his time between a medieval English village and California, where he was based as a Fleet Street foreign correspondent and columnist for more than 20 years.

The Dark Heart of Hollywood

Glamour, Guns and Gambling –
Inside the Mafia's Global Empire

DOUGLAS THOMPSON

MAINSTREAM
PUBLISHING

EDINBURGH AND LONDON

FOR JANE KLEISER

This edition, 2013

First published in Great Britain in 2012 by
MAINSTREAM PUBLISHING COMPANY
(EDINBURGH) LTD
7 Albany Street
Edinburgh EH1 3UG

ISBN 9781780576107

A catalogue record for this book is available
from the British Library

Printed in Great Britain by Clays Ltd, St Ives plc

3 5 7 9 10 8 6 4

'There's no business like show business.'
                    – Annie Oakley (Ethel Merman) in
                          Annie Get Your Gun, 1946

ACKNOWLEDGEMENTS

'Oh Lon, when I think of all those awful people you come in contact with – downright criminals – I get scared.'
'Oh, there's nothing so different about them. After all, crime is only a left-handed form of human endeavour.'
– May Emmerich (Dorothy Tree) to crooked lawyer Alonzo Emmerich (Louis Calhern) in *The Asphalt Jungle*, 1950

A PROPER SALUTATION TO THE MANY WHO HAVE contributed directly and indirectly to *The Dark Heart of Hollywood* is a complex undertaking, as it involves friends, colleagues and, most pertinently, contacts, some of whom trust to anonymity for their well-being. All the usual suspects are involved. And some significant others, who have helped separate strands of the myth from what actually went – and goes – on in the business of Hollywood and organised crime. One in particular is in delicate health and I hope he holds out for many more visits to Santa Anita racetrack. And the winners' window.

From my early days reporting from Hollywood, I've found that of all places in the world it's there that what you know *and* who you know are both required to survive. It's too easy to go the wrong way, to assume and presume, if you don't understand the unique etiquette. Never more so than in the twilight world, where what's going on isn't going on, and vice versa. Or maybe it is. The puzzle is very much part of the intrigue.

John Peer Nugent was an experienced and edifying force from day one. He'd been there, done that and was generous with his education. I shared that with my talented friend John Hiscock, who now has his own library of knowledge and is a constant and positive sounding board.

My friend Bobby McKew, who has transatlantic knowledge of the subject matter, was again generous with his time and his introductions. As again was Dino Cellini Junior.

I will always be indebted to the newspapers and magazines that indulged the reporting which allowed me first-hand interviews and encounters with many of the eclectic cast, star and cameo performers in *The Dark Heart of Hollywood*, especially Marvin Mitchelson, whose memory lives on during my regular talks with his widow Marcella. Others pertinent to these events stretch from John Huston, Robert Mitchum, Lloyd Bridges, William Campbell, William Holden, Zsa Zsa Gabor, Judith Campbell Exner, Frank Sinatra, Peter Lawford, Robert Wagner, Jill St John, Sammy Davis Junior, Angie Dickinson and Coroner Thomas Noguchi MD to the lovable George Raft, gentleman Cary Grant, monster Mickey Cohen, the incorrigible President Richard Nixon, Robert Vesco, Bernie Cornfeld, Jackie Kennedy Onassis, Aristotle Onassis, Joe Louis, Muhammad Ali and beyond. In addition, I'd like to note the many throughout America – especially in Phoenix, Arizona, Hollywood, Las Vegas and Miami – Macao, Hong Kong and Europe who would not thank me for name checks.

As ever, the marvellous Bill Campbell and the company cavalry at Mainstream Publishing made the difficult part enjoyable, while the sharp-eyed Debs Warner kept excellent editorial order.

I'm always asked who is the most exceptional Hollywood personality I've met. Most of them are larger than life – yet Robert Mitchum and director John Huston could tell stories about post-war moviemaking like few others. They never stinted on the colourful. Mitchum especially. He claimed Huston killed Clark Gable by pushing him too hard while making *The Misfits* (1961) with Marilyn Monroe. He also told me about filming *Heaven Knows, Mr Allison* (1957) in Trinidad and Tobago, in which Huston directed him and Deborah Kerr. Mitchum said he once happened upon Huston masturbating a monkey.

Mitchum asked him why.

'He likes it, dear boy,' Huston told him. 'He likes it.'

Hopefully, as I do, the monkey said, 'Thank you.'

'When the action starts, it may not go the way you planned, and you're down to your reflexes. That's where your roadwork shows . . . If you cheated on that in the dark of the morning, well, you're going to get found out now, under the bright lights.'

– Joe 'Smokin' Joe' Frazier, 1973

CONTENTS

PREFACE

HANG 'EM HIGH

'Nobody's perfect.'
— Osgood Fielding III (Joe E. Brown),
Some Like It Hot, 1959

IT WAS AFTER 28 STICKS OF DYNAMITE SENT HALF HIS HOUSE and, with it, his shredded collection of bespoke silk suits fluttering like confetti into the California sky that Hollywood's longest-serving mobster Mickey Cohen figured he should do a little more to protect himself. It was his friend and Al Capone's surviving accountant from Prohibition days George Demetris who put him onto the idea of a bulletproof car.

The dapper gunsel didn't make it sound like an epiphany, more an interesting idea: 'I began to see that in my line of work an armoured car might help. We went over to Hillcrest Cadillac in Beverly Hills – Cadillacs were the best on the road. It was important to me to be able to get away quick.'

Cadillac it was, then.

A chassis was ordered and all the protective paraphernalia. Coachcraft, the auto bodybuilder over on Melrose Avenue in West Hollywood, were engaged to make it bulletproof. One of the Coachcraft partners, Burt Chalmers, set up a private area to keep the engineering work under wraps.

'It was the goddamnedest thing you'd ever seen,' reported Cohen. 'The bottom of the car was flat – bombproof. It felt like a tank. The glass was made so you could shoot out but killers could be standing by the windscreen blasting you and nothing would come in.'

Coachcraft ran endless tests on the car's protective shield, including having it fired on by California Highway Patrol high-powered rifles. They didn't penetrate. The Cadillac went on to be 'test driven' by everything but a bazooka and survived intact.

Cohen spent the equivalent of $250,000 on his personal tank. Then he was told he couldn't drive it. Such protection was licensed only for the cops and the FBI, and a few VIP commercial business concerns, which excluded working in murder and extortion, loan-sharking and staging successful stick-ups at new-fangled theft-proof venues.

The bootlegger and bodyguard, purveyor of mayhem and mischief, followed through in the American way and in 1949 demanded his rights – his day in court. His legal team received a sympathetic hearing from the judge, who said he understood their client's needs, given all the bombings and clattering shotguns aimed in the gangster's direction. He'd make a deal. Mickey Cohen could drive his bulletproof Cadillac if he told the court who had given him permission to have the car tested at the gunnery range of the Los Angeles Police Department (LAPD).

But Cohen was no stool pigeon. He'd rather not say.

'I couldn't keep the car. Certain political friends and officials gave the OK. They're the proper people you buy for that sort of business. Where else were we going to test it? The cops are there to help people. The gunnery range was perfect. You couldn't shoot at the Cadillac in the street with .38s and Magnums, for Christ's sake. People would think we'd declared war. There were enough people being shot at already . . . me, for one. Around here somebody is always trying to make a point, to steal something from somebody – or kill 'em.'

President Manuel Roxas of the Philippines, who was having a spot of bother with riots in Manilla, offered to buy the hopefully revolution-proof car. Cohen couldn't do the deal, as only an hour earlier he'd sold the custom Cadillac cost price to a Texas car association.

When I met Cohen in Los Angeles in 1974, he was physically past his prime. He was not long out of prison, having served time for tax evasion, and was suffering from a paralysis brought on by a bang to the head during a jailhouse dispute in Atlanta a decade earlier. But he was a feisty, if condensed, character. He was all mobster-speak as he stalked with difficulty around his apartment.

What had brought about this renewed interest in him were, as always, his Mafia connections and his boast that he had information about the kidnapping of newspaper heiress Patty Hearst earlier that year by the self-styled terrorist Symbionese Liberation Army.

His claim didn't lead to much, but it nevertheless put Mickey Cohen back where he'd been most of his life – in the Hollywood headlines. He smiled at all the attention. He didn't have much energy, but he acted as if he was in one of those jerkily filmed Warner Brothers pre-Second World War gangster shoot-'em-ups. He found a mellow pleasure in it, like happening upon an album of treasured photographs from the past. He was back under the bright lights.

Cohen had been in the Mob from his teenage days. He was in Hollywood – or prison – most of his adult life. In either place, he was a leading man.

He asked me whereabouts in Los Angeles I was living but then, without waiting for an answer, shrugged on his hoodlum persona full-size and snarled: 'This place is all about serious money. It doesn't matter where it is, they'll go to hell and back to get it. Don't ever think this is some friggin' Disneyland.' That was the story, of course. It's always the story of Hollywood – who makes the money and who controls the business.

PROLOGUE

GOLDEN LAND

'All right, Mr DeMille. I'm ready for my close-up.'
— Norma Desmond (Gloria Swanson),
Sunset Boulevard, 1950

It was the movie that spoke so little that made most noise in an evening of warm nostalgia at the 84th Academy Awards. When they handed out the Oscars at the Hollywood and Highland Center on 26 February 2012, time-tinted memories floated against the happy applause for some of the silver-haired guests in the audience.

For many others watching the ceremonies on television around the world and at the black tie parties throughout the golden triangle of Beverly Hills, Holmby Hills and Bel Air, thoughts reached back to simpler days. Golden days, said the crowd at an unofficial Oscar gathering in Hancock Park, sitting in a sharp dip south, down from Sunset Boulevard and over Fountain Avenue in Los Angeles, providing expensive homes for those fond of tradition. And this was a traditional crowd. They adored *The Artist*, the nearly wordless black-and-white romance that was awarded five Academy Awards for celebrating Hollywood's formative era. The late 1920s provided a moment of perfect synergy, when time and place merged into prosperity, into an upward momentum that was irresistible. Especially to the Mob.

When the good times came to California, the bad guys rolled into town as regularly as the breakers along the Pacific

Coast. It was appropriate. There is little indigenous on the Hollywood landscape other than cactus; coyotes were the original interlopers. Los Angeles County is studio-issue badlands, a desert blocked between the San Bernardino Mountains and the ocean, an endless terrain poorly punctuated by impossible and often impassable canyons.

The twenty-first century picture is a knitting pattern of sweeping freeway interchanges, with the towns and neighbourhoods in the largest linear city developed since the invention of the motorcar squeezed in between. From the sky, southern California serves up like a triple-decker concrete sandwich.

When the Mafia discovered Hollywood all those decades ago, they partnered up in an enterprise that, like a good movie, was cash register gold. It was – and is – home, a power base, to the one industry that provides a safe meeting place for the complex forces that control our lives: money and politics and crime.

The inter-relationship between the people who head these forces is carefully guarded; the public spotlight rarely exposes it. But they are secretly in contact through selected intermediaries. And the one neutral area where the leaders of these groups can see one another – an acceptable meeting place and a glamorous one – where movers and shakers can make deals, threats, exchange views or come to arrangements, is within the world of show business.

Back in the day, the unorthodox business endeavours were double-barrelled and loaded. Today, things are slightly more subtle. They can potentially be as lethal, but, like *The Artist*, not much is said.

While the 2012 Oscars were being handed out and the Hancock Park crowd were recalling how only a decade earlier a couple of Las Vegas headaches had been cured the old-fashioned way, by sending some medication – Vincent 'Vinny Aspirins' Congiusti, whose cordless power drill dispatched all pain – several time zones away contraband was being dispersed.

The consignments throughout Europe, China, Japan,

South Korea, Malaysia, Paraguay, Brazil, India, Pakistan and Russia included counterfeit copies of *The Artist* – it didn't even need subtitles – along with other 2012 Oscar movies such as *The Iron Lady* and *The Help*; the balance of the shipments were action movies with provocative guns-and-cleavage packaging.

If a film wins an Oscar, people want to see it – and why wait? With counterfeit DVDs, they don't have to. If a film opens to rave reviews in New York or London, its fans, from Rio to Reykjavik, want it *now*. With an 'event' movie like Daniel Craig's third appearance as James Bond in *Skyfall*, versions stamped out in Malaysia for fifty American cents sell immediately in London's West End for £5. Within a week of the film's release, fans can get them for £3 a time.

Film piracy has a higher profit margin than any drug; the mark-up is three times more than for Iranian heroin and four times that of Colombian cocaine. It is also lower risk than other criminal enterprises. It provides what Al Capone always liked – '*an opportoonity*'. The immense profits from the piracy of those make-believe romances and adventure tales bankroll people- and drug-trafficking, extortion and all-inventive, illegal endeavour. Money makes money. Film crews are bribed almost daily to provide new films for copying. Hollywood has never been more popular with the Mafia. And both are in global sales. With different sorts of overseas distribution partners.

A Shanghai production facility openly flew thousands of DVDs at a time into City Airport, London. It's easier than transporting people, who have to be watered and fed. Yes, they're smuggled too, but by land, with Spain as a European centre; many thousands likewise originating in China. You can send DVDs by courier or an airmail stamp. Then the smuggled human cargo sells them for you.

The Mafia's export and import carousel, its reach around the girth of the planet, continues to astonish, even in this era of high-tech. The murder in early 2011 in Staraya Square in Moscow of a young computer geek was a warning to his film piracy bosses in the Ang Bin Hoey triad (organised crime association) in Malaysia, who were laundering American Mafia money in Russia. The crime was not investigated, as the Moscow gangsters were paying off the police, who were also employed as enforcers against their Estonian rivals. Chinese and Taiwanese triads are linked into Italy's 'Ndrangheta (the Calabrian Mafia) and the Camorra in Naples to repackage Hollywood product back to America, to New York and Miami and Los Angeles, where it all begins.

Once upon a time . . .

It is a bewildering coincidence – Technicolor Hollywood happenstance – that superstar mobster Charles 'Lucky' Luciano was born in the same year, 1897, and place, Lercara Friddi in Sicily, as the magical film director Frank Capra. With the American Mafia, Luciano helped create the world's most powerful crime organisation. Meanwhile, Capra, whose best-known film, *It's a Wonderful Life*, was made the year Luciano was deported back to Italy, promulgated the fantasy and romance of Hollywood.

From early on, Hollywood became a brand name for wealth and instant success; gratification *du jour* served up all over town. A place where Marilyn Monroe complained, 'They pay you $50,000 for a kiss and 50 cents for your soul.'

What has changed during the century-old relationship between the Mafia and Hollywood is the geography. *Hollywood* is no longer one place – it's an idea. It's global. The whole world wants to be a star. And so easily can be. What has not altered, as Mickey Cohen told me those disquieting number of years ago, is the motivation: money. The rest – power, political influence – follows. As, of course, does greed. Almost everything, people and principles, can be corrupted if the price or the pressure is correct.

America's Mafia hierarchy always followed a corporate structure in New York and Chicago, but much of the money – and the myth – was generated via the sound stages of Hollywood. The Mob and the movie moguls connived, and it was those in the middle, being fed fantasy, highs and hope, who paid. That has never changed.

The Mafia influence is cyclical and cynical. The illicit trade in DVDs was a niche profit winner as the twenty-first century got its legs, but it will be overtaken by more sophisticated ways of getting the action to the consumer using electronic communication. What will not change is the increasing development of the drug and gambling markets.

With the turbulent world economy, the Asian casino business is not so much a temptation as an outright invitation to the Mob – an expected $58 billion in total revenue in 2012. That compares with $6 billion in Las Vegas in 2011.

In 2010 in Macao, gamblers, many from mainland China, high-rolled $600 billion, which is about the same amount withdrawn from bank cash machines across the United States in a year. That's a lot of cash – even in a world that talks trillions in national debts.

Yet, as Asia is being squeezed – Japan, Korea, Taiwan, Vietnam, Cambodia – for all its gambling potential, the next Las Vegas is being planned in Europe. In fact, there might be two of them, both in Spain. The 'Europa Vegas' concept, which is projected to be complete by 2017, involves a dozen casino-hotels in Barcelona and Madrid. There are more planned for the UK and throughout the Continent. The feasibility thinking is that ailing national economies will welcome any project that makes money turn – like when the state of Nevada, desperate for tax dollars during the Great Depression, legalised gambling in 1931. And the investment return in Europe, as in Asia, is conservatively touted as 'tens of billions of dollars'.

And there are tremendous funds in euros and yen and sterling and Swiss francs in pension funds everywhere. While the innocent grafters wait for it to pay for their retirement, the investments created by the world's gangsters and business titans return to them *legal* dividends in the most beneficial currency *du jour*. These are astonishing, bank-bulging record amounts – never mind the quality, count the zeroes; what would have seemed mythical money to the flamboyant gangster Benjamin Siegel when he drove with the sun behind him into the Nevada desert from Los Angeles in 1942.

Ben 'Bugsy' Siegel was inured to the unexpected. When he arrived in Hollywood by train in 1937 – Mickey Cohen was appointed his backup and bodyguard – all the rackets he and his Syndicate partners operated in New York, New Jersey, Cleveland and Chicago were flourishing at high profit in Los Angeles. But this Hollywood, this wonderland out on the West Coast, was a very different place.

The police were running all the scams. The cops were the bad guys. They weren't *fighting* crime, they were the ones *organising* it. Everything was not as it should be. It was upside down. As, so often, was the distinguished-looking actor William Boyd. Siegel's boyhood hero, and star of *Hopalong Cassidy*, the early cowboy movies and television's first western series, Boyd was apparently often too drunk to stay aboard his horse Topper. Still, Siegel had no illusions. As the out-of-towner got to know his way around Sunset Strip with movieland friends such as Cary Grant and George Raft, he discovered how fantastic some of the fantasy was.

You could never tell what he was really thinking behind those watchful blue eyes, but he knew *he* was a straight shooter. There were plenty dead bodies to prove it. Of course, others also lacked illusion. And could also be charming and deadly and shoot with just as much bull's-eye accuracy. The Wild West was playing at the movies *and* in the streets of the place the Spaniards called the City of Angels. It remains one of life's more fanciful misnomers.

BOOK ONE

WONDERLAND

'Oh, but I don't want to go among mad people,' Alice remarked.
'Oh, you can't help that,' said the Cat. 'We're all mad here. I'm mad. You're mad.'
'How do you know I'm mad?' said Alice.
'You must be,' said the Cat. 'Or you wouldn't have come here.'

— Lewis Carroll, *Alice's Adventures in Wonderland*,
1865

1

THE DON OF HOLLYWOOD

'Morning, gentlemen. Nice day for a murder.'
– Rocky Sullivan (James Cagney),
Angels with Dirty Faces, 1938

IN THE BEGINNING, HOLLYWOOD WAS THE KEYHOLE TO America. By the twenty-first century, the rest of the world had joined the cast, the product and ethos of the place becoming as important and dazzling – arguably more – in Beijing and Barcelona than Burbank.

In the 1960s, the New York smug suggested that, one magical night, America had been turned on its side and all the nuts and bolts rolled into southern California. The nuts, they said, were happy there. It was their kind of place. Whatever happened, it worked.

Maybe it was the law of supply and demand, for in the early days that was the only one being paid any attention. Possibly, it was the Mediterranean climate. Good ideas and bad guys flourished like ivy on the white and pink stucco bungalows spreading across turn-of-the-last-century Los Angeles; it was where the action was. Even then, the characters, including the first Mafia don, seemed to have stepped from a neatly written script.

Vito Di Giorgio had the Central Casting name and the pedigree. He *was* an olive oil importer. He was born in 1878 in Palermo, Sicily, the island home of the Cosa Nostra, where he learned the family business. He arrived in America in 1904 and by the time he was running Los Angeles in 1912 he'd robbed and killed his way through New York and New Orleans. His reputation got to the West Coast before him, but he quickly caught up and enhanced it. He survived a couple of assassination attempts, including one on his family as they were returning from a Sunday at the beach to their home on East 21st Street in central Los Angeles. In those days, the violent settling of disputes was disorganised, a circus of wham-bam-and-scram incidents with ancient weapons as likely to misfire as hit the target.

Don Vito Di Giorgio was better than that. A member of the feudal and imported Black Hand Gang, the template of the American Mafia, an organisation expert in the Sicilian specialities of extortion and blackmail, he established a network of connections throughout Los Angeles County, up the coast to Santa Barbara and San Francisco, and down it to San Diego and the always useful Mexican border. He also enjoyed backup from the heavy-hitters in Denver, and especially Chicago, the gangland hub of America.

The local authorities gave Don Vito's crime empire a profitable boost in 1916, when, with California trending as ever, they brought in anti-liquor laws to conserve alcohol for wartime purposes – almost four years ahead of the Volstead Act and nationwide Prohibition, which also banned beer and wine, and for so many put as much edgy fun as profit into drinking.

With that headstart and a thirsty Hollywood crowd, the illegal booze business became lucrative and competitive; with 840 miles of Californian coastline to navigate, the consignments of liquor from Mexico and Canada were offloaded at several key beaches, often just north of Santa Barbara, from where shipments could be trucked in customised compartments to San Francisco and Los Angeles. The 'Hooch Highway' stretched all the way from Tijuana to Vancouver. The drivers were given 'stimulants', including tiny packets of cocaine, to keep them alert for the journeys, which for some must have turned into quite a trip.

By the time of Prohibition proper, the network was annually supplying more than four million illegal gallons of high-proof alcohol. It was rough stuff. By the early 1920s and the popularity of the movies in Hollywood, however, tastes had become more sophisticated: clients liked to keep the first drink down. Good Scotch, about 200,000 cases a year, with a mighty mark-up, was being imported, giving the Mafia bootleggers the equivalent 2012 income of $45 million every year (until Prohibition's historic constitutional repeal in 1933).

People were arriving too, speeding along Route 66, the magnet being the prospect of a better life, of finding work, a home and a future. Some just couldn't wait to do it in that order and used their previous jailhouse incarceration to boost their CV. Within this workforce, lack of a prison term was a sign of weakness. Or, if looked on kindly, as genius.

The attractive booze business lured adventurers like Anthony Cornero, who was born in 1895 in a village on the outskirts of Milan. His farming family prospered until his big-gambling father lost his farm and livelihood on the turn of a Queen of Clubs. The Cornero clan emigrated in 1904 and the youngster who'd become Tony 'the Hat' Cornero took to the streets of San Francisco. He was ambitious, but by age sixteen had got ten months in reform school for improving his spending habits by stealing. On release, he became a taxi driver in the city and got a taste of how the better-off lived, seeing the luxuries for which they'd casually pay well. He'd spend his lifetime providing pleasures until he himself had one drink too many.

He moved to Los Angeles in 1922 and invented himself as Tony 'the Admiral' Cornero, smuggling quality whisky across the Canadian border and selling it to top-end Hollywood nightclubs and emerging 'star' spots, such as the Beverly Hills Hotel, and the high-rollers of the fledgling film business. Cornero, like western movie star Tom Mix, sported a white Stetson, which he accentuated with cream gloves; his bodyguards carried the guns.

Purportedly running a shrimping business, Cornero started

with a fleet of small boats and ran rum from Mexico to Los Angeles, his freighters missed by the US coastguard, who were short-staffed and also paid to glance the other way. The waterline heightened with his enterprise and he bought the SS *Lily*, a merchant ship that could transport around 4,000 crates of bonded Scotch a time to beyond the three-mile limit from Los Angeles' San Pedro harbour. The Scotch was then unloaded into speedboats, which delivered it to ever-changing coastal points.

But it wasn't plain sailing for the Admiral. He was in at the deep end in the constant and often vicious struggle to be the Mr Big of the underworld; across the spectrum, from the scallywags to the killers, there were no illusions. The most effective way to better your odds was to kill off your rivals. Cornero was aware that Don Vito was a victim of these brutal politics. The Don had been caught off guard while out of town for a 'made men' conference in Chicago. He wanted to look his best, but it didn't work out when two bullets smashed through the back of his head as he relaxed in a leather chair in his hotel's barber's shop.

And criminality can't abide a vacuum. Albert Marco, who'd arrived in America from Bogliasco, near Genoa, through Ellis Island, was an accomplished pimp by the time he began working out of Seattle in Washington state, the jumping-off point for the 1898 Alaska Gold Rush. There he met Charles Crawford, who, as a young man, set up a business providing 'home comforts' to the prospectors heading for the Klondike. Together they created the city's best prostitution network. City officials were bribed, and their business was more reliable than digging for gold, it's just that they extended themselves and blatantly leased a 500 'crib' brothel to accommodate their around-the-clock teams of busy freelance girls, who themselves were paying $10 a week rent, which was collected for Crawford by the Seattle Police Department.

Charlie 'the Wolf' Crawford got out of town with 'decent people' outrage baying behind him and headed south to Los Angeles. His associate Marco slipped back into bootlegging and the backwaters.

But these men were pioneers. Crawford got himself the Maple Bar (drinking and plotting, downstairs; girls and gambling, one floor up) smack at the corner of Maple and Fifth Street, and a close association with the 'City Hall Gang', a bunch of corrupt officials operating with the collusion of the Los Angeles Police Department (LAPD). The main player in this game was Kent Kane Parrot (he pronounced it *Poirot*, as in Hercule), who had manipulated himself into being the indispensable Chief of Staff for Mayor George Cryer, himself a few pages short on the ethics handbook.

With dry-cleaning and laundry shops throughout the city used as fronts for the illegal booze business – thus money being 'laundered' – Charlie Crawford masterminded supply along the Hooch Highway. But he used Albert Marco, who had grown into a wily and superbly connected Mafia operator. Through Crawford, the corporate-thinking Marco also partnered up with another bootlegger–gambler, the generous Milton B. 'Farmer' Page, who was known for buying associates a drink before killing them.

Tony Cornero found himself swimming in crowded waters. With Vito Di Giorgio assassinated and his underboss Rosario DeSimone – probably the most intelligent of the Hollywood Mob – respected and quietly running operations his way in Los Angeles County, the badlands territory came under the control of Albert Marco.

It was open season on Cornero. The Parrot–Crawford–Marco–Page combination used the LAPD to keep constant pressure on the self-styled Admiral, while they ran booze, the city and the newspapers. Kent Parrot was a charismatic character known as 'the Boss'. He was a big man with lots of bulk on his 6 ft 2 in. frame and he used it to give presence to his point of view – lavishly underwritten, along with Mayor Cryer's political campaigns, by seemingly eternal bootlegging and prostitution profits.

The Admiral first fought back in the quietly intelligent Mafia way – he tried to buy himself out of trouble. He invested $100,000 in Mayor Cryer's second re-election campaign, but the City Hall Gang simply smiled, took the money and kept the pressure on. While they encouraged their man 'Farmer' Page, they made Cornero's life and business more complicated – and deadly. The Cornero bootleggers were constantly being caught – not by the law but rival booze runners. Consignments would be hijacked at gunpoint, while his bodyguards and growing band of gunsels were regularly rousted by the cops.

In benevolent contrast, the City Hall's hard men were allowed to thieve and kill as they pleased. In April 1925, Albert Marco pistol-whipped an LAPD uniformed officer and was fined $50. Then was given his gun back. When he was arrested by a rookie patrolman, having 'marked up' a couple of his girls, two detectives got the charge down to disturbing the peace, although Marco was also carrying a revolver. He had a concealed weapons permit, but as a non-citizen was not entitled to it. Los Angeles County's longest-serving sheriff, Eugene Biscailuz, had granted it and argued that he deserved the licence. The Los Angeles City Prosecutor agreed. Cornero's frustrations burst over the edges.

A gambler like his father, he staked everything and retaliated in the summer of 1925 after a Page pirate crew had rammed one of his ships at sea and stolen 1,500 cases of rum.

He ordered one of his latest henchmen, the good-looking Italian Johnny Rosselli, to do what he did most every night in Hollywood – get a girl. As instructed, Rosselli talked a little too much and 'leaked' the time and place of Cornero's next booze shipment.

The set-up was arranged on the Pacific Coast at Wilmington, not far south from what would become Los Angeles International Airport (LAX). On 3 August 1925, all that was in the sky and on the wind in the late evening were seagulls and impending trouble.

Seven hoodlums, three shotgun specialists and four henchmen with snub-nosed pistols were deployed by Page around the rum shipment's landing spot. A sedan had been parked at a sharp angle on the access–exit road to the marshy beachland. As they sat anticipating their prey, Cornero's team with Thompson machine guns opened up from bushes behind them. The black sedan took 88 bullets. A gunman called Jake Barrett was also riddled with them, but, like the others, survived the haphazard hail of gunfire. The LAPD had Cornero brought in, but he shrugged off their accusations. No one was talking, but the Admiral was still plotting.

Eight months later another Page henchman, the absurdly violent Walter Hesketh, was taken out at the corner of Spring Street in downtown Los Angeles. He was strolling back to his apartment when a black sedan swerved towards him and a fusillade of bullets put him to the ground. As the weeks went by, there were more street accidents in which bodies and bullets collided.

Cornero and Rosselli were hauled in for police questioning, but the Admiral was never detained. Rosselli spent only one night on the metal bench of a Central Jail cell in downtown Los Angeles, charges against him for holding two unregistered revolvers being dropped for no official reason.

Someone in Chicago had 'spoken' with Kent Parrot about the future of the suave sociopath Rosselli – 'Johnny Handsome' in the wonderland of Hollywood. Short in stature at 5 ft 8 in. on account of his tuberculosis, he came across as quiet, respectful and neatly turned out. A main-chance man, he had moved out West with the blessing of his going-places mentor Al Capone and the Chicago Outfit.

Rosselli had started life as Filippo Sacco, born on 5 June 1905 in the rural village of Esperia, just short of 70 miles to the south-east of Rome. He arrived in America illegally half a dozen years later. After his father Vincenzo died in the 1918 flu epidemic, he settled in the crowded tenement streets of East Boston with his mother Maria. Like many young immigrants, he was a teenage street kid and quick to see the chances of easy money operating for the neighbourhood Fagins. The youngsters acted as runners for the bookies and, more haphazardly, the dope peddlers.

Drugs – morphine, heroin and cocaine – were widely used and readily available. At a price. Even movie heroes were addicted. In 1916, Douglas Fairbanks, an athletic and high-fashioned Broadway actor turned Hollywood leading man, starred in *The Mystery of the Leaping Fish*. His character Coke Ennyday was billed as 'the world's greatest scientific detective'. This was a crime-fighter lauded in the film notes as 'gifted with not only a brilliant mind and great deductive talents, but also the ability to consume huge doses of drug without any problem'. They continued: 'Ennyday's life wouldn't be the same without his constant injections of cocaine, as whenever he feels down or needs energy, his loyal syringes will get him high and laughing again.'

For Filippo Sacco, supplying drugs was shameless. Morphine was available legally on prescription, though its distribution by the street gangs was such a social problem that City Hall had a police task force working to eradicate it. Of course, most of the cops on the beat looked the other way and got their dollars and drugs in return. Such was the corruption that federal authorities were brought in to police the problem. And it was to an undercover federal informant called Fisher that the 17-year-old Filippo Sacco sold a quarter ounce of morphine and found himself indicted on narcotics charges. He made bail and fled town before his court case. But only after making the informant Fisher vanish as well. Fisher's remains were never found.

Filippo Sacco, who by now had become Johnny Rosselli (after the Florentine painter Cosimo Rosselli), would go on to be charged with many crimes but not that of murder.

Having made his connections in New York, and then in Chicago, with brothel entrepreneur Johnny Torrio, Rosselli was soon mixing with rising Mafia stars such as Frank Costello, Tony 'Joe Batters' Accardo and the subtly malevolent Paul 'the Waiter' Ricca. A teenage killer in Naples turned Chicago waiter at the Bella Napoli Café, where the owner 'Diamond Joe' Esposito introduced him to some guys from the old country, the always softly spoken and elegantly dressed Ricca became the Chicago Outfit's strategist. It was a title Johnny Rosselli admired. Still, however effective, his cruel crudity was ever present. He'd order a murder with the throwaway comment: 'Make'a him go away.' And his psychotic hit men would do just that.

Rosselli learned from all of them, especially Al Capone – before he became *Al Capone* – when he worked as Capone's driver. The mobsters liked Rosselli and because of all his coughing and spluttering it was Capone who recommended he be sent from the wet and damp of Michigan out West and onto the high seas with the Admiral.

Tony Cornero was still being harassed in his bootlegging operations – even the US coastguard had rounded on him. He was aboard his yacht *Donnarsari* not long before Christmas Day 1926, having offloaded 2,000 cases of Canadian whisky into speedboats. Rosselli was at the wheel of one of them, when he spotted the coastguard. He went for the shore and escaped. Meanwhile Cornero was arrested, though he jumped bail and went into hiding until Rosselli delivered the profits from that particular smuggling operation. With the cash, the Admiral bribed his way into Canada, but the country quickly bored him.

He paid Rosselli back with an enthusiastic reference to Abner 'Longy' Zwillman, the highly respected and entrepreneurial gangster who, along with Meyer Lansky and Benny Siegel, comprised the 'Jewish Mafia' leadership. Lansky and Siegel had carved out a reputation as fearless killers for hire and, along with Lucky Luciano, organised bootlegging along and down the American East Coast. Zwillman controlled *everything* in New Jersey, including a string of restaurants and nightclubs. He adored show business. And showgirls.

Zwillman bankrolled his indulgences, including a high-profile and passionate romance – red roses and a red Cadillac – with Hollywood's tragic and turbulent 'blonde bombshell' Jean Harlow, by smuggling even more booze out of Canada using First World War army trucks and conniving his influence into labour racketeering. His business plan was to control money – his turnover was $4 million in 1928 – and men. With Lansky and Luciano, he was behind the 'Cleveland Conference' of 1929 in which the unholy alliance of Jewish and Italian mobsters, which within two years would become the powerful and infamous National Crime Syndicate, aka *The Mob*, *The Outfit*, *The Syndicate*, emerged.

The Syndicate was the more accurate description, although in essence it remained the Mafia, but with an ethnic twist – of your neck, if you weren't careful. And part of it always had an appetite for glamour, as well as an unlimited capacity for cash. It was all very much cash and carry.

By 1929, Tony Cornero had decided he'd rather be in jail than in Canada. He walked into custody in Los Angeles and got a two-year federal prison term in McNeil Island penitentiary in Puget Sound in Washington state, where he contemplated what profits could be derived from the Stock Market crash. This left his seagoing sidekick Johnny Rosselli clear to join in with Jack Dragna, a nasty, calculating criminal who'd kill for a cigarette or a favour. Any timidity Dragna ever showed was for his own safety. Born in Corleone, Sicily, in 1891, Dragna always got a bad press for his inadequacies when compared with the activities of the Chicago and New York hoodlums, but he was a Hollywood survivor, as familiar with Sunset Boulevard as anyone.

For Johnny Rosselli – and many others – the arrival of 1931 was important. Cornero got out of jail that year and went into the gambling business, opening the Green Meadows casino out in Nevada at a place called Las Vegas. He offered good odds and waitresses who liked to be friendly.

At the same time, Joseph Ardizzone, the 'thought to be too old-fashioned' head of the Los Angeles crime family, was having discipline problems. His men had twice tried to assassinate him. He said he was retiring. They didn't believe him and on 15 October 1931, while out driving – a .41 revolver in his hand on the car's driving wheel – he disappeared. His body was never found. While Don Ardizzone's chair in his office around the corner from the Maple Bar was still warm, the rather more bulky Jack Dragna slipped into it.

In the years up to that moment, Dragna had been president

of the Italian Protective League, which kept space on the 11th floor of the Law Building downtown. Officially, it minded the interests of its own community, however it made its profits by exploiting them and running rackets. It wasn't easy to operate the vice and drug rings; the City Hall Gang had a monopoly on the corruption of the cops. Still, some of the LAPD were happy to collect more than one pay-off. Dragna's syndicate had a small blackmail and extortion racket going and were constantly making contacts in the labour unions.

Dragna also had the actual and metaphorical muscle of Chicago working for him. His attraction for them was he always did as instructed, a soldier not a general in a business in which too much ambition could be fatal. Even in Hollywood he was content to let others put on a show. Especially Rosselli – Chicago's man on the inside – to whom Dragna delegated the movie business and community. Rosselli became Mr Hollywood. It was a ducks-to-water appointment.

Rosselli (Cornero saw him as 'a rattlesnake in a box – don't put your hand in') encouraged Dragna to be more adventurous, to kill a few rivals and encroach into the City Hall Gang domain. It became easier. Local politics helped – Mayor Cryer stood down and Kent Parrot lost his power base to a new political machine. Charlie Crawford remained a buffer to the Mob's ambition, but happenstance helped again. In the summer of that pivotal year, a corrupted assistant city attorney lost the plot ('couldn't take it any more') and shot down Crawford at his desk. There are some things you simply can't legislate for. The combination was unlocked.

Hollywood and all around it was flooded with booze; a bootlegged $60 case was now going for a third of the price. Supply was more than meeting demand, even with the soaring thirst that Prohibition had increased tenfold. At the same time, those who'd worked in nightclubs and saloons were now 'in the movies' doing myriad jobs for money their talents wouldn't fetch elsewhere.

Hollywood was living fast and easy. The sun came up day

after day after day in this public relations man's fantasy, acreage that began as an apricot and fig ranch that a Mrs Wilcox from Kansas City took over and named 'Hollywood'. There was now much more than fruit to be picked.

The world was watching as the first global moving picture stars were created. The shrewd Gloria Swanson went from *Keystone Kops* comedies to a Cecil B. DeMille leading lady at Paramount Studios, a Rudolph Valentino co-star and the mistress of the bootlegger-businessman turned Hollywood tsar, roguishly handsome Joe Kennedy, who was married with his own growing family. Swanson was star material. She was always ready for her close-up. The money shot was her wardrobe. She was tiny, a fringe over five feet tall, and would happily be weighed down by lavish gowns and beads, all manner of parts of walking and flying wildlife decorating her, setting off her carousel of dazzling jewels. Off-screen she was just as calculated in emphasising the image. A department store dress cost about $12, yet Swanson managed to spend upwards of $175,000 a year on clothes. She was photographed. She was copied. She was for a time, when it really was something to say, the most famous woman in the world. Yet there was fame to go around.

British-born Charlie Chaplin had started making movies in 1913 on $150 a week. Within two years, he was on $10,000 a week. Within a decade, Hollywood was seeing the highest profits in America and paying wages to match. In 1927, the 'film industry' – that is all assets, from talent to studios – was valued at $1.5 billion. That year the talking pictures began with *The Jazz Singer* – the Al Jolson vehicle smashed every record any nerd could think of.

By 1930, Warner Brothers Studios alone was valued at $168 million, with the brothers holding the majority of the stock. Moguls, indeed.

Warner Brothers Studios also began feeding the public fascination with gangsters. The films debuted in 1931 with the endlessly polite and patrician Edward G. Robinson as Little Caesar and the fast-talking James Cagney as *The Public Enemy*.

Cagney co-starred with mobster Longy Zwillman's girl Jean Harlow, but it's the scene where he shoves a grapefruit in Mae Clarke's face that's remained the most memorable. Even 50 years later, when he made his last film appearance in *Ragtime*, the citrus fruit was still with him: 'It was based on a real-life incident involving Hymie Weiss.'

Weiss was a renowned Chicago North-side gangster who shot up bootleg rivals, including Capone and Johnny Torrio, and originated the 'one-way ride' when he took a fellow gangster out for a drive and only he returned. Cagney put him in the movies: 'Hymie Weiss was listening to his girlfriend yakking away at breakfast. He didn't like it and he took an omelette she'd just prepared and shoved it in her face. Repeating this on screen would have been a shade too messy, so we used the grapefruit half. It sure was popular – especially with Monte Brice. He was Fanny Brice's brother and had just gone through an unpleasant divorce from Mae when the picture came out. Every time I pushed that grapefruit in Mae's face at the Strand Theatre, there was a guaranteed audience of one – Monte. He would come in just before that scene was shown, gloat over it, then leave.'

It wasn't this that upset some critics, and although it took much flak for 'glorifying gangsters', the popularity of *The Public Enemy* made it the first film to earn more than $1 million at the box office. They didn't have to wave a flag for the real-life mobsters to believe there was plenty of money to be made at the movies. Cagney himself revealed the arithmetic: the cost of the film was $151,000 and it took 26 days to make.

Rosselli was under pressure to bring Hollywood into line. He liked the films and the movie crowd. He'd work as an extra for the quick pocket money and the gossip. But what Chicago wanted wasn't small talk – they wanted a studio, they wanted control. They wanted their hands on the money. But, as always, it was events that controlled the game plan.

The Great Depression was biting. It was tough in union-free Los Angeles, where wages were kept low – and bread lines became longer. There were as many soup kitchens as speakeasies. But money could be made on the turn of a card or chance played for five cents a time – 'nickel bingo' – in hastily erected tents: because it was as reliable as work, gambling was the one business that attracted everyone. The Mob made money from the needy and the desperate, as well as the flush, much of it with the help of Rosselli's ocean-going partner Tony Cornero. By then Conero's Green Meadows casino, with its live entertainment and exotic interior, was a success, the model for all that would follow.

Rosselli was allowed to use the place as his own; likewise his friend's fleet of gambling ships moored beyond the three-mile limit off the California coast, which included the *Rex*, sitting in the water off Redondo Beach, with its $300,000 of luxury fittings. It had a crew of 350 (always friendly) waiters and waitresses, cooks, a full orchestra and gunmen. The first-class dining room served French food only.

Most evenings, around a couple of thousand onboard 'visitors' were accommodated, permitted to gamble, drink and dance as long as they pleased – or their money lasted. The *Rex* enterprise was a success, designed to lure an eclectic bunch of gamblers. After expenses, the operation was clearing $300,000 a night. Most often it was the movie crowd who glamorously populated the tables. They had the money. And the excessive inclinations.

Drugs were a huge business and sex of every possible variety was something of an artistic licence. And not just on the casting couch, which became obligatory at every audition. (The madcap Mack Sennett Studios – home of those fun guys, the Keystone Kops – had to be fumigated, plagued as they were by vast infections of venereal crabs. Mack Sennett Studios was also home to Hollywood's principal drug dealer; known as 'the Count', because he carried a cloak, heroin was his speciality.)

Prohibition was truly an experiment in temptation and, as America continued to drink, imbibers concealed their tipples in prams, hot water bottles, garden hoses and coconut shells. One enterprising individual who liked life sunny side up went to work on an egg: half a dozen of them were drained and filled with booze.

The Mack Sennett pusher had learned a few tricks, too. He provided bags of peanuts, the nuts having been removed and the shells filled with the drug of choice. The first bag was always free; after that users paid and paid. *Dope* did just what it said: it made users pliable – but it could also make them capable of performing.

Drug consumption often began as a result of peer pressure and naivety – cocaine was the coca in Coca-Cola until 1914 – but just as often from *need* and then addiction. The 'valley of the dolls' culture was there from the start – stimulants to get going in the morning, uppers, and mellow pills, downers, to allow sleep in the evening. Huge quantities of bootleg booze – the harsh, high-octane thirst-quenchers – racked up super-size hangovers. And there were pills for that in this circle of carefree self-destruction.

For the early film studio bosses, who required the cameras to keep rolling and the box office overloaded, anything that kept their stars – faces that became instant screen idols – happy and working was encouraged, prescribed by the studio doctors and dispatched from their 'on the lot' dispensary, which was usually next to the canteen/coffee shop. The drugs were for 'nerves', or as a 'tonic' to make overworked performers lively in front of the silent film cameras, but they made them victims of their own success.

Olive Thomas was only one of them: the original Ziegfeld Girl at age 16, painted nude by Alberto Vargas, silent screen star and wife of Mary Pickford's brother Jack at age 21, found spreadeagled and naked, dead from a drug overdose in the Hotel Crillon in Paris age 25. On 10 September 1920, Olive was staying in the Royal Suite. She had spent the previous evening buying drugs in Montmartre. In societies just putting their heads above the trenches of the First World War such waste of life was frightening and disturbing. Hollywood took the blame.

With 3D hindsight, you can see it so clearly. Hollywood lured youngsters from all over America who had one thing going for them – they looked good on camera. They'd never been taught how to deal with attention, let alone vast wealth and perilously corrupting fame. Marriages were studio-arranged; love affairs concealed. If there were problems, then 'human' stories were invented about the pressures of stardom and home life. Taboo was any mention of a star being homosexual – like screen lover Valentino, who American men wanted to be and American women wanted – and a star could not have an illegitimate child or an abortion. Otherwise, anything went.

For the flapper girls, the fashion was to wear sommelier-style spoons around their necks for their cocaine, tasters for their 'joy powder'. The star crowd buzzed like bees and maybe some wondered, like Eugene Wrayburn did about the bees in Dickens' *Our Mutual Friend*, if possibly 'they over-do it'.

The human pleasure cruiser Barbara La Marr – 'The Girl Who Is Too Beautiful' – certainly did. Dope caught up with her before she'd reached 30. She married five times, made dozens of films and said she was able to do all of it because she slept only two hours a night. The studios said she had been on too strict a diet.

Silent star Alma Rubens, who appeared with Douglas 'Coke Ennyday' Fairbanks in *The Mystery of the Leaping Fish*, lost her way with drugs, supplied by the Mafia's network of pushers organised and run by Lucky Luciano.

Every studio had their 'Count', a fixit or go-to contact, but the original source of this constant stream of recreational chemicals was always the Mob. During medical shortages, they were known to supply hospitals and private clinics.

There was no gender prejudice about who got to like it too much. Screen leading man Wallace Reid (D.W. Griffith's *The Birth of a Nation*, 1915) died, aged 31, in a clinic after morphine – prescribed to keep him working but to which he had become horridly addicted – ruined his mind and body. An all-American star leading the all-American life, Reid was more popular than Douglas Fairbanks and Mary Pickford, and more swooned over than Rudolph Valentino. Such was his stardom – and box-office appeal – that after he was buried, in his favourite tweed suit, the gossips of Hollywood were certain he had been 'put down', helped to his death, by the studios, to stop him being a walking advertisement for depravity. The studios failed to hide the truth – that his life had ended with him a drug-induced lunatic in a padded cell – but for the largely puritanical nation it was another gross example of Californian sin. What fanned the 'public outrage' that punctuated all the well-read scandals was that this behaviour was a tunnel to hell and there was no light showing.

Still, the show, as ever, had to go on.

The new money was flaunted, and it was spent on mansions and servants and just about anything you could gold-plate or diamond-stud; bling was the thing. It was all about perception – what the public saw and what they believed they knew. The Mob–mogul associations became so entrenched with the Hollywood authorities – the LAPD and the city prosecutor – that it appeared part of law-enforcement policy to cover up any murder or dodgy death, even if a movie star wasn't involved. A star could be dropped from their contract if their sleeping around became public, but if someone died, that was part of life: it happened. It certainly did for Virginia Rappe.

The very good-time girl died following an encounter on 5 September 1921 with Roscoe 'Fatty' Arbuckle, who that year had become a history-making one-million-dollar Paramount Studios contract player. The holiday weekend party that Arbuckle hosted at the St Francis Hotel in San Francisco was a raucous affair. Everybody was having a good time, and Virginia Rappe's screams and squeals from a bedroom suite were thought to be part of it. The story was that Arbuckle had raped the showgirl and when he was spent had used a champagne bottle on her. She died in hospital.

For Arbuckle, at the time 33 years old, the location was wrong. The coroner's office in San Francisco was contacted by the hospital and the cover-up instigated by Paramount executives (private detectives helped by a hospital orderly were prevented from destroying medical evidence at the hospital) was stopped mid-track. The San Francisco District Attorney

Matthew Brady, who was building an election campaign to be California governor, wanted a trial – and as big a one as possible. He got three.

A tremendously popular actor-comedian, Fatty Arbuckle was known for wild sex parties, but bribes by the studios had kept his lurid good times out of the newspapers and the star out of jail. This time, however, the tragic results of his bad behaviour couldn't be disguised.

His lawyers blamed the victim. She was an actress, and a model, and therefore a bad person. The first trial jury voted 10–2 for an acquittal but a mistrial was ruled. The second was 10–2 for guilty, but was dismissed. Arbuckle was third time lucky, with a full acquittal in April 1922. There was outrage: Hollywood people could get away with murder wherever they were.

But Arbuckle's Hollywood life was over. While he still had curiosity value to be exploited, he appeared in a play titled *Baby Mine* in 1927 at Chanin's Forty-Sixth Street Playhouse in New York, but he died destitute and drunk a couple of years later in 1933. Arbuckle's co-star, who didn't speak to him throughout the production, was the just-starting-out and painfully priggish Humphrey Bogart.

Hollywood's first blockbuster scandal, 'the Arbuckle Affair', was a warning to the film community and studio bosses, and to the Mob. They didn't want an investigative spotlight. But they got it – time and time again in those early years.

William Desmond Taylor, the 50-year-old Paramount director with a penchant for sex and young girls (and vice versa) was discovered dead in his home study on 1 February 1922. When his butler found the body, he alerted a neighbour, who telephoned a doctor and Paramount Studios. The police were not alerted. Executives arrived and went through Taylor's home, supposedly removing coded love letters written by, among others, the 20-year-old star Mary Miles Minter, who had made her first film, *Anne of Green Gables*, for Taylor.

But news of the affair between the ingénue and the ageing director got out and Hollywood got more screeching headlines.

What no one got was a killer. Taylor's death was initially ruled as being brought on by a heart attack.

Later, a reluctantly performed medical examination showed two .38 bullets had gone through his back. Those had stopped his heart. There were suspects and suspicions; circumstantial evidence pointed to a Mob execution in return for Taylor's temerity to reject its financial investment in a movie – but there was never a conviction.

Nor was there ever one in the shooting to death of Hollywood bigshot Thomas Harper Ince in 1924. It is one of the most remarkable incidents at a time when the powers of film and business were learning to live with organised crime and collaborate in what served the interests of both: none of that needless nonsense with police and arrests and trials. As the wheels of graft turned, everyone but the handsome Ince profited from his death. Press tycoon 'Citizen' Hearst certainly sold many more newspapers.

Hearst, a multimillionaire from his press empire and silver mines, was keen to sign off on a film deal with Ince. To do so, he invited him to celebrate his 42nd birthday aboard his 280-foot yacht *Oneida*. Hearst, his mistress Marion Davies – for whom he'd created his film company Cosmopolitan Production Studios – and their guests, including Hearst's movie people, his local newspaper columnist Louella Parsons, Charlie Chaplin and Dr Daniel Carson Goodman, a physician turned screenwriter, were joined by Ince when the yacht anchored in San Diego harbour on Saturday, 16 November 1924.

Marion Davies liked to drink, especially champagne, while Hearst was a total abstainer. So it was Davies who organised liquor, delivered to Hearst's San Simeon Castle up the coast from Santa Barbara by Al Capone's distributors. Her link to the Mob deliveries was Hearst's friend and Capone's bootlegging partner Joe Kennedy. Hearst looked the other way to indulge his guests and Marion, who was allowed *almost* everything she wanted.

On the Sunday evening of 17 November 1924, there was plenty of drink and food at Ince's birthday celebration. But his birthday went very wrong. The story, as it came out – in Hearst newspapers – was that Ince became ill and was taken ashore by water taxi. Dr Goodman went with him. From then, it is a confusion of accounts of events over whether Dr Goodman took Ince to a hotel or a hospital or to his Benedict Canyon home in the Hollywood Hills. That Ince was taken to his home and died there of heart failure was the Hearst line. It was endorsed by Ince's doctor, Ida Glasgow, who signed the death certificate. The Los Angeles District Attorney accepted it.

There was just the bullet in Ince's head to be concerned about. The *Los Angeles Times* – for one afternoon edition only – shouted the banner headline: 'Movie Producer Shot on Hearst Yacht'. Then the story was pulled and it vanished.

As did Ince's body.

At his wife Nell's request, he was cremated. Nell Ince was awarded a lifetime financial endowment by Hearst, who also helped others deal with the trauma of the death of their friend. Louella Parsons, who began her cruise on the *Oneida* as a columnist for one newspaper, left the vessel as a syndicated gossip star for every Hearst outlet. With her fame, which made her the queen of newspaper malice in wonderland, she never found space to report on the events on the yacht. But then, how could she? She told the police and anyone else who asked that she wasn't aboard.

The most predominant version of events – official archives of the case do not exist – is that Hearst, a renowned sharp-shooter, shot Ince either by intention or mistaking him for his real target, Charlie Chaplin, who was a regular lover of Marion Davies. (Chaplin most certainly had a way with the ladies: actress Joan Barry once broke into his house at 1 a.m., lectured him at gunpoint for an hour about his morals and then slept with him.)

Hearst ignored Davies' dalliances with other men so long as it did not reflect on his dignity. She had apparently got a little too close to home with Chaplin and their friendliness, fuelled by champagne, had been much too obvious on the yacht. Chaplin and Ince were similar in look and hairstyle. Or maybe it was Ince and Davies who had turned Hearst into a jealous gunman with their impropriety. Only one thing is certain: Ince was dead and gone. William Randolph Hearst had the power to cover up the death.

Not long afterwards, D.W. Griffith was asked about the death of his friend. 'All you have to do to make Hearst turn white as a ghost is mention Ince's name,' he said. 'There's plenty wrong there, but Hearst's too big.' Which is what Hollywood had become.

By the late 1920s, the Hollywood population had jumped from a turn-of-the century 30,000 to 250,000, but the people who made the movies worked behind the towering high walls of the studios, gated and protected from reality. Drugs, bootleg booze and casual sex were the games of choice, which for any exploitative gangster reads like a good business plan.

What almost everybody who got involved with the Mob failed to realise was that any person or project was instantly dispensable. The money-making machine was all that ever mattered. Whatever threatened profits was eradicated, be it star-makers or star-fuckers or the stars themselves. The Mob made and broke careers, destroyed lives, and it was always business related. People who stuck an elbow out of their allowed parameters were just a little collateral damage. Watch and control was the Mafia way.

Even when they played, movieland people had their own Mafia-shared zones. There were more discreet spots like the Clover Club off Sunset Boulevard, a little west of the Chateau Marmont, which had a private red-velvet gaming room on the second floor. On an evening of cards, usually poker, players could lose ten or twenty thousand dollars while outside people queued up for cups of watery soup. There was a string of more public places: the Cotton Club in Culver City on Sunday night; Monday at the quaintly spelled Cocoanut Grove; Tuesday at the Club Montmartre; the Roosevelt Hotel on Wednesday; Thursday driving out of town for 'weekend fun'.

Resorts over the border in Tijuana became Hollywood getaways. The Agua Caliente Resort offered 20-hours-a-day gambling and *anything* else clients craved. There was a Gold Room with gold table services for gourmet food and big gamblers. There was also a horseracing track that hosted some of the richest races available. There were the odds at the Tijuana track . . . and the odds at the bookies. Apparently, there was a syndicate that could cater for lavish wagers.

Studio boss Carl Laemmle, one of the most important movieland pioneers and a founder of Universal Studios, used the services of a highly personable gambling go-between, a young man who always seemed to be around. Johnny Rosselli took the bets from Laemmle and other big players, such as Joe Schenck (who, with Darryl F. Zanuck – and investment from 'the Brain', the gangster genius Arnold Rothstein – founded Twentieth Century Pictures, which merged with Fox Corporation in 1935 to establish 20th Century Fox) and his new great friend, the extravagant wagering producer Harry Cohn. It was heavyweight business: these were the Kings of Hollywood; Rosselli's other friends, Chaplin and Clark Gable, were heirs apparent.

Yet Rosselli and his Mob masters wanted more than moguls and movie stars under their control: they wanted the film industry, the business. They wanted to run Hollywood. Which, of course, is what the studio chiefs wanted, too.

It's always been a fight over which monsters were winning in the sunshine and shadows.

2

PLAYLAND

'I don't know nothin'. I don't see nothin'. I don't hear
nothin'. When I do, I don't tell the cops. Understand?'
— Tony Camonte (Paul Muni), *Scarface*, 1932

HARRY COHN, THE BELLIGERENT BOSS OF COLUMBIA
Pictures, idolised Benito Mussolini, which was most
appropriate given that they were both dictators. The best said
of Mussolini was that he got the trains to run on time; Cohn
made some good movies, which ran on average 105 minutes.
He also made a great deal of noise. Some of those who'd
worked with him, the grand Lloyd Bridges especially, told me
they believed the bluster from the man they knew as 'King
Cohn' was simply a protective weapon: 'He was the one guy in
town who didn't want to know unnecessary secrets. He felt
that knowing too much could get you shot. I was a young guy
making pictures and wasn't going to argue. Not many people
did. He had connections – and a good intimidation act.'

After he met the Italian dictator in 1933, when he produced
the documentary *Mussolini Speaks*, which was narrated by
Lowell Thomas, an early 'new media' star, Cohn had his
Hollywood office turned into a mirror of Mussolini's. Like *Il
Duce*, he had his desk mounted to give him a vantage point
over his visitors. Cohn got to that towering position from the
Upper East Side of New York, where, like the mobsters he
worked with, he learned to at least appear tough and gloried in
a vulgarity of speech and behaviour. There wasn't a skirt he

didn't want to put his hand up – something else he shared with Mussolini.

After scuffling around his hometown, playing piano at the silent movies, stealing and scamming, he moved West and found a gofer's job at Universal Pictures, where his brother Jack was working already. The two then teamed with anxiety-sufferer Joe Brandt, a former advertising partner of Jack Cohn, to form Cohn, Brandt and Cohn (CBC). Their product didn't even rate the description 'low budget'. It was breadline material. Lloyd Bridges said the rising star Clark Gable was responsible for renaming CBC 'Corned Beef and Cabbage'. That sort of thing did not help the raw relationship between the Cohn brothers. Jack liked it quiet and organised financially in New York. Harry was Hollywood, and a profane and nasty piece of work: a bully when he was allowed to get away with it. The more sensitive Joe Brandt couldn't take the storm of stress between his partners.

When the newly named Columbia Pictures began to prosper, he announced he was selling out – to the first brother to give him half a million dollars for his third share of the business. Cash. Jack canvassed his bank contacts in New York, but they were as unyielding as the Depression. Harry, however, had better luck with his gambling partner Johnny Rosselli, who was now under orders to make a daily report to the Syndicate in Chicago.

When Harry Cohn told him of the buy-out possibility, Rosselli had a crackerjack evening bulletin. He realised, as did his bosses instantly, that this was a 'legitimate' way into Hollywood. They'd bought politicians, cities, towns, real estate and law enforcement – now they were purchasing a movie studio.

With an ironic nod to the business at hand, it was Jean Harlow's lover Abner 'Longy' Zwillman who provided the $500,000. Zwillman's private secretary arranged a meeting with Harry at the apartment he rented full time at the Garden of Allah villa-bungalow complex at a corner on Sunset just before it leaves West Hollywood and runs into Los Angeles.

They both wanted to do business, but Zwillman was in the cash-is-king negotiating spot. Harry Cohn offered an IOU and top-heavy interest on the loan. The mobster declined. Cohn could have the money in return for the shares in the studio and that was the deal. In 1932, organised crime in America controlled the majority of stock in a Hollywood studio. Or, put another way, the Mafia owned Columbia Pictures.

Which went like gangbusters. Only two years after the mobster and the mogul concluded their arrangement, the studio released *It Happened One Night*, a romantic comedy starring Claudette Colbert as a flaky heiress and Clark Gable as an adventurous newspaperman. Colbert and Gable may not have clicked off-screen the way he had with Joan Crawford, Marion Davies and Jean Harlow, but the Frank Capra movie did. It was the first film to win all the big Academy Awards, receiving Oscars for Best Picture, Director, Actor, Actress and Screenplay. Even Harry Cohn was pleased. He and Johnny Rosselli became closer and closer. The link, of course, was money. And the smooth-talking mobster's access to 'the wire' – the interstate transmission of racing information – which could make a good day better or not when customised by the Mob.

Rosselli appeared more the mogul than Harry Cohn. He was a regular visitor to Columbia Pictures. He turned down a salaried job offer from his friend but shared times, tennis and swimming pools with him at Cohn's homes in Hollywood and Palm Springs. Cohn's gambling became more and more an obsession. Rosselli arranged for a 'wire' to be set-up in Cohn's office to receive instant racing results.

In 1934, racing came to southern California, with the opening of Santa Anita Racetrack, which was then a short drive out east from downtown Los Angeles. In 1938, to the south of the city in Inglewood, came Hollywood Park Racetrack, which put Cohn in horse heaven.

Rosselli provided the betting tips and Cohn supplied the cash. It was, if you like, combination betting. And it wasn't all one way. There was a fondness between them, according to a survivor of Rosselli's circle, who was enjoying late years' retirement in Nevada in 2012. He confirmed the story that Rosselli had had two identical ruby rings made, one for himself and one for Harry Cohn. Yet, he said, what no one realised was that Longy Zwillman was paying Rosselli 'expenses'. He explained the apparently kind gesture of gifting the ring to Cohn as 'keeping the fish on the line'.

Columbia Pictures never lost money during the tenure of Harry Cohn and his silent partners, with a string of early landmark films, including *Lost Horizon* (1937) and *Mr Smith Goes to Washington* (1939). Nor did the Mob – in Hollywood or beyond.

When Prohibition ended on 5 December 1933, the corporate development of the Mafia was already in place. Some old-fashioned thinkers had been disposed of, but there were employees who were trained in such matters. The thinkers remained – and thought Hollywood a cash cow.

By 1931, when a machine-gun debate concluded the power struggle, and the lives and ambitions of at least 60 Mafia men, the boss of bosses was Charles Luciano. The Sicilian Salvatore Luciano emerged as a charismatic, clever, wily and lethal leader of a multi-ethnic criminal conglomerate. He'd had an impressive adviser.

As a nine year old, he'd started a protection gang working in and around the Lower East Side. He offered little Jewish boys the choice of paying up or being beaten up. Most handed over nickels and dimes. Maier Suchowljansky, who'd not long arrived with his family from Grodno in Poland, where he was born in 1902, wasn't taking any such nonsense. His reply to Luciano's suggestion he pay ten cents a week was a rapid fuck-off. Luciano attacked. It was in his brutal nature. But his opponent fought back just as hard – he didn't know any different. The fight ended, but it was the starting point of a dark friendship between Luciano and the boy he came to know as Meyer Lansky.

About the same time, Lansky became friendly with another young tearaway, Brooklyn-born Benjamin Siegel, the son of

Russian–Jewish immigrants, who began his gangster career, like so many, trading protection for dollars. Together they formed the Meyer Bug Gang, dealing in muscle and murder for the bootleggers operating throughout New York and New Jersey.

Siegel was a psycho-pistolero, a cowboy of a monster with a vampire's blood lust who wanted to be in at the kill, if not pulling the trigger himself. Yet, as did Luciano, he listened to the counsel of Meyer Lansky, who, although as much a killer as his associates, ran a corporate brain inside his head. Lansky, they said, could see round corners. He could also cut them. With Luciano and Siegel, he worked with the addicted gambler and genius Arnold Rothstein, a New York mastermind who was always cold and calculating. The nationwide crime organisation was the brainchild of Rothstein. It was an idea he talked about with his students, who also included the older (by ten years) Francesco Castiglia, who, as Frank Costello, was the greatest corrupter of politicians, policemen and judges – those known as *the foreign dignitaries*.

Costello had worked as a bootlegger alongside Joseph Kennedy, and later said Kennedy and Rothstein were the only men he ever admired. Rothstein – teetotal, non-smoker – saw his life and future as a spreadsheet. 'The Brain' appeared in F. Scott Fitzgerald's 1925 novel *The Great Gatsby* as Meyer Wolfsheim, who wore human teeth as cufflinks. Wolfsheim fixed baseball's 1919 World Series, but the fact from the fiction is that Rothstein probably only profited greatly from it. He only followed hot horses, those that always, always won: it was fixed. He was an able tutor and his class was eager, hungry for knowledge and opportunity. He taught them about forming organised groups, affiliations for no other reason than business; of 'looking after' politicians at local and national level; that the dollar was non-denominational and its nationality was profit. Money and the making of it was, he said, an international business.

Have gun, will travel, was crucial to the job description. So too was utter allegiance to profit. When Rothstein was shot in Room 369 of the Park Central Hotel in November 1928, age

46, a single bullet went through his custom-tailored Harry Beck silk shirt, blasting a hole where the initials A.R. had been hand-stitched. It was a nasty gut-shooting and Rothstein died the next day. The murder, which was never truly investigated by the New York authorities, was dismissed as a falling out over gambling debts. Rothstein, the great fixer, had protested that the game was fixed. He died in that belief. His students were never brought into inquiries about their mentor's passing.

In gangland politics, it was a landmark moment – like the Stock Market crash was for the straight world in October the following year.

Rothstein's students had learned well. What happened outside their world was of no importance. They had their own agenda. When the battle for gangland dominance was over, with a couple of final assassinations in New York in 1931, it was a diplomatic coup that Luciano was the controller. He kept the Italian factions content, while his quieter – and privately equal – partner Meyer Lansky brought in the Jewish mobs who, unknown to the Italians, outnumbered them. With the Syndicate in control, gambling, prostitution, graft, corruption, numbers, loan-sharking, hijacking, criminal receiving, counterfeiting, pornography, smuggling, white slave and narcotics trafficking and all the other nefarious and profitable activities on the wrong side of the street were about to prosper. The savagery, the unconscionable number of deaths fostered by Luciano and Lansky to establish point position, sped a high Richter rumble across gangland America. The old had been shaken out by men who had grown up faster than anyone could remember, a bunch as young as they were single-minded and ruthless.

The New Deal gangsters also established an enforcement arm: Murder, Inc. It recruited rub-out men from the Meyer Bug Gang and comprised a bunch of made men, including Siegel himself, Louis 'Lepke' Buchalter and Albert Anastasia, the Lord High Executioner. Still, no task for Murder, Inc. was taken forward without the personal approval of Meyer Lansky. He signed off on every deal, as it were.

Other triggermen included Martin Goldstein and the colourful if nervy Abe 'Kid Twist' Reles, who killed from a sweet shop known as Midnight Rose's. The hit men got a salary and a sliding scale in dollars per successful death. Enjoying that sort of cash was Gaetano Tommy 'Three-Finger Brown' Lucchese. The one legitimate job the Sicilian had taken cost him his right index finger in a mangle machine. He decided such employment was too dangerous. A cop who later booked him nicknamed him 'Three-Finger Brown' after the Chicago Cubs pitcher. It was appropriate, for Tommy Lucchese loved sports, especially boxing. In 1931, he talked it non-stop with the Mafia soldier who worked alongside him in Murder, Inc., Frankie Carbo. He spoke just as much sporting business with Johnny Rosselli.

With Al Capone sidelined (in the US Penitentiary in Atlanta, Georgia, in 1932 for tax evasion before transfer to Alcatraz in 1934), the ingratiating Rosselli remained the Mob's solidly established link to Hollywood. His other clever tactic was to collect and distribute 'business profits' himself. He didn't franchise out that job, as he did killings. This way he avoided others skimming before the cut and causing trouble back east. It also undermined the authority of Jack Dragna, which was generally believed to be no bad thing.

Rosselli was perfect: rat-like cunning with a plausible manner, suave when necessary, horribly violent when required. Rather good credentials for a multimillion-dollar Mob shakedown of the financially vulnerable Hollywood studios – and the perfect match for Willie Bioff, one of the most remarkable – and evil – walk-on players in the history of Hollywood. The mission was to control the movie unions.

Bioff was a clever kid. At nine years old on the streets of Chicago, he was on commission (plus tips) from a group of brothels in the Levee. This red-light district on the Near South Side of the city was 20 square blocks of illicit relaxation: there were 500 bars, the same number of whorehouses, about 50 pool rooms and a dozen or so gambling joints. There were peep shows and cocaine parlours. It was an area where any pleasure or disease was cheaply available. A Democratic politician called Mike Kenna was overlord of the enterprises. They called him 'Hinky Dink'.

This area was home to young Willie after his father disowned him when he was eight years old. He'd pick out men and explain his mother was out but his attractive sister was at home and feeling lonely. The interested got the message and others just brushed the little kid away. But Willie Bioff grew up and so did his ideas.

He got married to the equally twisted Laurie Parkin and opened his first brothel on their wedding day, 7 August 1924. When he wanted more girls, he and Laurie went into the white slavery business. They roamed the farming communities of Illinois and lured young girls with tempting tales of money and glamour. They'd pay the girls' way to Chicago, then put them to work locked into the brothels.

Al Capone had taken over the Outfit in Chicago, Johnny Torrio having retired following a shooter's failed attempt on his life in January 1925. As the wars for control of the city made the front pages and the obituary columns – Hymie Weiss went down in 1926 and half a dozen of the 'Bugs' Moran mob in the St Valentine's Day Massacre in 1929 – Willie Bioff did some muscle work for the gangsters. Through his payments, he met Capone's trusted financial man Jake 'Greasy Thumb' Guzik (on account of the tens of thousands of used banknotes he counted) and, in time, Frank 'the Enforcer' Nitti, then finally Capone himself. They all saw each other in one another.

The economy was bad and getting worse; the Depression a fact of everyday life, even for the gangsters. Guzik had advised Capone that Prohibition could not last and the Outfit fought and bruised their way into other profitable enterprises, as did the nationwide Syndicate, expanding drug markets, labour unions, gambling and business racketeering. The infrastructure for all this had been created during the lavish Prohibition era. Political and police corruption was a way of life and the Mob had the influence to do anything it wanted in and around Chicago. It was left to the federal government to bring down

Capone, and although they claimed to have broken the Mob as well, that was a little colourful – Hollywood, you could say. Like the myth of gangbuster Eliot Ness.

Underboss Frank Nitti took control as the largest fiscal stream, the illegal booze business, ended. Under Capone, they had 'lost' almost all their rivals. They were the only player in town.

Jake Guzik was partnered with Murray Humphreys, a Welshman with a deceptively lilting voice, to give the gangster business a more corporate structure. Humphreys, an enforcer for Capone, was the equal of any fire-spouting Hollywood studio boss. He was tougher too. He'd been called a 'gentleman' by two American presidents (Eisenhower and Truman) but was a heartless man. This well-mannered – 'cultivated', said the White House – gentleman scarred women and children and had taken a knife to the genitals of union workers who opposed him.

The violence may have been old-fashioned but the foundations of corporate gangster-hood were arguably established the day the Prohibition profits dried up. In New York and New Jersey, it was Luciano–Lansky–Siegel–Costello–Zwillman; in Chicago, a more temperate chairman than Capone, Nitti.

A clever businessman, especially in a declining market, Nitti delegated with flair. 'Greasy Thumb' Guzik and Murray Humphreys took over the local unions and gambling throughout Cook County by muscling in on the existing operators; they spread their own bookie and casino outlets without fear of any legal intervention. With Paul Ricca as his underboss, the wily Nitti kept everything low-key. An achievement, given the notorious operators on the payroll: 'Joe Batters' Accardo, Claude 'Screwy' Maddox and 'Tough Tony' Capezio, Rocco 'Mr Big' DeGrazia and the meanest of them all, the low-handicap Sam 'Golf Bag' Hunt – the only links he knew were the ones on a set of handcuffs.

Yet, federal agents, in particular Eliot Ness, spun that, with Capone gone, Mob rule in Chicago was over. The FBI bought the message and agreed organised crime was finished. It wasn't. It had stretched.

Nitti's operations moved into Milwaukee and Madison, Wisconsin, Rockford and Springfield, Illinois, Kansas City and Hollywood, where loan-sharking – loans with terms not as favourable as those Harry Cohn had received – became a valuable component. Legitimate businesspeople who had been spurned by the banks were 'validated' by the Mob and were then penalised in interest and extorted for influence. But it was the big, hit-making studios that really got turned over. Nitti had just the boys for the job.

Paid-for sex became too much of a luxury for many during the Depression and Willie Bioff found he could make up his losses by violently extorting shop owners in the Fulton Street district of Chicago. He took to terrorising Jewish shops, leaving his opposite number, George Browne, to work the same trick on the other stores. In time, Bioff and Browne (B&B) became a business. They demanded increased dues from union members and slipped the cash into their own pockets. It was such easy money they then put the bite on Barney Balaban, the owner of Chicago's biggest cinema chain, Balaban and Katz Theatres. Balaban and Sam Katz were nickelodeon boys who had produced some of the first silent films. And they'd grown up tough. When B&B turned up and demanded extortion payments, Balaban roughed them up and ejected them.

They bounced back with a new tactic: if their demands were not met and $20,000 paid over immediately, all the projectionists, good union members, would go on strike and Balaban and Katz cinemas would be dark. The money, they lied, was for unemployed union members. Bioff was cute enough to know that if Balaban gave the $20,000 to charity, the company could write the money off their corporate tax bill and win public admiration at the same time. Barney Balaban was shrewd as well. He knew there would be no written account of their arrangements.

So, yes, they'd donate $20,000 to a union soup kitchen but

tell the IRS they'd given $100,000 – skimming $80,000 off for themselves. And B&B couldn't complain. The $20,000 in cash was delivered to B&B by Balaban's lawyer, Leo Spitz, who, before handing the money over, reached into the suitcase and pulled out $1,000 and stuffed it in his pocket 'for carrying charges'.

The pair of happy hoodlums went off to the Mob-controlled 100 Club inside the Chicago Loop. It was a high-jinks joint watched over by Nick Dean Circella, who worked for his cousin, Al Capone's former hit man Frankie Rio. Willie Bioff played roulette and lost about $1,000 in half a dozen spins of the wheel, as he constantly doubled up his losing bets. Rio and Circella pondered where the hapless pimp had got his cash. They investigated and a couple of days later, on a Saturday morning, the hung-over pair were invited out to Frank Nitti's mansion. George Browne thought he was going to be executed, while Willie Bioff knew it must be an opportunity – if they'd really done something wrong, they'd be dead already.

After 30 minutes, they were escorted into the front room, where Nitti sat in a large antique leather chair, with Paul Ricca and 'Cherry Nose' Charles Gioe in velvet easy chairs to either side.

'Where'd you get the money?' asked Nitti. Then, studying B&B, said: 'And don't you fucking lie to me.'

Bioff outlined the operation. Nitti got it before he'd got halfway through: there were thousands of cinemas in Chicago and the state of Illinois, more in other states north and south, east and west; the whole damned United States of America had cinemas. Nitti explained to Bioff and his still-silent partner George Browne that the Outfit was now their partner and Nick Dean Circella their points man – it would be 50–50 from now on. As a start.

When Capone was still around, he and Nitti had drawn up plans for making a move on Hollywood and now Nitti announced: 'The goose is in the oven, waiting to be cooked.' It was, of course, a golden goose. Los Angeles city and Los Angeles county were the Wild West for the gangsters; there, the currency was bribes and bullets. You could buy a sheriff's department badge, which opened all doors, for just $5. The police chief was a laugh, the District Attorney was bent, the mayor rigged elections and had his own spy network working in all branches of law enforcement. As for Hollywood – now you were talking corruption.

Nitti, who followed the financial pages, saw the film industry was a goose to be plucked. The Depression had taken a toll on the fledgling industry, which did not have the depth of assets to easily deal with negative cash flow. Yet the movies were among America's ten biggest-earning businesses, with millions being generated every day. The gangsters happily believed they had permission to pilfer and pillage wherever they could.

The movies were primed for a shakedown. All the Mob needed was control of the nation's entertainment unions. Nitti consulted with Lucky Luciano, and it was agreed that it was time for them to join up and invade Hollywood properly, with all guns blazing, as it were. The arrangement made sense: Luciano's New York conglomerate and the other New York families already controlled the East Coast Stage Workers Union and the local branches of the projectionists' union. It was a straightforward tactic.

In move one, Willie Bioff was ordered to shakedown Barney Balaban for a 20 per cent increase in pay for the projectionists. As expected, Balaban laughingly turned it down.

Move two saw the Chicago and New York mobsters arranging a general strike against the Balaban cinemas across the Midwest and East Coast. The projectionists went without pay and in some weeks the cinemas were close to closure.

Move three saw Nitti send in George Browne as a peacemaker: the strike ended and the workers got a tiny increase in salary. George Browne as a star – to both sides of the dispute.

As planned by Nitti and Luciano, he became national president of the International Alliance of Theatrical Stage Employees (IATSE) in June 1934 at the union convention in

Louisville, Kentucky. The election was a clean one; it was announced to newsmen who were banned, along with the public, from election proceedings at the Browne Hotel on Louisville's Broadway. Union delegates were met and greeted by Luciano, Meyer Lansky, Longy Zwillman and his 'staff' from the Syndicate's heavy mob, Murder, Inc., including Buchalter and 'Kid Twist' Reles. There were two other contenders for the president's job, but when they strolled into the convention hall they had second thoughts. There were ranks of men holding oiled machine guns side-by-side around the brightly lit hall. An aide whispered to the rivals that Browne was going to win the vote. They, most graciously, dropped out of the election.

It was an Ethel Merman moment for the Mafia. They had control of American show business.

The remarkable Willie Bioff was named the IATSE president's 'special representative' and the shakedown artists B&B went off to California to do in Hollywood what they did best – extortion. It wasn't the smartest move for a group working to establish a corporate criminal empire in America, but they were putting down markers, the slickness and the silk suits, and determined underworld controllers were pausing in the wings.

George Browne regressed and spent his time drinking beer in an office that was a lot smarter than the Chicago dives he was used to. Bioff was like a rat on fire. In bundles of cash – always wrapped in brown paper parcels – he picked up more than $500,000 in 'peace negotiation' money from 20th Century Fox, Paramount and Warner Brothers studios. It was easier than anyone involved could have imagined. And the reason was simple: like the mobsters, the power players in Hollywood were only interested in money. Not culture.

For all the money the studios paid out to the gangsters, they saved upwards of $20 million in costs they would have had to pay out in increased wages and better conditions had the demands of those actually making the movies been met. As virtual co-producers, these silent business partners also kept union activists, the Communist infiltrators, in line. Films were made on budget and on time.

It was little known, but there was a more subtle operation in play by B&B to help the movies prosper. By getting more money for workers in live theatre and for opera and concerts, they edged up ticket prices, which in turn made the movies much more competitive. It wasn't just following the money, it was chasing the greatest amount.

Bioff's visits to studios became more and more regular and in time even the grand finances of film were being stretched. It was Johnny Rosselli's gambling buddy Joe Schenck, now chairman of 20th Century Fox, who devised a plan to solve the drain on the studios' fortunes. They'd spin Willie Bioff's game back on himself – tempt him with more loot. He told Bioff that he could be the go-between 'agent' for the studios and Dupont, who supplied raw film for the movies. He'd get a 7 per cent commission and his annual pay-off would never be less than $50,000 (it was three times that in 1930s dollars). Bioff all but chewed Schenck's hand off to accept. On one condition: not a word was spoken to Johnny Rosselli.

Yet by then Rosselli, the Mafia's main man in town, was linked to all the players. Still, everyone in the web was happy. They were being paid and the movies were being made without trouble. Like most of them did eventually, Willie Bioff *went Hollywood*. He thought he was a star. He began to look as if he'd dressed in the dark, expensively. He flashed gold business cards with inlaid diamonds. He had Joe Schenck launder $100,000 cash for him so he could present a legitimate cheque on a ranch in the San Fernando Valley, which he filled with a swimming pool, antique furniture, Chinese vases and his seven children, who weren't allowed to touch anything.

When Bioff attempted to put the bite on the Screen Actors' Guild (SAG), the president, the fiercely political Robert Montgomery, started asking questions about the union organiser's financial affairs. And those of the studios who were hiding their pay-offs in a balance sheet of euphemisms like 'Christmas gifts for critics' and 'overseas guest entertaining'.

It would all bring too much attention – just as Lucky Luciano was realising that he wasn't paying enough of it to Hollywood. He thought Chicago was getting too much of the profits – and control – now that the Mob had the lock on the world's film capital. He started making regular trips West and became involved with the girl they called 'Hot Toddy'.

Thelma Todd had always wanted to be a star, but the girl from Lowell, Massachusetts, took a circuitous route. She started out as an assistant schoolteacher and in the summer worked as a model, and a good one, at local theatre shows. A lot of 'movie men' tried to help her with the original 'I can make you a star' – and her sexual fantasy of a strong man taking charge of and looking after her every need – but it was a high school photograph that granted her access to the silver screen, sent in by a classmate who nominated her Miss Massachusetts, 1925.

And she became just that. Before she was 21 years old, Thelma Alice Todd was in Hollywood, in Paramount's 'Stars of Tomorrow' Acting School. There was one snag. Thelma – blonde, bountiful, funny and certainly having that special star quality – liked to eat. At first, diet pills helped; then more and more amphetamines, washed down by good bootleg booze.

She looked the part – and got plenty of them, working with Laurel and Hardy, Buster Keaton and appearing in *Monkey Business* and *Horse Feathers* opposite the Marx Brothers. She was an instant star and gained a reputation as a wisecracking comedian – 'the Ice Cream Blonde' – but could do drama, too. She showed that in the 1931 original screen version of Dashiell Hammett's *The Maltese Falcon*, playing Iva Archer, the discontented wife of Sam Spade's murdered partner.

In the curious carousel of Hollywood, she became involved with another newcomer, Pasquale DiCicco, former bootlegger and pimp, friend of Lucky Luciano and now a film agent, which was a title many of the Mob's men in town deployed. In the vivacious Thelma he saw a stunning and very funny, needy woman. She saw her fantasy man. They eloped in Prescott, Arizona, on 18 July 1932, but as husband and wife were a disaster. 'Pat' DiCicco enjoyed other women and kept his business affairs quiet, while she mixed her tranquillisers, jumping into boxes of pills and bottles of booze and pulling the stoppers after her. She had so many car smashes the studio ordered her to have a full-time driver. She also became involved, although it's never been clear if it truly was a sexual relationship, with the director Roland West. Officially, her marriage ended on 3 March 1934 – by then she'd made 70 movies – with Thelma citing cruelty and incompatibility, which DiCicco did not object to within court precincts.

During her marriage, she had met Lucky Luciano. DiCicco, the cousin of film producer Albert 'Cubby' Broccoli, had been reluctant to introduce the sexually charged couple, but he did. And they were. Luciano was smitten by Thelma Todd and, although she was wary of his Mafia credentials, she enjoyed him and the endless supply of drugs he provided. Luciano catered for an all-around need.

Roland West offered Thelma a business deal, as well as care and attention. He opened a seafood restaurant in a three-storey building only a pedestrian bridge away from the beach at 17575 Pacific Coast Highway, Castellammare, between Santa Monica and Malibu, which became Thelma Todd's Sidewalk Café. One floor up was their private nightclub, named Joya's, where a select group of the Hollywood crowd could gamble privately. There was a bandstand and a dance floor. Thelma was the attraction, even on the drinks menu: *Thelma Todd Knockout* – $1, *Thelma Todd Milk Punch* (gin base) – 45 cents, *Thelma Todd Rickey* – 45 cents. Minus the Thelma glamour, it was: *Gin Fizz* – 35 cents.

The actress had an apartment at the top of the building, but she had nothing to do with running what was quickly a popular hot spot at the beach. She was the show. And the Mob wanted part of it. There was pressure on Roland West regarding the restaurant business – who would supply napkins, food, drink, laundry services – and also directly from Luciano, who wanted to open a proper gaming room in the upstairs club. Thelma Todd rebelled. She put the picture of Mob extortion together:

if they didn't leave her alone, she'd take her complaints to the District Attorney.

Of course, the usually perspiring DA Burton Fitts was connected; two of Luciano's men worked in his office. So when superstar Todd made an appointment for a meeting with the District Attorney on Tuesday, 17 December 1935, it didn't seem a problem. But it was.

Thelma knew a lot just from being around DiCicco and Luciano, and the District Attorney couldn't just ignore her: she was too high profile and would make a lot of noise. He couldn't prosecute the Mob, as that would be prosecuting himself. And he'd be dead before he got started. It would be much simpler for all concerned if Thelma Todd was the one who was dead.

The evening before that solution was reached, Thelma, in a mauve and silver gown, a mink and a Crown Jewels starter kit, was driven by chauffeur Ernie Peters to a party at a former speakeasy, the Café Trocadero on Sunset Strip, given by British actor Stanley Lupino and his talented daughter Ida. Pat DiCicco had asked Ida Lupino if he could be seated next to his former wife but turned up late with actress Margaret Lindsay and all but ignored Thelma, who proceeded to get drunk and argue with him. They were in a cordoned-off VIP area – the concept and attraction of the 'velvet rope' behind which only beautiful people could party began at the Trocadero – but guests at the club had a good view of Thelma and, although she was boozed, she was laughing and happy. She certainly wasn't acting in any way suicidal.

Still, that was how it looked on the Monday morning at 10.30 a.m., 16 December 1935, when her maid Mae Whitehead found her lifeless body slumped in the front passenger seat of her chocolate-coloured 1934 Lincoln Phaeton convertible in the two-car garage of the cliff-side mansion. The car's engine had been running. Thelma still had on her evening gown.

Roland West had locked the restaurant at 2 a.m. Thelma had left the Trocadero just before 3 a.m. Limo driver Ernie Peters had dropped her at the Sidewalk Café, he recalled, at around 4 a.m. The drink had put her choreography a little askew, but he said she had made it up the staircase to her apartment. The *Los Angeles Times* front-page headline read: 'Body of Thelma Todd Found in Death Riddle'. If it sounds like a Raymond Chandler thriller, it certainly became part of one. Chandler was a neighbour, living in Pacific Palisades – his view over the ocean is one of the most spectacular in the world – and *Farewell, My Lovely* (published in 1940) contains many elements of the demise of Hot Toddy.

Yet, the 'death riddle' beloved of the headlines, which became an ongoing debate, had a simple explanation, given the times and the place and the ambitions of those with whom Thelma Todd was involved. She was in the way, and she was about to make trouble. And she was dead on deadline, exactly 24 hours before her appointment with District Attorney Burton Fitts.

There were many theories. Her death certificate said she died from accidental carbon-monoxide poisoning, but that was on the LAPD detective squad assertion that she had been running the engine to warm the car for driving or herself. There was an autopsy, but after her funeral her body was quickly cremated, with the paperwork signed off by the District Attorney's office. And why not? Thelma had died accidentally.

This left no opportunity to medically examine the body and give reasons for her broken nose and the blood coagulated on her face and splattered across her dress and body. Or her missing teeth and two fractured ribs. Many stories were circulated implicating Pat DiCicco and Roland West in her death. There was a rumour about another lover and an intruder. And it came around to suicide again. Some who had primary information on the case maintain she was knocked out with a blow to the face, beaten and placed in the front seat of the car, where she was killed by the carbon monoxide, which turned her face crimson. That could have been done by any of the three men who had been present at a corner table at the Trocadero at the Saturday night party. The men were all known associates of Thelma's lover Lucky Luciano.

As such, an explanation was not required. No one was ever arrested in connection with the death of the 29-year-old film star who never did get to testify about the Mob in Hollywood because no one required that either.

3

THE BEST OF ENEMIES

'Well, if I were you, I'd have that money back by seven
o'clock tonight.'
'FUCK YOU! Lookit me, FUCK YOU! And if I was you, I'd
shut my fuckin' mouth and watch my step! Yeah, you,
Smiley! Or would ya like me to blow your fuckin'
Adam's apple down your spine?'
– Benjamin Siegel (Warren Beatty) to Mickey Cohen
(Harvey Keitel), *Bugsy*, 1991

BENNY SIEGEL ALWAYS WANTED TO BE IN THE MOVIES, BUT
he never made it when he was alive. It wasn't for the lack of
trying. Mickey Cohen, who knew his limitations, wanted to
marry a movie star but accepted dating a girl who specialised
in exotic snakes. And film-making. Their friend George Raft
was a star. And he introduced two of the most colourful killers
of the twentieth century around Hollywood, where they met
everyone on the headliner casting list.

Raft, originally Georgie Ranft from New York's West Side,
established himself as a screen hoodlum in *Scarface* (1932) and
was an actor on the up and up when Siegel got to town. Raft,
a likeable man but one who always seemed withdrawn in his
own world, had been a successful nightclub dancer in New
York (Fred Astaire rated him). But it was as the coin-flipping
partner to Paul Muni's 'Scarface' that he became a star and
coined his coin-spinning. His circle was Jean Harlow, Clark
Gable, Cary Grant, Gary Cooper and a baker's dozen of

starlets – 'It's always good to have an extra,' believed Raft – and they became part of Siegel's social roster, too. It was an intriguing world for him.

The crowd he now ran with had graduated in an 'anything goes' world. He dived straight in at the deep end. Lee Francis was a Madam who'd learned the prostitution business in houses in Reno, Nevada and San Francisco before moving down the coast to 8439 Sunset Boulevard in Hollywood. The House of Francis was a grand building, with girls on most floors, who could be visited there or, if preferred, could make home or hotel visits. The rival cat house was Mae's, which offered the same amenities but the girls there were duplicates of the movie stars of the day – Ginger Rogers, Marlene Dietrich, Jean Harlow, Joan Crawford, Claudette Colbert; the studios supplied the costumes worn by the real stars in their movies, such as Colbert's *Cleopatra* ensemble. Mae's was run by the actress Billie Bennett on behalf of MGM, giving the studio the added benefit of knowing which of its performers were popular.

Jean Harlow was a willing star on and off screen, and particularly at the House of Francis, where she paid for girls whom she took home with her and also, if the mood took her, rented customers for herself. The out-call service was $500 at the House of Francis of which half went to the cops and politicians, who looked the other way. Sex, of course, sells and that made some of the easy-living stars and starlets easy targets.

Joan Crawford had been arrested on prostitution charges in Detroit before moving to Hollywood and becoming a grand femme fatale. On the way, she appeared in a series of explicit 'stag' films, one of which was being used to extort her. Johnny Rosselli was asked to intervene. He was a superb negotiator: he took the $25,000 from MGM as a pay-off and kept it. He then met the blackmailers and told them he would murder them all if they did not destroy the film negatives. They agreed after he pushed a pistol into one sorry extortionist's ear. Although the story, as it went around Hollywood, was that it didn't stop the sex.

Benny Siegel's new friend Clark Gable happily admitted to being a regular at the House of Francis, parking his custom-built Duesenberg coupé at 8439 Sunset. Benny Siegel loved it all: the glamour, the sex, the power – and the money.

The gangster, who'd carried out at least 20 hits on behalf of the Syndicate, came to Hollywood at the indulgence and insistence of Meyer Lansky and Lucky Luciano. His instructions were to play it cool but to take over as many of the illegal Californian operations as quickly as he could. Siegel roared down the roads driven by avarice as if he'd inherited them.

Siegel was the Mob's investment in the heart of Hollywood. He had more than half a million dollars in 'seed' money, but first he spent it on renting opera singer Lawrence Tibbett's Beverly Hills home, which was all neat lawns, hand-operated sprinkler system and pretension on McCarthy Drive. He gambled thousands of dollars at Santa Anita and hosted lavish parties; his hand-cut suits were made by the dozen and he had his wife, Esther Krakower, and their two daughters, Barbara and Millicent, kept distant from his more flamboyant activities at a sprawling house in Holmby Hills.

The generous (with other people's money) gangster loved Hollywood and vice versa. He was called a 'sportsman', which was a neat euphemism for a gangster. He was also a gangster's gangster. He was part of the assassination squad that took out Joe 'the Boss' Masseria, allowing Luciano's Mafia takeover. In Thanksgiving week 1932 in New York, he and two others had pumped four bullets into Tony Fabrizo, who had announced he was going to name names in a book about his mobster life. Siegel also took out a few of Dutch Schultz's triggermen, also 'Pretty' Amberg, who specialised in cosmetic surgery with a table fork on the faces of those he didn't like.

Yet in Hollywood, it was insisted, the good-looking, free-spending Benny Siegel was a 'sportsman'. He followed his orders, not his instincts. He didn't kill Jack Dragna; he tolerated him. His other Mob contact was Johnny Rosselli. The Italian provided connections with the inner circle of the studios: Jack Warner, Louis B. Mayer and Harry Cohn. Deals began rolling in.

Rosselli came to Siegel with a share of the Agua Caliente racetrack in Tijuana, which had been closed down in 1935 but was up for grabs again by the Mexican authorities. For a flat fee of $100,000, they would allow eight weeks of racing, with all profits going to the organisers. Harry Cohn also went in with Rosselli and the venture did nothing but cause profit for all. It was the beginning of a wonderful friendship between Siegel and Rosselli. Money was the bond.

Siegel was also going about his master's business: he mirrored the Mob's extortion set-up with the unions of the New York garment industry, but in Hollywood he set about organising the 'little but necessary people'. The main unions were already controlled, but the extras, the walk-ons and walk-offs of every film made, were open season. Siegel had them and he'd approached actors and studio chiefs with: 'I've put you down for ten grand for the extras.'

'Extras? Nothing to do with me . . .'

'I'll explain,' the gracious Siegel would begin. 'Suppose on your next picture the script has been finished, the director is ready to go, the stars are ready, the stagehands, everybody is drawing a salary, and when you shout "Action!" the extras walk out.'

It never had to be spelled out more than that and Siegel was conservatively receiving $500,000 a year in what he called 'friendly loans'.

Mickey Cohen is the closest I got to Benny Siegel, other than a fleeting conversation with Siegel's daughter, Millicent Rosen, who in 2012 was operating the Odyssey Lighting business in Las Vegas and still in touch with the families of Meyer Lansky and his gambling tsar Dino Cellini. She said her father was hot tempered, but she was a little girl growing up not in but very much out of his shadow. He didn't bring his work home.

In 1975, Cohen was working with my friend John Peer Nugent, a former *Newsweek* correspondent (Vietnam and the like) and then a magazine writer in Los Angeles. In those days, early evenings were spent in the King's Head pub in Santa Monica, where 'Nugent', who was never known by his first name, would smoke his pipe, sip one of many glasses of California red wine and play back Mickey Cohen on a rattling tape recorder. I hadn't met Cohen face to face at the time and it was eerie hearing what seemed, those many years ago, to be a voice from the past, from the dead, which I suppose in many cases is exactly what it was. And it was quite a voice – and a story.

Meyer Harris Cohen was born on 4 September 1913, the sixth child of Russian Jews, in the Brownsville area of Brooklyn, and his father's funeral followed eight weeks later. His mother Fanny still had the pioneer spirit: she put four of her children with relatives and headed west with her new baby boy and his sister, Lillian. She settled and opened a grocery store in Boyle Heights, which was a little like putting down roots in no-man's-land. On the eastern side of the Los Angeles River, it was a rainbow community – Germans, Russians, Japanese, French, Finns, Jews, Italians – with some striving for the pot of gold, while others rotted in putrid poverty conditions.

Mickey Cohen grew up with multiculturalism. The family business prospered and his brothers Harry, Sam and Louie, and his other sister Pauline, joined them in Los Angeles. They all worked, the young boy selling newspapers on street corners. Mickey got caught stealing nickels from a news-stand when he was three years old.

Harry and Louie Cohen opened a chemist's shop and employed their little brother in the afternoons. The police raided the pharmacy and caught Mickey supplying home-made booze out the back. He didn't give up without a struggle, assaulting one of the cops with a hot plate. He was seven years old. And Mickey learned a lesson. Harry called in a favour, the 'fix' was in, and the matter was never heard about again. Mickey believed from then on that everything could be 'fixed'. Of course, it couldn't.

Especially when he was caught just after robbing the

Columbia cinema in Los Angeles at noon. His 'persuader' was a heavy club. As he was about to get away with the cash, the police grabbed nine-year-old Mickey. He went to Fort Hill reform school, where he was beaten every day during his year there. He got to fight back. A condition of his release was that he had a 'big brother' to watch over him and lucky Mickey pulled Abe Roth, who was a boxing referee. From there, he got into the world of boxing, where he was so useful his brother Harry became his trainer and they went off to New York to try for a ring future at Lou Stillman's legendary gym on West 57th Street. Stillman charged 25 cents for outsiders to watch the training. He encouraged them to smoke, as he said the choking tobacco fumes toughened up the guys in the ring. The equally legendary author and fight authority Budd Schulberg – whose film producer father B.P. Schulberg gambled tens of thousands of dollars off Sunset Boulevard at the Clover Club – said Stillman had a 'garbage disposal voice'. He used it to explain his tactics in training Mickey Cohen: 'Big or small, champ or bum, I treat 'em all the same. If you treat 'em like humans, they'll eat you alive.'

The West 57th Street gym was a connected place. Arrogant, overbearingly wealthy men in cashmere overcoats would watch the action through clouds of Havana. It was a tough world – at least a dozen of Stillman's fighters went to the electric chair – and many, like Mickey Cohen, joined the Mob.

Mickey had to leave the fight game. There wasn't much money in it and, for a man with an obsession with cleanliness (OCD), there were a lot of smells and sweat and he had to spend hours in baths and showers after training. Instead, he decided to go to Cleveland, where he figured pursuing a career in armed robbery would be more lucrative and less sweaty. The Ohio city was still ruled by the Italians and this new 'Jewboy' from the *Kosher Nostra* was dismissed as surplus to requirements. But Mickey did what he always did best: he put a gun in his hand and shoved the pistol in someone's face.

Suddenly, all of underworld Cleveland knew the style of this crazy stick-up guy. On Nugent's interview tapes, Mickey sounds so proud. It transcribed: 'It made me equal to everybody. Even as small as I was when I whipped out that big .38, it made me as big as a guy standing 6 ft 10 in. tall.'

With this remarkably induced self-esteem, he hit card games, brothels and cafés – anywhere there was cash to carry – and he was in action every night of the week. What Mickey never admitted to on the Nugent tapes was killing anyone. You can read between the lines, but for a poorly educated man he knew one thing for certain: 'Hey, there's no statute of limitations for offing a guy . . .'

He was careful; in Cleveland, he'd been offered and accepted a job as a hit man for the local outfit and as a franchised killer who would take himself and his gun out of state to earn his retainer. But Mickey wasn't always clever when he desperately wanted money, which throughout his life was all the time. He once stuck up a Cleveland café popular with the local office workers and those at the 105th Street police station directly across from the scene of the daylight heist. The Ohio Outfit liked Mickey, but he was too 'unpredictable', so he moved over to Chicago.

There had been trouble at one of Capone's gambling joints on the North Shore and Mickey was put in to protect the place. He did it his way. A trio of the rivals were walking up to the casino with only a plate-glass door between them and machine-gun mischief. Mickey started shooting before they even reached the door. Two died, one fled. Mickey told the cops that the taller of the dead guys was pulling out a gun, so he had blasted him in self-defence. It didn't go – at first. He was charged with murder but released the following morning after the problems had been 'fixed'. The jailhouse officials were reluctant to free Mickey Cohen – *accused murderer* – 'just like that', but the Mob representative, a young and clever Chicago lawyer called Sidney Korshak, asked them for a moment so he could make a call to the police precinct boss. Chicago was indeed a 'fixit' kind of town and Capone's latest triggerman was freed 'just like that'. It was a metamorphosis for Mickey: 'I wasn't a punk kid any more. I was someone who had done something to justify the favour of Al Capone.' Which he got in a big way. He never talked about doing the actual killings but put it in this roundabout way: 'I soon found there were lots of older guys willing to teach me about how to grow up and be good at a particular piece of work I wanted to get to know about.'

Mickey Cohen learned to kill professionally in Chicago. He knew he was a crook and a shootist, the people around him were gangsters, but he also learned, the revelation, that there were more bent people in City Hall in Chicago, the federal government, the police and the FBI than any good American citizen could ever imagine. He was 'disappointed'. So much so he increased his stick-up routine to two or three robberies a day.

Short and pudgy, with a face like a well-used anvil, he invited attention by buying cream Stetsons. He paid $50 a time and after a few days he'd get fed up with the head gear and throw it away. As soon as that happened, his crew knew another robbery was on the way. Mickey never used his own cash to buy a hat. When he wanted one, he took out his .38 revolver.

His future took a dramatic turn when he got into an ongoing row with another hoodlum. Mickey pistol-whipped the guy, who, when he recovered, went out and got drunk and brave and stuck a gun in Mickey's back. Mickey grabbed the gun – and both men had hold of it. They went to a café to ponder their dilemma. Mickey picked up a sugar bowl and smashed it over the other guy's head: 'His head split open like a melon and blood flew all over the joint.' After that there was nothing but chaos and cops.

Mickey scrambled the gun away in the basement, but it was found and he was looking at an attempted murder charge. That nice young lawyer Sidney Korshak sorted matters out. Mickey Cohen was asked to leave town. Which he did.

He went back to Hollywood, where he belonged.

The triumvirate of Meyer Lansky, Lucky Luciano and Frank Costello all wanted Mickey Cohen in Hollywood as a strong arm for Benny Siegel and also to keep an eye on 'the Bug'. But Mickey remained his own maverick.

He was in the right place at the right time. The era of proper, bespoke corruption of the Hollywood studios and the stars was the fashion. It was a deadly game. Mickey hired three full-time bodyguards. He was regarded as a buffer between the Los Angeles Mafia boss Jack Dragna and the March hare antics of Benny Siegel. But Mickey didn't see any politics – he wanted to have fun and told Nugent on tape:

'When I was told to come out here, and that Benny was out here, I actually wasn't told that I was fully under Benny's arm. I figured I'd come out here and do whatever pieces of work I wanted to do on my own. My understanding of it was I would be with Benny if necessary, if he had to call upon me or vice versa. I understood that Benny was sent out here by the Outfit to put his part of the country in line with the way of doing things back east. I really don't consider the Mafia the only strength. It's an organisation. It is what I would refer to as a syndicate. Particularly in the days of my operation, this was a very strong organisation. The Italians were all powerful, as were the Jews in those days – the days when Lepke was in power. Of course, they were in power on different things, like union-wise. The Italians were powerful with gambling, liquor licences and everything. So it was an organisation, but it wasn't the Mafia. Being Jews, Benny and me, and even Meyer Lansky, couldn't be a real part and parcel of that.

'I was supposed to call Benny right away when I arrived in Los Angeles. But I says to myself: "Let him look for me. If I get in touch with Benny too quick, he'll lock me up right away and I won't be able to go on no scores. I have to get a hold of some money and I have some things to do."

'Actually, we never even gave a fuck about Benny. We were just rooting, taking off scores. I was out with ten different broads every night and I was in every cabaret they could ever have in the town. When we needed money, we always had two, three scores in advance. We always had tipsters waiting for us to get together with them.

'I didn't want to work and that's what being with Benny

would be like. I didn't want to get involved where I had to keep records, keep people in line, be involved with politicians and all that bullshit.'

But Benny Siegel soon knew Mickey Cohen was in town. Big time.

The gangster has always seemed proud of this particular announcement of his activities. It was the day he nailed Dago Louie, who ran a bookmaking operation, an elaborate affair where other bookies worked and where deals were made and only $500-plus bets were taken.

Of course, Dago Louie and his City Hall partners had protection – two Los Angeles County Sheriffs on the door. Mickey, the new boy in Hollywood, got one of the cops to open the security door and stuck his .38 in his stomach: 'You cocksucker, you move and you're gone.'

There were a couple of dozen punters in the betting room at 9 a.m. When Mickey waved a sawn-off shotgun at them, they waved their arms in the air. He had no idea what the bookie looked like – 'I don't know Dago Louie from a coat hanger' – but he found him. And lots and lots of cash, about $15,000, which was a big pay-off, as well as the gamblers' rings and jewellery. He took Dago Louie's diamond stick pin.

Mickey wanted more. He decided to wait for the main man Morley Orloff. The chief bookie was already there and stayed silent, but his nerves got to him and he revealed himself to Mickey, who was marching around with his shotgun. The pause was just enough time for Davy 'Little Dave' Schneiderman to arrive – with $32,000 in cash.

Schneiderman worked with Johnny Rosselli and Jack Dragna through Dago Louie. He knew the cash would be safe; no one would dare rob this connected joint. But Mickey had – and went off 'cabareting' and spending the cash. Three days later Benny Siegel sent word that he'd like to see Mickey at the YMCA in Hollywood.

Siegel confronted him: 'I heard you were a fucking nut but goddamn, how crazy can you be? You took off Jack Dragna's goombah. Ya took off little Davy Schneiderman, Johnny

Rosselli's partner. You're gonna have to kick that shit back.'

Mickey retorted: 'Let me tell ya something right now. I don't give a fuck who it is or what it is. When I go on a score, I put up my life and liberty on this score. I wouldn't kick back to my mother.'

Mickey left Siegel wrapped in a towel in the YMCA gym. Hours later they met again in downtown Los Angeles at the offices of Siegel's lawyer, Jerry Giesler, who also represented Charlie Chaplin and Errol Flynn. Johnny Rosselli was there and, according to Mickey, was an unwanted mediator. One issue was Dago Louie's stick pin, which Mickey recalled was a 'family whoreloom'. As a favour to Benny Siegel, he 'kicked it back' to Dago Louie.

The two gangsters came to what Mickey Cohen never called more than a 'mutual understanding', but it was enough to make them the top mobsters in Hollywood. He said they became as close as any Italian and Jew could in the underworlds.

Jack Dragna was old-fashioned, only the Italians could be the leaders of the gangs – certainly not Jews like Benny Siegel and Mickey Cohen. But the Jewish boys made a corporate order that Mickey easily explained: 'Benny's attitude was *Fuck Dragna* – and he did.'

With the introduction of a more delicate touch – 'gangster light' – the ill-gotten gains could be reinvested smoothly. Teams of lawyers and business advisers showed how to steal legitimately, using legalese not Brooklynese. But for Mickey and Benny it was the old saw – you can lead a horse to water . . .

Benny Siegel had control of the extras' union and was expanding his influence all over southern California. He forced bookmakers in California and Arizona to subscribe to the Syndicate's wire service, which reported racing results throughout the USA. He organised prostitution rings from Seattle to San Diego. Some of the girls were drug 'mules', carrying narcotics along the pipeline he'd established to and from Mexico. Millions and millions of dollars worth of heroin and opium were being smuggled into America. He gave no thought to what or who was in the way. There were no parameters to his perfidy. He was following instructions and taking control of the state, from the oceans to the mountains and back again.

He called a meeting of the Hollywood gaming club organisers and explained that they would have to split their take 50–50 with the Syndicate. The problem was an old-timer called Les Bruneman, who ran a string of gambling joints in a string of beach communities south of the city. He didn't want to share. In fact, he had futile aspirations – in themselves, a suicide note – of taking control of the West Coast gaming scene.

In July 1937, Bruneman visited one of his clubs in Redondo Beach, leaving in the early evening to take his favourite hostess out for dinner. They were on the oceanfront boulevard when San Diego triggerman Frank Bompensiero – appointed by Johnny Rosselli for the job – pumped three bullets into his back. Bruneman survived and the girl was unhurt, but as he recovered it became known that he was planning to enlarge his business from the coast inland to Palm Springs. It was decided he should be killed again, as it were. Properly this time.

Frank Bompensiero was to be the lookout man, while Leo 'Lips' Moceri, veteran of Detroit's Purple Gang, finalised the business.

On 25 October, Bruneman and a different blonde had dinner at the Montmartre Grill in Palm Springs before going on to the Roost, a late-night drinks spot. Gunman Moceri came in and put 16 bullets in Bruneman. One of the bar staff ran at the shooter but was killed with three shots.

Moceri was furious that Bompensiero hadn't stopped the barman. In later court evidence, he is attributed with this version of the hit:

'I've got a .45 automatic and the place's packed with people. I walk right up to his table and start pumping lead. Believe me, that son-of-a-bitch's going to be dead for sure this time.

'Bomp's supposed to be by the door, watching my back to make sure nobody jumps me. I turn around and I see this football player coming at me. Bomp's nowhere in sight. Now,

I'm either going to clip this guy or he's going to knock me on my ass. So I blast him and run out, and there's Bomp already in the fucking car . . . waiting for me. Shit bag.'

The killing had added benefits for Benny Siegel. In the public outcry about lawlessness, the city authorities cracked down on Tony 'the Admiral' Cornero (his friend Los Angeles Mayor Fletcher Bowron apologising to him that needs must) and he abandoned his offshore gambling fleet for Nevada. He joined many of the City Hall Gang in Las Vegas, where they believed they could rob and steal without interference from bigger crooks and killers.

Sweet – it was sugary sweet in Hollywood.

Benny Siegel didn't ever make it as a movie idol, but he got himself into high-standard home movies. With the help of his movie-connected friend Al Smiley, he bought a set of professional camera equipment and would re-enact scenes he'd seen on the movie sets played out by George Raft while his 'assistant', Moe Sedway, worked the cameras. Siegel bragged he always did the acting 'better than Georgie' and no one, including Raft, disagreed with him. Although through Smiley he put word around about these 'screen tests', it was all diplomatically overlooked. Sedway, who'd run bootleg booze with Siegel and Lansky, and was one of Lansky's important lieutenants, kept his counsel for the ears of different critics.

While Sedway kept Lansky and Co. in constant touch on progress, Siegel got more intimate with Hollywood fame by dating stars such as Lana Turner and Ava Gardner, and raising hell along Sunset Strip and around the bordellos and nightclubs with George Raft.

At Santa Anita racetrack on a day out with Johnny Rosselli, he hooked up with Countess Dorothy di Frasso, who had money, class and a husband in Italy, plus a former lover in Gary Cooper. He began to be seen all over town with her. And on the French Riviera, where they met up with George Raft, who was there wooing the actress Norma Shearer. It was such a good time that Siegel arranged to stay for three more weeks

– but vanished the next day. The catalyst for his swift departure back to America was a cable he received from New York.

Harry 'Big Greenie' Greenberg was a big problem for the Syndicate. And now he was a big problem for their man on the West Coast. Greenberg had worked with many mobsters, including Siegel and Buchalter, and as an original player in the fellowship that created the national Syndicate, he knew a great deal of its business. Greenberg had been convicted of racketeering and was deported back to Poland, his homeland, but he was soon on his way back to America via Canada, where he let it be known that if his old associates didn't help him, he'd do a deal with the federal authorities. It was a clear offer – pay up or I'll start talking.

Greenberg had got out before Buchalter's two hit men got to him, and now he had been tracked down in Los Angeles, living as George Schachter. He had a wife, Ida, and was keeping quiet. But that was not the point, agreed a Syndicate board meeting in New York. This time Longy Zwillman sent two killers to take out Big Greenie, but they too failed to make a hit.

The angry and frustrated Benny Siegel decided to take care of the matter himself. He'd take time away from his celebrity associates and mix with those whose modus operandi he understood rather better. Shrugging off his matinee idol guise, he went along to make an evening of it the night before Thanksgiving, 22 November 1939. A telephone message had been given to Greenberg, saying there was a package for him at the pharmacy near his 'safe' house off Santa Monica Boulevard in West Hollywood.

As he was parking his Ford convertible on his return, an old pal walked out of the darkness and towards the car. Expert gunman, the underworld boss of boxing Frankie Carbo put five bullets in the head of Big Greenie. Across the street Benny Siegel stood by one getaway car, while boxer Champ Segal was in another – the one that quickly took Carbo north to San Francisco, where he jumped on a flight back to New York.

A young researcher at Paramount Studios, Peggy Schwartz,

heard the gunshots as she was walking outside Greenberg's home. Moments later she saw Carbo, a cigar clenched in his teeth, running from the house. Another witness, a prominent lawyer, identified Carbo and Bugsy Siegel as the kill team. It seemed like an open-and-shut case. Still, the wheels of Californian justice took some remarkable spins in the months before it reached Spring Street and the Los Angeles courts.

By then, Carbo had slipped away to Pennsylvania, outlaw country, then down to Florida and over to Cuba. Siegel was similarly unavailable (although in town) until finally his butler gave the cops entry to his stunning new mansion at 250 Delfern Street in Beverly Hills. Siegel was taken downtown and charged with Greenberg's murder. It was at that point Siegel asked for the return of $100,000 he had donated to the election campaign of John Dockweiler, who in the summer of 1940 had replaced Burton Fitts as the head lawman of Los Angeles. With the money returned – and with much embarrassment – Siegel used the funds to pay for his defence.

While the cash was being conjured up, Siegel enjoyed the facilities at Los Angeles County Jail. He paid an inmate to be his valet, slept in the prison doctor's room, had a round-the-clock telephone service and was allowed out to lunch with his girlfriends, such as British actress Wendy Barrie. On his lunch dates, he was under the watchful eye of a deputy sheriff who, just like Siegel's driver, was always waiting for instructions.

Yet the prosecutors were certain they had the evidence to send one of the American Mafia's most powerful men to the gas chamber. They'd arrested Syndicate hit man 'Kid Twist' Reles, who, in return for mercy, was talking. And singing more than anyone so elevated in the Syndicate had ever done before. The authorities had no concept of the extent of the killings Reles had been involved in. After one candid conversation they'd 'solved' forty-nine murders in the borough of Brooklyn. The rest of New York and America followed; it was astonishing arithmetic, almost 1,000 killings for 'business reasons' by members of Murder, Inc. to protect the interests and freedom of the Syndicate's board of directors.

Reles was known as 'Kid Twist' because of his expertise in strangulation. He had strong, pliable fingers. One of life's enthusiasts, he was adept at getting the last breath out of his victims. The target was trussed up like a turkey, with the head pushed down onto the chest, legs folded into it and the hands in between, a rope around the neck and under the feet. With every little movement, the rope tightened around the throat. Finally, after a long, drawn-out death, by which time the killers would be many miles away, it was all over. If speed in killing and disposal were required, however, then ice picks were employed to do the job.

Kid Twist ran up a whodunnit of an indictment. He seemed to enjoy talking and was proud of his lethal achievements, of the icings and especially the sadistic strangling. After he'd killed, he'd go out early the next morning to get a newspaper to find out who he'd killed. He was only ever given targets, not names. Yeah, he said, he took an interest in his work.

As did the authorities. They had Reles under 24-hour protection in a room on the sixth floor of the Half Moon Hotel in Brooklyn's Coney Island. He had a constant team of six guards with him. He was cordoned off so well that the DA's office said the precautions 'would've made the Queen's Crown Jewels safe in Jesse James's parlour'. That was optimistic. Especially for Kid Twist. He was flipped out of the window and smacked into the roof of a hotel extension. He died on impact.

They said he jumped. That he tried to escape with roped sheets. That he'd slipped. That the maid had pushed him. They never mentioned a butler. The body landed 27 feet from the Half Moon – that's remarkable jumping. There was an elaborate cover-up and an investigation, which offset each other. Few knew that Frank 'Mr Fixit' Costello had distributed $100,000 among the New York Police Department (NYPD) for Kid Twist to take a high dive and become legendary: 'the Canary Sang but Couldn't Fly'.

With his demise, Benny Siegel walked away, his shoulders leading, from the murder charges: Kid Twist was no longer around to link him to Big Greenie's shooting. And without

Reles's testimony, Frank Carbo got the benefit of a hung jury. The Los Angeles DA muttered it would have been better to have 'hung' the jurors in a more literal sense.

Mickey Cohen gave the view from the other side; he was forthright on the Nugent tapes: 'I don't profess to be no angel, so when I call a man a rotten son-of-a-bitch I got reason for it. The organisation knew that Reles was a violent, ratting-rat bastard from the very go. The guy had no decency in his whole body. And the best proof of the pudding is that my guy Neddy Herbert called a turn on him years and years ago and told the outfit that he was a sadistic, rotten cocksucker that couldn't be trusted. They wouldn't listen to Neddy or me. But they believed us later. That's why Reles was thrown to his death from a hotel window in Coney Island.'

The killing of Reles was effective but noisy. It frustrated and annoyed officials, who believed they were being taunted by Siegel and the Syndicate. The reality was that the Mob thought they could get away with anything, that the 'fix' was always in. And they had reason for their optimism.

The authorities had seen off Al Capone to Alcatraz on tax evasion and now the Internal Revenue Service (IRS) – feared in America as the guys who took away a debtor's iron lung – were looking closely at the hoodlums in Hollywood, where there was an amazing dollar turnover but few taxes paid. It was the early days of 'creative financing', when even the most successful film at the box office never seemed to go into profit.

Willie Bioff was still being flash with his cash. Hollywood was worldwide. Movie stars were easy to extort and compromise – drugs, sex, illegal dalliances and perversions – but there were the potentially damaging headlines if matters went wrong. Meyer Lansky had his own file on the FBI director J. Edgar Hoover (gambling, sexual orientation), so there was influence all the way to the top of federal law enforcement. Local authorities were much more cheaply bought. But Hollywood was unique. The stars were idolised. Newspaper columnists were not all afraid to offer fact and innuendo in a clever mix. It was an open bank, but a dangerous one.

Still, Bioff had the arrogance of stupidity and the other way around. SAG President Robert Montgomery had investigated and discovered the union agitator had bought his 80-acre Woodlands Hills ranch with a pay-off from Joe Schenck; his private investigator also provided a copy of the cheque that Schenck had made out to Bioff for $100,000. Robert Montgomery reported the deal to the IRS and eventually Schenck was indicted for tax evasion. The Fox Studios boss said the money was a loan and the quiz went back and forward. Eventually, he cooperated in return for a lighter jail term. It was lighting the blue touch paper.

Joe Schenck outlined the entire scam. He was convicted and given five years, but within twelve months had received a full presidential pardon and was free – Schenck had contributed $500,000 of Mob money towards President Harry S. Truman's triumphant election campaign.

By then, the fire he'd started was blazing. Rockets were going off. A grand jury issued subpoenas for all the major studio heads, but the government had little understanding of the extent of George Browne and Bioff's extortion scam or that the Syndicate through Nick Dean Circella were so heavily implicated. It was one of the Warner Brothers, Harry, who helped them with that. It put many people in jail. And killed a few others. Some escaped, but only to catch a few more breaths.

All the Syndicate's Hollywood team were in the frame, as well as the Chicago Outfit and Frank Nitti, who'd sent B&B out West in the first place. A lot of favours were called in. Johnny Rosselli was moving behind the scenes. Bioff was engaged in meetings with Sidney Korshak, the pleasantly spoken lawyer who'd got Mickey Cohen out of trouble and Chicago. He was now based in Hollywood as a kindness to 'Joe Batters' Accardo, who'd asked him to settle there on behalf of himself and his colleagues as their mouthpiece of first choice. It was a damage-control challenge for the man already known as 'Mr Silk Stockings' – like them, he was so smooth he'd get clients off charges in a moment – and not an easy one.

B&B were indicted for taking the major Hollywood

studios – MGM, Fox, Warner Brothers and Paramount – for millions of dollars in extortion money. Willie Bioff had been carefully briefed by Rosselli that Korshak spoke for Chicago. He must do whatever Korshak said. Korshak gave him $15,000 for 'legal costs', although Korshak was that cost. Like all things Korshak, it kept the books straight. He also tutored Bioff, but his client didn't pay attention to the lessons.

B&B pleaded not guilty, which meant a trial and exposure for Rosselli, Paul Ricca, Frank Nitti and others. It also got Bioff a ten-year jail term and George Browne eight years in the slammer. Nick Dean Circella went on the run, but he too was arrested, hiding out with his girlfriend Estelle Carey, who was one of the '26' girls – you got a free drink if the throws of the dice made that number – at the Colony Club. She was a fun girl. It was her gruesome death that marked the end of the beginning of the Mob in Hollywood and opened the way for a brand new game plan, one that made the world of black and white, good and bad, an amoral grey hue.

With Nick Dean Circella in jail alongside B&B, the Syndicate was nervous. There was word Circella was going to talk. They wanted to send a message to the trio to keep quiet – and when it arrived, it was a brutal one.

When Estelle Carey had been on the run with Circella, she'd dyed her hair black; now he was in jail, she'd become a redhead and was sharing an apartment at 512 Addison Street in Chicago. The one-time model had gone back to work as a waitress and was staying away from her usual haunts. However, the mobster who killed her on 3 February 1943 – going by the name Joe Russo, but more commonly known as Marshall Caifano – only had to knock on her apartment door to carry out his orders. Estelle was on the telephone to her cousin and hung up to find out who the caller was.

Her face was cut with a bread knife and she was beaten with a rolling pin, an electric iron and a 10-inch blackjack club. She was stabbed with an ice pick and a broken whisky bottle. The frenzy of violence left a trail of blood in the kitchen and living area. Estelle was still alive when she was bound to a dining table chair, petrol splashed over her and a match lighted. She died from the burning of her body.

It was the first known Mafia hit of a woman in the history of organised crime in America. It was a reaction of madness and panic, and it revealed the absence of cognitive thinking and planning of Frank Nitti and his fading organisation. Next George Browne's wife got a message that she would vanish into the boot of a car if her husband said a word.

Circella crumbled. Bioff, little Willie the Pimp, went ballistic. Women were off limits. You could kill a guy, beat a guy, but this? He went heroic. He contacted US Attorney Boris Kostelanetz from a jail house visitor's phone and got right to it: 'This is Bioff . . . what do you want to know?'

First, Boris Kostelanetz wanted to know why Bioff was talking. The reply was immediate: 'We're doing time for them. They're killing our families.'

Boris Kostelanetz quickly found out who 'them' were. Willie Bioff fired off names and facts like a machine gun: Johnny Rosselli, Frank Nitti, Paul Ricca, Ralph Pierce, Phil D'Andrea, Louis Kaufman, 'Cherry Nose' Gioe, Frankie Diamond, Louis 'Little New York' Campagna. He outlined everything for Kostelanetz – times, dates, places, names and amounts. Of course, he'd first worked a good deal for himself. In exchange for his testimony, the US Government was to agree to let Bioff keep the money he had stolen over the past decade – and walk away from any charges against him. Bioff talked and talked for three weeks after which folders packed with indictments were handed out.

Frank Nitti felt disgraced and betrayed. He suffered from extreme claustrophobia and the fear of another term in a prison cell was a burden too far. The day after the charges were brought he began a booze binge, slugging down whisky. He had a bottle in one hand and a .32 revolver in the other when he was seen staggering beside the railway lines near Illinois Central Station. He waved the gun and the bottle about. He fired the gun and a bullet went through his snap-brimmed Fedora. He had another go and put another hole in his brown hat. The third shot blew his head off.

The racketeering trial began on 5 October 1943. By 22 December, all were found guilty of conspiracy to extort more than $1 million from Hollywood. George Browne and Willie Bioff received new identities and vanished into a witness-protection programme. After spending Christmas with their families, the mobsters were sentenced on New Year's Eve. The Chicago mobsters and Johnny Rosselli got ten years each and a $10,000 fine. They were sent to do their time in Atlanta Penitentiary, which is a bad place to even drive by.

An editorial in the *Chicago Herald-American* newspaper announced that the trial had brought about 'the total demolition of the Chicago Syndicate', but it was very much wishful thinking.

Against strong political forces, Mr Silk Stockings, the now ever-present Sidney Korshak, used contacts in Washington DC to have the mobsters moved to the saner and safer confines of Leavenworth Penitentiary in Kansas. The head of the Federal Parole Board also became a very wealthy man at this time. In fact, a great many people did.

Paul Ricca began the manipulation using Louis Campagna's wife Charlotte as an outside go-between. Louis was seriously connected, nasty and forthright. (When the under-siege Willie Bioff had asked the Palermo-born Campagna if he could resign from the Outfit, he was told: 'Anybody who resigns, resigns feet first.') Charlotte Campagna was no less determined. She worked her way to a Missouri lawmaker called Edward 'Putty Nose' Brady to get to his connection, a lawyer in St Louis. Paul Dillon was a veteran Mob mouthpiece who had worked for the Swansea-born Murray Humphreys defending two IATSE union thugs after they were charged with a great deal of grievous bodily harm to a cinema chain owner. Dillon was involved with Missouri's leading gangsters, but it was his political friends who were required. In 1934, he'd worked as Harry Truman's campaign manager during the President's first race for the Senate. He said Dillon could visit him at the White House any time.

Dillon was most helpful with regard to the plight of Mrs Campagna's husband and his colleagues, providing a price list for using his White House influence to engineer the release of each of the imprisoned men. In addition, $15,000 would need to be paid to Bradley Eben, a lawyer whose mother worked in the Truman White House as a liaison between the President and Attorney General Tom Clark. Clark was the key player in the corrupt equation. He was known for doing 'favours' for the Mob.

All were paroled exactly one week after an application was lodged on 6 August 1947. The authorities howled in protest, judges and prosecutors wrote to Tom Clark, but a Federal Parole Board had voted unanimously for release without the normal paperwork. They hadn't even seen the notes on the case or the records of the hoodlums. One legislator challenged the move, asking if it was true the Parole Board had taken half a million dollars in return for the gangsters' freedom. The charge was never denied. Or, of course, admitted.

The House Expenditures Committee recommended that the gangsters be sent back to prison. The keenly worded report suggested the paroles had been granted in questionable circumstances and identified Paul Dillon as being a personal friend of President Truman and Attorney General Clark. Yet it said it could find no evidence that anyone had been bribed, only that 'a Good Samaritan' had spent money to help the release.

That Good Samaritan was 'Joe Batters' Accardo, who had made certain that the $200,000 in taxes and fines due were paid as 'goodwill'. His main mobsters were instructed in detail to take cash to Paul Dillon's office and to 'drop the money on his desk and leave'. When this had been done, it allowed Dillon to tell the parole hearing that 'a bunch of strangers and good and concerned citizens donated the money'. When Lou Campagna was asked about this by the Congressional Committee asked to investigate, he said he didn't know who any of the 42 strangers were.

'Do you believe in Santa Claus?' he was asked.

'Yes, yes. After all this, I suppose I do . . . I mean, if you were me, wouldn't you?'

The Committee offered in its report: 'The Syndicate has given the most striking demonstration of political clout in the history of the Republic.' And indeed it had.

On 13 August 1947, after less than three years in jail, they were all released on parole – on condition they stayed away from organised crime figures. Paul Ricca, who'd taken over from Nitti, put 'Joe Batters' Accardo in the leader's chair. But 'the Waiter' still placed it where he wanted it. It was an effective partnership and a clever if evil line-up bolstered by the support of Ricca's favoured henchman, Sam Giancana, who was tight with Lou Campagna. It would be Sidney Korshak who would guide them in Hollywood, and even give advice and help to wildcat Mickey Cohen, who was now running Hollywood on his own, fighting the LAPD's just as rough and violent Gangster Squad, formed in 1946 to keep the East Coast Mafia out of Hollywood.

Johnny Rosselli was also in search of new areas and starlets to exploit, including the Nevada hot spot Las Vegas. It was wide open there, as it was in Los Angeles, now that Benjamin Siegel was dead – another piece of collateral damage at the beginning of the Mob's new era in Hollywood.

4

A BADLANDS' BOUQUET

'How could I have known that murder could sometimes smell like honeysuckle?'
— Walter Neff (Fred MacMurray),
Double Indemnity, 1944

WHILE JOHNNY ROSSELLI AND HIS HOLLYWOOD EXTORTION associates were languishing in prison, Benny Siegel was playing his part in Meyer Lansky's masterplan to control gambling worldwide. He was helping create Las Vegas: the snag being he was a gambler, not a developer. Details were not his speciality; he could do murder and extortion, but architects' drawings often left him baffled and frustrated – and very angry.

He was under enormous pressure. The Syndicate had gambling operations in place along the East Coast, in the Midwest and in Florida. Cuba was a Mafia-controlled island. Siegel had got himself much kudos with the success – more than $8 million a year – of the radio transmission horse-racing service that fed results to illegal bookies and their customers. Success wasn't a word you'd throw around southern Nevada and early Las Vegas, with its worn-out gambling halls along US Highway 91 and thousands of acres of desert going all the way to the horizon. Yet the wiseguys were there; they could see potential. Gambling was legal, which is always a plus for businessmen, as it allows for 'tax-free' profits through skimming. A casino makes $50 million, you declare $14 million. It is done in the books and physically, with suitcases of cash being removed from the casino 'cages'. An early Las Vegas trick was for a high-roller to win big and walk away with a pile of cash that would later be 'laundered' with all the rest of the money. And, of course, big winners made good advertising.

It was Siegel's job to make the Mob the biggest winners of all in Las Vegas. With Moe Sedway, he moved into town, taking rooms at the El Cortez Hotel. Others, such as Tony Cornero, were already there, but the Lansky team moved quickly – although it fell at the first fence: Siegel tried to buy into the El Rancho gambling set-up but was rebuffed. Other investors created the Last Frontier, which was the future: a resort with a swimming pool and tennis, and air-conditioned rooms. The Syndicate then bankrolled Siegel and Sedway to take over the El Cortez and the two were operating it in person by Christmas 1945. The war was over and money was more available; real estate was booming and in August 1946 the El Cortez was sold for $600,000.

Benny Siegel had cash. And dreams. An often lethal combination. He also had Hollywood. And he'd been smitten by one of history's great femme fatales, the enjoyably amoral Virginia Hill of whom Longy Zwillman had remarked she 'didn't look too hard to know'. She wasn't.

Hill had arrived in Hollywood via honky-tonk bars (shimmying for $20 a week) and dance halls in her hometown of Alabama ('I left because enjoying life was illegal') and many towns en route (hooking for 50 cents to $5). She said she was 27 years old when she met Siegel.

Along the way, she'd spent time with the Fischetti brothers, Rocco and Charlie, 'Joe Batters' Accardo, the Franks, Costello and Nitti, Murray Humphreys and Joe Adonis. She got around. She'd also had four husbands: a Mexican rhumba dancer, an Austrian ski instructor and two others whose employment details she'd forgotten. Her one steady relationship was with money. But still, there was never enough.

When Siegel arrived in Hollywood, the top racing service was James Ragen's Continental Racing Services, which supplied results to thousands of bookies between Chicago and

Los Angeles, each of whom paid Ragen between $100 to
$1,200 a week. The Chicago-Irishman lived up to his breeding.
He was his own man, who shot and cut up people who got in
his way, and he did the work himself. Which was understandable,
for he had turned Continental into an enviable money-making
machine. It had a monopoly on the transmission of minute-
by-minute information from local racetracks to bookies
throughout America.

The US Government described Continental thus: 'Through
distributors it gets its news by wigwag or telephone from the
tracks, flashes it by Western Union teletype throughout the
country. It supplies last-minute news on track conditions,
horses scratched, changes in jockeys, last-minute odds at the
parimutuel (betting) windows. Big-time bookies must have it
to lay off bets when a "hot" horse gets a dangerously high play,
to get the results of a race 1,000 miles away in a matter of
minutes and to keep a winning customer on the hook for the
next race. In effect, it takes betting out of the racetrack and
makes it a nationwide operation at countless bookie outlets.'

And it was worth millions a year. It made Frank Nitti go
green – and he didn't like Ragen's solo act. With Paul Ricca, he
organised the rival Trans-America wire, with their men across
the nation controlling local outlets and pressurising Ragen's
business. Siegel, with the help of Jack Dragna, was ordered to
run Trans-America. Ragen became difficult and was gunned
down in a noisy ambush on a South Side Chicago corner. He
survived and was taken to hospital but never left. A Mob nurse
injected him with mercury when he showed signs of recovering.

Continental Racing Services was carved up – and Siegel's
rival, Jack Dragna, was named to run the California office. All
Siegel received was a visit from Murray Humphreys, who told
him to shut down the Trans-America wire service. Siegel told
Humphreys where to go – back to Chicago, to tell Nitti and
Ricca that for him to close Trans-America in Nevada, Arizona
and southern California it would cost them $2 million. In cash.
The Chicago Outfit became concerned about Benny Siegel.

Paul Ricca told Charlie Fischetti to get someone close to

Siegel. Virginia Hill was perfect. She'd worked with Charlie and Joe Fischetti, who ran American prostitution; she'd been 'adopted' by 'Greasy Thumb' Guzik and his wife. They'd offered her a madam job, running a couple of dozen Chicago brothels, but she said she wanted to go 'up in the world – not up and down all the time'.

Guzik then introduced her to Joe Epstein, a shy mob accountant who was his number two money man. He was Central Casting: everything about him was mild – except his habits. He liked his vices and he very much liked Virginia Hill, who became his – handsomely paid – mistress. She also worked for him as a courier, bringing suitcases full of dirty money from Chicago, Kansas City, Cleveland and Los Angeles to Syndicate-owned and run banks in Cuba, Mexico, the Dominican Republic, France and Switzerland. There, the money was laundered, usually at a price of ten to twenty cents on a dollar, and then invested in legitimate businesses.

The financial Mata Hari was now sent to Hollywood as an under-the-covers spy. And, of course, she wasn't so hard to know. She reported her conversations with Siegel to the Fischetti brothers in Chicago, although they never trusted her either. So bad was the paranoia that Paul Ricca ordered Johnny Rosselli to start an affair with Virginia Hill so he could 'bug' her, as it were. She knew Siegel had tried to recruit Dragna and Jimmy Fratianno, as he was planning his own organisation in Nevada. Siegel was a regional problem at a time when the Mob was intent on going worldwide with their grandiose schemes for profit. He was a dinosaur. He should be extinct.

When she had the time – which might seem improbable – Virginia was also a lover of and an international courier for Lucky Luciano. All that cash had to go somewhere and Meyer Lansky had a network of friendly banks headquartered out of Geneva and Paris, where Hill would pick up the latest styles on her 'fashion trips' after making her financial deposits. She wore availability as if Chanel made it: effective at customs and immigration in London, Rome and Paris; downright enchanting in the safe deposit world of Zurich and Geneva. She played her role to perfection.

Benny Siegel never knew how connected she was, but it was her contacts, through Luciano, that helped him establish the Mob's Mexico–Californian drug connection, a useful weapon in controlling Hollywood. Drugs had always been Lucky Luciano's money maker of choice.

Co-creator of the Syndicate, Luciano had been set up and convicted by the crusadingly ambitious special prosecutor Thomas Dewey in 1936 and received a jail term of from 30 to 50 years on cleverly conjured prostitution charges. He went to prison but ran the Syndicate from there, giving orders through Frank Costello. Luciano was an absentee boss – *away at college*, in the patois – but continued to have great influence and receive equally great payments. He consulted from Dannemora Penitentiary in far upstate New York, where his favourite Sicilian dishes were prepared for him.

Luciano then got truly lucky. American military intelligence ruled that he could help in the war effort, with his Sicilian connections, and supply intelligence that could thwart enemy attacks. He was moved to Great Meadow Prison in Comstock, near Albany, New York, and the deal was agreed that at an appropriate time he'd be freed. With the war over, 4 January 1946 was found to be appropriate and the same man who put him away, White House aspirant and now Governor Thomas Dewey of New York, commuted his sentence.

The cruel news for Charles Lucky Luciano was that he was going home, to Italy, back to Sicily where he'd started nearly 50 years earlier as Salvatore Lucania. That detail was non-negotiable, Luciano, Lansky and the boys found out. But Luciano had some cheer about the deal, for he and Lansky had mapped out Cuba and that was only 90 miles from mainland America.

Luciano went on a road trip of Italy following his return to Palermo. After Rome, he moved on to Naples and it was there he received a rallying call, a note reading: December, Hotel Nacional. Which is where he was on 22 December in 1946.

He'd bed-hopped around Venezuela, gone from Caracas to Mexico City, and Aerovias Q Airlines took him to Havana. He was met by Meyer Lansky. The two men were playing hosts to some of the giant gangster figures of the world, about two dozen of them, including clever killer Albert Anastasia and the New York boss Joseph Bonanno. Moe Dalitz and Syndicate commission member Longy Zwillman led the hugely influential Jewish mobsters. Also very present were Carlos Marcello out of New Orleans, and Santo Trafficante Junior, who'd moved to Cuba from Tampa, Florida, that year to watch over his family's slice of the island's gambling action created by his father. All the major Mafia families were represented at the official meetings on the two top floors of the Hotel Nacional. It was like a reformatory school reunion amid intriguing architecture on the spectacular Havana oceanfront: with extracurricular, explicit personal entertainment, sex and menace. And a singer. Frank Sinatra.

Sinatra, the first modern pop superstar and wannabe Mafia man was the cover for the Havana Conference. The story went that the guys had got together simply to hear him sing. Lansky's gambling tsar, Dino Cellini, claimed they paid him *not* to sing.

Things almost went sour from the start. Sinatra had arranged for a friend, showgirl and aspiring actress Dorothy Lyma, who called herself Alora Gooding, to meet him there. Sinatra was 31 years old and cockily confident, but not so much as to refuse to appear for the wiseguys. But he wanted some fun too, and Alora, who had spent time in joints around Reno, Nevada, was a lot of fun. She'd worked for Benny Siegel and been around with some of the boys. She knew how to look after herself, having been brought up by a gun-crazy father in the California farmland. Sinatra had met her on the set of the 1941 film *Las Vegas Nights*, when he was singing with Tommy Dorsey's Band. Their affair had run around his performance schedule since then. Happy and excited, Alora drove down from her home in Sacramento to Los Angeles and flew from there to Miami and on to Cuba.

There was edgy, newly customised private security around

the Hotel Nacional, especially the areas blocked out for the conference. Most of the guards were off-duty policemen or army officers. They had instructions to keep everybody but the VIP American visitors out. Alora was in her suite with Sinatra when a crashing noise made her jump out of bed. She rushed over to the window, which overlooked a large courtyard filled with coconut palms and a mini-forest of soft-leaved vines. The high black entrance gates were open and two men in jackets and ties were running towards their part of the hotel. They had something in their hands.

She yelled at the half-awake, startled Sinatra: 'They've got guns. They're coming to kill us.' A hunting rifle was leaning against the wall on the other side of their room. Sinatra began scrabbling through a suitcase. He pulled out a revolver but hadn't turned around when there were shouts at their door and the men burst in.

Alora had the rifle expertly armed and pointed at the door. She fired. The man on her left, wearing a dark-grey, striped suit fell to the floor. A second shot rang out, from behind the intruders, and the other business-suited man fell backwards into the hallway. Both were dead. Now, other men in suit trousers and dress shirts were suddenly all over the hallway and crowding into the bedroom, which now smelled of cordite.

'You killed that guy!' said Sinatra, lighting a cigarette.

Her voice shaking, Alora protested: 'But they had guns. They were coming to kill us.'

'Those weren't guns. They were walkie-talkies.'

Alora collapsed on the floor and began screaming. Sinatra sat on the bed and said nothing. The two bodies and any fuss were swept away by the time Alora was moved out of Havana the next morning to a lifetime of invisibility. Sinatra still had to sing for his supper.

The bizarre incident was not allowed to disrupt the conference schedule. It was not even generally discussed. When Sinatra even mentioned it, he was shut up: 'Leave it, forget about it.'

As always, it was Mr Fixit, Johnny Rosselli, who was brought in to look after Sinatra. He showed him around. They had their picture taken – by agents from the US Federal Bureau of Narcotics. There was another federal happy snap of Sinatra with his arm around Luciano on a balcony of the Hotel Nacional. There was another of him carrying a suitcase into Cuba, but he always said you could never get $3 million into such a small bag. Rosselli had told the Syndicate for some years that Sinatra was a weak and greedy guy, that he had a voice and a big cock but no balls. But he was and would be useful.

Luciano was given a tribute from the gathering, $200,000 in crisp bills, but before the talking proper began the delegates were invited to indulge in all the delights of Havana, in and around the hotel. The tasty, mild Bacardi rum and the giant cigars put a little pep in the salsa for the crime convention. The idea was for them to see how wide open a town it was, a place for vast investment of time and money, of anything goes.

One big question on the gathering's agenda was whether Benny Siegel would have to go. Maybe he had too many stars in his eyes, for it hadn't gone well in Las Vegas for the Mob – and *their* money.

It was at the Café Trocadero on Sunset Strip that it all began to go wrong for Siegel, just as it had for Thelma Todd. The nightspot was owned by Billy Wilkerson, founder of the *Hollywood Reporter* daily magazine, and it was there Siegel had met him on a night out with Virginia Hill. Wilkerson had talked about his dreams of a lavish casino in Las Vegas. He'd have all the gambling and the drinks and the glamour, but he'd also have Hollywood. He'd bring in star entertainers and bankroll famous faces to play the tables. Hollywood would be Vegas, and Vegas would be Hollywood in his hotel-casino of wall-to-wall starlets. There would be no clocks, even to tell you the time. Or anyone to whisper how much you were losing.

An addicted gambler, Billy Wilkerson had the same dreams as Benny Siegel but was running out of cash to make them come true. On the Syndicate's behalf, Siegel solved that worry, taking 67 per cent of the project to create the Flamingo Hotel-Casino for $650,000. He and Wilkerson believed it might take a couple of hundred thousand more – $1 million tops. The money vanished, as did the next investment, as building costs rose uncontrollably. Contractor after contractor walked in the front door of the Flamingo and drove a Cadillac out the back. Bugsy spent money wildly. He had a fourth-floor master suite with side exits, three-foot-thick concrete walls, trapdoors in the wardrobes leading to the basement garage – and an always fully fuelled getaway car.

He had Virginia Hill in the master suite with him, Countess di Frasso in another room, and actress and wartime pin-up Marie 'the Body' McDonald in another. Along the corridor was Wendy Barrie. The English actress put up with a great deal from her lover – and his other lover, Virginia Hill, who in the Flamingo lobby used her useful right hook to dislocate her rival's jaw.

The flamboyant gangster's business life was even more complicated. It wasn't just a personal spending spree that was doing runaway arithmetic with the construction budget; he was paying top dollar because of hangover wartime shortages: he'd get black market material delivered during the day, which was stolen in the night and sold back to him the next day. A suicidal way of doing business.

By October 1946, the money spent stood at more than $4 million. The Syndicate asked for an accounting and a panicked Siegel raised money on non-existent stock and spent more and more, to a final upfront money total of $6 million, to have the Flamingo open for Christmas and the holiday season. Still, the rooms wouldn't be ready for occupancy. Gamblers would come – and go somewhere else to spend the night and their money. It was a bad, bad business, with other people's investments.

Which is what Lansky and Luciano, Benny Siegel's childhood friends and fellow teenage monsters, were looking at that December in Havana. They were in every sense blood brothers. Lots of people had liked Benny. OK, he'd been a pain in the ass at times, but that was the pistolero he was. But their quick-tempered and frenetic friend had lost his and their control. He'd also been making a noise about setting up his own Mob. Business was business. Lansky voted for the death sentence, Luciano gave the go ahead.

Their friend had wasted money and skimmed a fortune in construction funds cash, which now rested, delivered by Virginia Hill, in the calm of Switzerland and points east and west. Whatever boyhood loyalties existed in the room at the Hotel Nacional, it was decreed that Bugsy must die and the Syndicate's business interests and its massive investment put on a level footing. Frankie Carbo, who'd killed with Siegel and was respected for this kind of work, would do it; if there were any mishap, he would never mutter a word to the authorities.

The hapless Flamingo Hotel opened on Boxing Day 1946 in some of the worst weather Nevada had known. It rained in a desert. The air conditioning didn't work. George Raft was his faithful self and was present amid a few other celebrities and the decorators' debris. In the showroom, Xavier Cugat and his band worked with Mob favourite Jimmy Durante and other acts. It was all summed up rather well by another flashy character, the white-suited, dandyish author Tom Wolfe, in *The Kandy-Kolored Tangerine-Flake Streamline Baby* (published 1965) in which he reported:

> For the grand debut of Monte Carlo as a resort in 1879, the architect Charles Garnier designed an opera house for the Place du Casino. For the debut of Las Vegas as a resort in 1946, Bugsy Siegel hired Abbott and Costello, and there, in a way, you have it all.

Wolfe didn't explain that Abbott and Costello were not even top of the bill; that evening and into 1947, the casino lost $300,000. And there weren't many laughs in that either.

Siegel closed down the Flamingo and reopened it with habitable rooms and the Andrews Sisters as a crowd-pleasing attraction on 1 March 1947. It all began to work, but far too late and he knew it. He'd drive down to Beverly Hills every couple of weeks and on his return have the locks on his Flamingo suite changed. Every time. He had chairs brought to him and sat in the hotel corridor with Virginia Hill, watching the locksmith complete the work. Outwardly, he displayed no other tics of fear. All he could do was wait. He knew.

On 8 June 1947, Virginia Hill was telephoned from Chicago by the Mob bookkeeper Joe Epstein, who told her to tell Siegel she was going to France to seek out wine for the Flamingo's cellars. The accountant met her at Midway Airport in Chicago and gave her $5,000. She flew on to Paris.

Frankie Carbo used a US Army rifle to take Siegel down, as he sat by an undraped window at Virginia Hill's place in North Linden Drive up from Santa Monica Boulevard, in the richer reaches of Beverly Hills. Benny Siegel was contently reading Braven Dyer's column on baseball in the *Los Angeles Times* sports pages when he was killed.

Moments before he died he asked his dinner companion Al Smiley who was in the room with him: 'Can you smell the flowers?' There were none. If you can smell blooms and they're not present, superstition says, however irrationally, death is in the air.

Two pinpoint accurate .30 bullets shattered his face. The close-up fireplay that followed by Carbo's two regular associates was redundant and made needless, extra mess of Siegel and the room. It was instructions: there was to be no lingering in his death. One steel-jacket shell crushed his nose at the right eye. The other went straight through his right cheek and out his neck. The instant, intense internal pressure punched his right eye from its socket, like a passenger being sucked out of a punctured jet plane. It was found nearly 15 feet away from his body when the police discovered him sprawled, thrown back with the impact of the bullets, on a sofa, a shiny chintz luxury Virginia Hill had bought from a store at the corner of Beverly and Wilshire Boulevards.

That Carbo did the job was no surprise to Mickey Cohen.

Carbo liked Siegel, but this was business: 'That guy would do it to you just as fast as you'd do it to him. Some guys rose faster and faster in the racket world because they were willing to do things asked of them. I knew that Benny's Vegas propositions and the Flamingo took off very bad. It makes people think if the right thing is being done, especially if you've been bankrolled the way Benny was by the organisation.

'The day before the put-out on Benny, he called me over. He didn't seem to be extra nervous or anything like that. He talked a little bit staccato anyway. He says: "Ya got armament? What kind of equipment have you got?" I was his caretaker for equipment. It was like him having it, but it was in my control. I had certain stashes, certain farmhouses and ranch places, which were like his. I says: "Whatever you want. I got whatever you need."'

Cohen then arranged for Siegel to meet up the next day with his team's best shooter, Hooky Rothman, for a little extra protection: 'There's no doubt that Benny felt that there was some kind of come-off going to take place. In things like this, you know sometimes an order is given and you don't have any choice. It's one of those things. There was no other way it could go for Benny.

'Certain people are called by certain people to turn a certain trick, it's an honour for them to be able to do this piece of work. And to do it to perfection is a great thing to them. For the job itself, there was probably no pay whatsoever. If you got to pay somebody to do a particular piece of work, that's a dangerous situation. If you can't do it yourself or the people with you aren't faithful enough to want to do it as you or as part of you, it's worthless. Because you're always in fear of what they've got on you.

'It's like you pick up the newspaper and some poor ignorant bastard has went to hire some two-dollar hoodlum for $2,500. I used to get letters: "I want to get rid of my husband. How much would you charge for this?" It's silly and ridiculous.

'Power's a funny thing. It's strong at a time and then it

wanes. Somebody calls your hole card and it's like a dam – one little hole can blow the whole thing . . .'

Mickey Cohen had reluctantly stayed out of the way on the direct orders of the one man he would listen to: Meyer Lansky. Virginia Hill was, of course, conveniently out of town. She was in Europe. She told the police an elaborate story: she'd had a lovers' tiff with Benny, gone to stay with her generous friend Joe Epstein in Chicago and then flown to France for the fashions. She was travelling with a full four-set of luggage and a wardrobe trunk. She'd gone from Paris to Geneva on a specific schedule set by Lansky. Hill was in everything she did for money, not love. She, like Lansky, knew that if Siegel had to die, he would, and it was business. Happily, she could afford to mourn her lover in some style. The Los Angeles' Coroner's Report 37448 said he'd died of a cerebral haemorrhage, but she knew the cause of it all was megalomania.

A telephone message is said to have been recorded after the killing. It was to Jack Dragna: '*The insect was killed.*' The tape recording has never been found, but it remains part of the story of the death of 'Bugsy' Siegel.

Within an hour of Frankie Carbo pulling the trigger, the safe in Siegel's suite at the Flamingo was opened and emptied. The intruder had the combination, which was known only to Siegel and Virginia Hill, but she, of course, was out of town. As fast as the safe was cracked, the new management moved in.

Bookmaker Gus Greenbaum, a gregarious alumni of the Lower East Side, operated out of Phoenix, only a short, bumpy cartwheel of a drive away in Arizona. He was unpacked, showered and strolling the casino in a tuxedo before anyone knew about the new boss. By his side were Morris Rosen and the clever, closed-lipped Moe Sedway.

They didn't erect a sign telling gamblers *Under New Management*. But the Flamingo, like Las Vegas, most certainly was. The Syndicate had the Thunderbird (Rosemary Clooney gave her first Las Vegas performance there), the Stardust, the Desert Inn, the Sahara and a silent piece of every new build before the foundation was laid. Jimmy Hoffa from the

Teamsters Union invested in desert developments, gambling many millions of dollars of his members' pension fund. Sidney Korshak, counsel to large corporations, associate of important political figures, was a major influence in Jimmy Hoffa's Teamsters Union. The casinos began making legal riches beyond dreams, all of which was carefully counted by the hierarchy and then millions immaculately and illegally skimmed off in suitcases and trunks and even Greyhound-style buses adapted for the job with false compartments for the cash. The country was travelling too, into Eisenhower's 1950s, to an anthem of renewal, towards a post-war boom and the American Dream of prosperity for all.

The Mafia's Hollywood didn't share such democratic dreams. Mickey Cohen wasn't up for any Musketeer's code. He was all for one – and only one. Himself. That was always the priority. A connected gangster now retired to Nevada believes that Cohen set up Siegel's assassination. He knew Siegel's schedule and his routine when he was in Hollywood. Cohen's man, Al Smiley, was with Siegel when he was gunned down. The big drapes over the windows of Virginia Hill's front room were open, giving the shooters a clear view of those inside. While in the target room, Smiley wasn't even marked in the hail of gunfire. It was a theory the LAPD followed when they called on Cohen. They quizzed him, but he 'knew nothing about it'. And why should he? He and Benny were close. Of course, in later life, he'd say: *There was no other way it could go for Benny*.

There was also no other way for the cops to go. They had no evidence. Although that wasn't something that overly bothered the Gangster Squad. After all the years of corruption within the police department and City Hall, this 'new broom' had no grasp of how strong a grip the Syndicate already had on the film capital. And they were squeezing ever tighter. There was just a little local feuding – and blood – spilling over into their plans.

With his nemesis Benny Siegel dead, the always two-streets-behind Jack Dragna saw one of Capone's *opportoonities*. The only obstacle to his taking over the city was Mickey Cohen. It was way beyond time that he was wasted. Still, Dragna was as Mickey Mouse as they all said he was. Cohen was not willing to relinquish any of the rackets or the war, so the 'Battle of Sunset Strip' was on. And on the fringes of it stood the LAPD's supposedly untouchable Gangster Squad.

As a legal front, Cohen had several businesses, but the main one was an upmarket men's clothing store called Michael's Haberdashery on Sunset Boulevard, which he used as an office. On 18 August 1948, stick-up man Jimmy 'the Weasel' Fratianno, with his wife and daughter, visited Michael's Haberdashery to collect tickets to see Ethel Merman in the Hollywood run of *Annie Get Your Gun*.

Cohen had worked with Fratianno in Cleveland; he'd also helped the prolific killer to relocate to Los Angeles after a spell in prison. But Fratianno – who Frank Sinatra told me in February 1981 was 'a little fink' – was in with Dragna. As part of the Italian Mob – *Italian* – Fratianno, like Dragna, didn't like the idea of a Jew running Hollywood crime. That was an Italian's job.

The plan was that after the group had left the shop, a hit team, with Frank Bompensiero, Fratianno's best friend, as the lead shooter, would be waiting. It all went Disneyland.

Fratianno shook hands with the owner as he left Michael's Haberdashery and immediately Cohen went to wash his hands in the back bathroom, where there was also a toilet cubicle. He did that 50 or 60 times a day, so obsessed with cleanliness was he. Fratianno signalled and the shooting started.

'Slick' Snyder was sitting at Cohen's front desk and was shot. Cohen heard it: 'They shot Slick first. They thought he was me. I fell to the floor and put me feet up against the toilet door. I heard another blast. Jimmy Rist got hit – they just shot off a piece of his ear.'

But it was the dumbly loyal Hooky Rothman who was killed. He'd been parking Cohen's Cadillac when he heard gunfire and ran towards the trouble. Bompensiero, wearing sunglasses and a white Panama hat pulled low over his forehead, stuck a sawn-off shotgun in Hooky Rothman's face. Hooky wasn't frightened – his boss had been shot at. He swung at the shotgun with his arm and it went off, obliterating his face and killing him instantly.

Neither Cohen nor his associates could identify the gunmen to the police. 'That isn't the way of the racket world,' he offered. 'The guys who did it aren't around any more. Hooky's brothers came out for the funeral and the oldest one said to me: "Hooky died the way he wanted to. He lived for you and he died for you, the way he wanted."'

It was another serious screw-up by Bompensiero. Hit men are supposed to check not only whether they've carried out their assignment but also if they've shot and killed the correct target.

Leo Moceri complained: 'It was Bomp's contract and he blew it. Listen, the others didn't know Mickey from a lamppost, but Bomp did. They go in there and blast away at Slick Snyder, thinking he's Mickey. Then they shoot him in the arm, for Christ's sake. While this is going on, Mickey's in the shitcan, standing on top of the sink. They didn't pump one slug through that door. Like a bunch of cowboys, they panicked and ran out instead of finishing the job.'

No one, it seemed, could knock off Mickey Cohen. By simply surviving, he was the King of Hollywood – Mafia branch.

He was also king with the stars. He lived off the story that he'd robbed Betty Grable at a nightclub before she was famous and that later they became friends. And he went around with Robert Mitchum, Dean Martin and Jerry Lewis, and he adored Judy Garland. Of course, he wasn't the kind of 'friend' you could easily tell to get lost. But it was all in some way part of Hollywood. It was OK. Mickey Cohen arranged things.

In 1951, he set up a celebrity dinner for fading singer Frank Sinatra at the Beverly Hills Hotel, which celebrated the centenary of its opening in 2012. It was in the same suite where they'd held one for H.G. Wells in 1935. Wells tempted a larger and better crowd. By then, the landmark pink hotel set on

Sunset Boulevard, just as you lose the cooling air of the Pacific, was the pivotal glamour spot, the starting gate for Hollywood. It's where a young actor called Robert Evans was 'discovered' poolside by Norma Shearer in 1956. The mad, bad and absurdly rich Howard Hughes kept a permanent set of bungalows at the hotel. It was a discreet place to be (Clark Gable and Carole Lombard had carried out their tragic affair in Bungalow Four) and to be taken, as Johnny Rosselli's friend Marilyn Monroe often was.

Cohen twisted easily between the glamour of Hollywood and his own complex way of making money for himself and the Mob. With muscle and an inherent cunning, he was a success: he had 500 bookies under his influence, all using dozens of telephones, for each of which he demanded $40 a week in return for protection. He found the Los Angeles Police Department a little too difficult to corrupt and had moved out into Los Angeles County to any other jurisdiction that would have him. His favourite was Burbank, home of the Warner Brothers Studios. In 1950, the Burbank chief of police bought a 56-foot yacht, cash.

The lanky actor-comedian 'Red' Skelton, an important star in the 1940s and '50s, was close to Cohen, as was Jimmy 'You Must Remember This' Durante, who had been under the Mob's control, it seemed, for ever. Skelton was a favourite entertainer of Johnny Rosselli's Chicago connection Salvatore 'Momo' Giancana, who had been one to watch from the start.

Sam Giancana was arrested for murder in 1925 but wasn't prosecuted, the main witness being murdered himself. He had been a driver-shooter at the St Valentine's Day Massacre and at other prominent Prohibition events, and while he had spent some years in prison, by Eisenhower's time the somewhat Jacobean figure was the controller of protection rackets, pinball betting, prostitution, numbers, narcotics, loan-sharking, extortion, counterfeiting and bookmaking. In getting all this power, he is said, in his FBI files, to have killed more than 200 people, many of whom were tortured. It was never a good plan to piss off Giancana, but some people never learn.

Momo was annoyed with Skelton's 'manager', a Mob appointee who got the comedian into the best nightspots and movies. He wasn't kicking back the correct amount of cash and so Giancana sent him a message via Cohen. It wasn't subtle. He was sitting in the Hawaiian-themed Sugie's Tropics restaurant on Rodeo Drive in Beverly Hills when Cohen walked in and pinpointed him. The gangster clambered onto the table and, as the startled victim looked up, kicked him almost to death. Cohen flipped one of those little drinks umbrellas at the unconscious figure as a final humiliation. Maybe he'd been watching George Raft films.

Giancana owned the Worldwide Actors Agency outright, but his 'casting' was never made public, although actors with political leanings such as Ronald Reagan – a president of the Screen Actors' Guild before he got the other presidential job – got help with their careers. Sinatra's early success owed much to him and Moe Dalitz, who, with his partner Meyer Lansky, controlled the Desert Inn, where Sinatra made his Vegas debut in 1951. Giancana was a devotee of Ernest Hemingway and had liked Gary Cooper in *For Whom the Bell Tolls* (1943); he met Cooper, but not to talk about the film – the conversation centred on Hemingway, whom Cooper knew well. There were such crossovers.

At that time, Marilyn Monroe, who'd walked on in *All About Eve* (1950) and sparked interest as the crooked lawyer's lover in *The Asphalt Jungle* (1951), was gathering a formidable following. She was one to watch.

The Mocambo nightclub was hesitant to hire singer Ella Fitzgerald because she was black, so Monroe telephoned the owner and said she would take a front table every night if they hired Fitzgerald. The deal went through. The jazz genius said she found Monroe to be 'an unusual woman – a little ahead of her times'. What was most unusual was that no strings were attached – it was a purely benevolent gesture. There were few of them in Hollywood.

For many stars, actors, directors and stage performers, the incredible money they could and would command had often to be shared with the silent guys. Many of Hollywood's agencies, like the unions, had Mob interest, if not control.

And everyone wanted to be making movies. Murray Humphreys, favourite Mob manager of two Presidents, was believed by Giancana to be 'the nicest guy in the organisation' but, of course, that wasn't saying much. Humphreys worked to educate himself, not to be a gangster. He learned what to wear, when to wear it. He practised his diction and improved his vocabulary. He adored expensive, well-made suits and wore them well. He was elegant and you'd bet he peed iced water.

His daughter Llewella said that in the autumn of 1952 she walked into the living room, where her father was entertaining several men. He asked her: 'What do you think of Eisenhower?' She said she'd vote for him if she was old enough. Dwight Eisenhower stood up out of the easy chair he was sitting in and said: 'Thank you very much, young lady.'

Humphreys went to Hollywood and enjoyed himself; there, he became friendly with the actor Fred MacMurray, one of the world's highest-paid actors. He'd reinvented his career in 1944, when for director Billy Wilder he starred as the insurance salesman Walter Neff in the Raymond Chandler-scripted *Double Indemnity* who goes along with wicked Phyllis Dietrichson (Barbara Stanwyck) to kill her husband.

The star-struck Humphreys convinced Giancana to make his own trip to Hollywood. Giancana regarded the movies and movie stars as exploitable commodities, but he liked the look of the girls – the voice of Phyllis McGuire, of the headline McGuire Sisters, particularly engaged him – and enjoyed the attention and status he was given. It was the first of many visits. The mobster asked producer Joe Pasternak to show his teenage daughter Antoinette around the studios and he introduced her to Jimmy Stewart, Walter Pidgeon, Spencer Tracy and Greer Garson, while Giancana met with Johnny Rosselli.

Llewella Humphreys and her mother Mary became Hollywood regulars. In 1941, they were keen to see the filming of director George Cukor's *A Woman's Face*, a courtroom melodrama built around Joan Crawford's starring role as a facially disfigured blackmailer: 'The studios had tours and we went to see the Joan Crawford picture being made. She was a very big star, at her peak then. She always worked on a closed set so that no one could come and see her. Mother really wanted to meet her. But this set on that particular day was especially closed because Joan Crawford had a scar on her face in the movie and didn't want anyone to see her.'

That wasn't going to be a problem for Mrs and Miss Humphreys. The head of MGM, Louis B. Mayer, best friend of gangster Frank Orsatti and (in 1937) the first person ever in America to be on a $1 million-a-year salary, intervened. He personally took the Humphreys over to meet his star. She wasn't best pleased, as Llewella Humphreys recalled: 'Joan Crawford stopped right in the middle of her scene and said: "Get those two out of here. I will not have it on my set. It's closed." The head of the studio went over to her and told her: "Either they stay or you go, and you are through in pictures." We watched her make the movie. That was the power at that level that Dad and the others had. Joan Crawford was very good.'

Which is more than she could say about many of the other people to whom her father introduced her. Johnny Rosselli's mainsteam reputation was tarnished. He was no longer only a handsome, rather mysterious man about Hollywood. He'd been fingered and convicted as a hood. He was on probation – legally – and back in Hollywood.

He'd spent the last years of his jail term in what was a 'country club atmosphere' of the 1940-built penitentiary in Terre Haute, Indiana. It was at the gates there that he was met by his long-time friend – and manager of boxing legend Jack Dempsey – the effervescent Jack Kearns.

Kearns was loyal. He looked after Rosselli, who'd spent his time inside learning Spanish, and drove him to Chicago, where he enjoyed his freedom for a few days. But Rosselli was anxious to get back to Hollywood.

The story goes that Kearns paid for his ticket, while other associates helped him get a second-hand Ford runaround and an apartment in Catalina Street, near the Ambassador Hotel on Wilshire in Los Angeles. Rosselli was playing a role. He had a pull on millions of dollars through the Syndicate, but for parole officers and Hollywood he was the little guy getting back on his feet.

The reality was Johnny Rosselli had bounced back into Hollywood following his unplanned time inside. He was once again the Mafia's leading man.

He never forgot showing Al Capone around 1927 Hollywood. Even in relaxed California, the big gangster's banana yellow suits and shocking pink silk shoes were outrageously over the top. Yet Capone enjoyed all the attention – which was the last thing the 'new' Johnny Rosselli wanted.

He worked his connection with Harry Cohn, who still wore the matching ruby ring, and around town, catching up with the starlets and the personalities, including Humphrey Bogart's favourite restaurant owner Mike Romanoff.

Rosselli hadn't lost his touch: dapper, debonair, the dedicated fortune hunter . . . in every sense, he was a perfect fit for the role. He could deal with them all: he knew how they all worked, how they thought. He even got a job – his only legitimate one – as an associate producer with the British-owned Eagle Lion Films, which operated out of offices on Santa Monica Boulevard towards the Pacific from the Samuel Goldwyn Studios. Bryan Foy (eldest of 'the Seven Little Foys'), who ran the place, lived over the hills in Encino and would drive in with his friend, Al Smiley.

Rosselli's other official source of income came from the Dupont Film Corporation, for whom he was a representative to Hollywood, replacing Willie Bioff. He knew nothing about film stock, but the Syndicate influenced and controlled the studios and if Dupont wanted to remain a dominant force in Hollywood it had to keep Johnny Handsome on the payroll. Dupont never complained since Rosselli had so much influence with the studio bosses; the company wanted to take the Hollywood film market from Eastman Kodak, who had a virtual lock on the market.

Rosselli was involved in the production of three films with

Aubrey Schenck, the nephew of his studio associate, Fox boss Joe Schenck. Amazingly, Joe Schenck, just out of prison himself as a result of the B&B extortion mess, had sponsored Rosselli for the job at Eagle Lion Studios. The first was *T-Men* (1947), about US Treasury agents who go undercover to bring down a counterfeiting ring. The next, *Canyon City* (1948), about a mass escape from Colorado State Penitentiary, then finally *He Walked by Night* (1948), a murder-hunt police procedural about a cop killer. With Rosselli's connections, this low-budget 'B' picture, which had the former serviceman killer hiding his rifle in a blanket, received the attention of a blockbuster, including a huge picture spread in *Life* magazine. In turn, the movie reviews were considerable and good, but Rosselli had more important masters than the critics. He answered directly to 'Joe Batters' Accardo, now the boss in Chicago, and the whispery-voiced, dead-eyes commander-in-chief Sam Giancana.

These men were going to allow him to establish the career of Marilyn Monroe and save the life and revive the career of Frank Sinatra. At the same time, they were going to let Mickey Cohen and the other street thugs enjoy their Gangster Squad war – a useful diversion for the authorities while they corrupted and compromised and plunged into the dark heart of Hollywood to put their man in the White House.

5

SHOWTIME

'See, that's federal property. This isn't. This is LA. This
is my town. Out here you're a trespasser. Out here I
can pick you up, burn your house, fuck your wife and
kill your dog. And the only thing that'll protect you is
if I can't find you. And I already found you.'
— LAPD Lieutenant Max Hoover (Nick Nolte),
Mulholland Falls, 1996

IN HOLLYWOOD, YOU ARE ONLY AS GOOD AS YOUR NEXT
deal. Or as dead.

It was the weight of the deal that the Mafia brought to town
that started the war. The *tourists* from the east were no Mr Ten
Per Cents, no nickel and dime agents. They wanted at least 30
per cent of the show – any show, be it movies, gambling, sex,
drugs . . . In fact, any vice or interest or perversion that could
turn a profit.

As always, it was about money. When they extorted
landmarks like the Mocambo Club and the Brown Derby at
Hollywood and Vine, the owners did not object, worried what
might happen to their business and their families. 'What are
you gonna do?' asked Jack O'Mara, who led the Los Angeles
Police Department's 'anything goes' ghost squad of detectives,
formed to take on these intruders. He answered his own
question by taking the mobsters up to Mulholland Drive,
which has the best views out over the Hollywood Hills and the
San Fernando Valley. 'We had a little heart-to-heart talk with

'em, emphasised the fact that this wasn't New York, this wasn't Chicago, this wasn't Cleveland. And we leaned on 'em a little, you know what I mean? Up in the Hollywood Hills, off Coldwater Canyon, anywhere up there. And it's dark at night.'

In that darkness, 'Mad' Jack would put a gun to one of their ears and say, 'You want to sneeze?' That was O'Mara's signature. The gun in the ear and a few suggestive words: 'Do you feel a sneeze coming on? A real loud sneeze?'

O'Mara saw the squad as a detergent as much as a deterrent. He called it 'wiping off the dandruff'.

When the squad got going after the Second World War, the organiser was a former US Marine gunner officer, Sergeant Willie Burns, of the LAPD. He was an inspired choice. When a group of hoods threatened his family, he called in the Marine – himself. And four of his cops. They went out and ran a drive-by shooting on the mobster's new Cadillac. All carried Thompson machine guns. All emptied their 50-round cartridge drums into the car. The mobster came around the next day. There had been a 'misunderstanding'.

Burns did not want that with his new team. They all had to know what they were in for. It was some time later, through grand jury testimony and affidavits given in court cases, that the full throttle of the pandemonium the Gangster Squad caused among the Hollywood Mob became known. Some of those on the receiving end, like Mickey Cohen, gave their version of events, and gangster lore has rather seen it from that side of the fence. The authorities have always tried to play down the antics because this was Dodge City – and the aim was to get the black hats out of Dodge. Any which way.

The squad didn't so much have an office as parking lot meeting points. They'd ride four or five to a car – broken-down Fords with holes in the floorboards to allow fluid to be poured into the master cylinders. Most of them smoked cigars and, with the car fumes, they were as much a hazard for the environment as the bad guys.

Willie Burns got the first 18 candidates from all across the city together near the Watts Precinct at 77th Street in

November 1946. He told them about Benny Siegel and Mickey Cohen and Jack Dragna and the rest. He told them about the shootings and the killings going on all over Hollywood, the drug jurisdiction feuds, the internal gunmen beefs and the regular gambling control killings. He pointed to the Thompson gun on his desk and explained that it was to be the weapon of choice 'to keep down these gangster killings and try to keep some of these rough guys under control'. With their Tommy guns, they'd get a carry case – yes, it was the double of a violin case – but they were cumbersome. They couldn't be left in a car; the squad had to keep them secure. O'Mara, as expected, slept with his under his bed. He was one of the seven officers who came back and signed on a week later. Including their leader Burns, they were now eight, with no office and two unmarked Fords.

The men still appeared on the duty rosters of their precincts, for where they served now did not exist. They were to be intelligent intelligence officers. The idea was to get the hoods out of the shadows and into the sunshine, then out of southern California.

The officers came in extra-large size – tall, muscled, former jocks and wartime fighters – but the image of dumb cops for hire was theirs to dispel. The LAPD had seen more scandals than bravery medals. One civic-leaning politician had attempted a clean-up campaign: he was dynamited in his car and left the city minus his left arm. The mayor and the chief of police brought in extra income by selling promotions. The rogue gene remained present throughout the LAPD, which is why Willie Burns and his guys were pretty much on their own. Which was just as well much of the time.

Jack O'Mara was 30 years old when the squad was set up. At the Police Academy, the one recruit he couldn't beat in the track events was Tom Bradley (the future Mayor of Los Angeles and a one-time potential vice presidential candidate). When he got fed up trying to outrun Bradley, he relaxed in the boxing ring. He did the usual young cop stuff of traffic patrol and the like before Pearl Harbor pitched him into the Second

World War. When he returned, he was a proper tough guy, inside and out.

In the first days of the squad, the recruits were sent an unofficial message. The barber at a Mob-controlled hairdresser who, along with hair, clipped customer's wallets as a bookie was trying to pay off police patrolmen to look the other way. O'Mara and a couple of the squad – Jerry Greeley, who was way over six feet tall, and the equally outsized Lindo Giacopuzzi – went round and gave the guy a haircut. They shaved his head with his own blunt open razor.

The rules were: there were none.

Mickey Cohen was hard to scare, but they had a go. They replaced their car number plates with out-of-state ones and, with the Illinois plates clearly showing, openly parked close to Cohen's clothing store. They pulled their hats down and their collars up and looked for all the world like hoods who'd just driven in from Chicago. Cohen's muscle kept wandering across the road from the car. To make the point, Lindo Giacopuzzi shoved the Ford in gear and drove towards them; as he swerved away, Jerry Greeley waved a Tommy gun in the air.

Part of the 'intelligence gathering' involved planting listening devices – multiple, multiple bugs – without a fuss. Or a warrant. When they listened in on Mickey Cohen, they heard him complaining about his staff and customers being rousted at Michael's Haberdashery. Willie Burns's wife received a bouquet of flowers shortly after that eavesdrop. It was a funeral arrangement. But Mickey Cohen – who only wore his suits twice and then sold them as new in the store – wasn't facing down bent vice cops or politicians on the take. But he was clever. He would claim he knew he was bugged and he fed out misinformation.

Still, there were several parties interested in getting Mickey Cohen out of the way.

He'd married the Hollywood studios freelance dance instructor Lavonne Weaver in 1940 – he got his pre-wedding blood test in his bookie's shop – and nine years later they were living on Moreno Avenue, which cuts down from Sunset

Boulevard to Wilshire Boulevard in Brentwood. It was a smart address, 513 Moreno, and was outfitted with automatic security lights. Cohen was arriving home to have dinner with his wife and George Raft. The floodlights flashed on as he came into his driveway and a gunman opened fire. Whatever they say about barn doors, the Jack Dragna shooter couldn't hit anything but the Cadillac.

Cohen drove off and returned home bleeding from shattered glass – but alive. George Raft said he looked 'a little mussed up', but the gangster insisted on supper, Raft's favourite of New York strip steak done rarely, followed by Lavonne's apple pie.

Death sneaked a little closer to Mickey Cohen on 19 July 1949. He had had dinner with Artie Samish, a powerful political lobbyist in Sacramento, putting on his sparkling show, dripping with bodyguards and starlets and members of the press, who knew he was always good for a headline.

The Los Angeles County Sheriff's Department had rousted Cohen and his men on gun charges. They were checked so often that they did not carry weapons. The California State Attorney General's Office (because of the Mob's connections) was protecting Cohen following the previous attempts on his life with the ever-present Special Agent Harry Cooper. After dinner, the crowd headed for Sherry's Café at 9039 on West Sunset Boulevard. By 3.30 a.m., Cohen felt he might go home. Sherry's owner and Cohen's friend Barney Ruditsky checked out the parking lot. It appeared clear. Two of Cohen's crew went to get his Cadillac. A valet car parker brought round Frankie Niccoli's Chrysler. At 3.50 a.m., the gunfire arrived in a smooth Remington crackle, a blast of automatic shotguns and a .30-06 super-powered rifle. The laughing partygoers fell to the ground. The evening's favourite blonde, Dee David, twisted her ankle in the melee. Colourful newspaper columnist Florabel Muir ran into the gunfire to find her story and got a blast of shotgun pellets in her backside as she turned away from the onslaught. Hoodlum Nebbie Herbert was riddled with bullets. Agent Cooper was staggering chaotically, waving his revolver and holding his bleeding gut.

Mickey Cohen, with his right arm hanging from him and bleeding, used his good one to get Cooper into the Chrysler. How the 5 ft 5 in. mobster got the broad-shouldered 6 ft Cooper into the car was, he said at the Hollywood Receiving Hospital, mind over matter. Cooper survived. Cohen had a bullet-torn shoulder. Nebbie Herbert died in hospital. It was open season on who was responsible. Killers like Jack Dragna's Jimmy Fratianno were mentioned. Big Frank Costello back east. Florabel Muir suggested the LAPD might have had something to do with it. Her theory was supported by forensics. Amid the detritus of the armed ambush were used shotgun shells that were regular LAPD issue.

The stand-off between Cohen and the cops turned into a mess for the authorities as the twentieth century reached its halfway mark. The LAPD vice squad rousted Cohen's henchman Harold 'Happy' Meltzer for illegal possession of a weapon, a revolver they themselves had planted on him. Cohen was telephoned with an offer from Sergeant Elmer Jackson of the LAPD Administrative Vice Squad that $5,000 would make the charge – and the gun – go away. He retaliated by appearing at Meltzer's trial with taped evidence of blackmail, extortion and pay-offs between the vice squad and Brenda Allen, the undisputed queen of Hollywood prostitution. She had 148 'pleasure girls' on her books who serviced the movieland elite. And special cops.

Madam Allen's lover was Sergeant Elmer Jackson. She soon turned on him, saying he and other vice officers took pay-offs. It went from the mayor's office to the chief of police until finally a grand jury investigation was ordered. It led to the resignation of Police Chief Clemence B. Horrall and a group of other officers indicted for perjury. Sergeant Willie Burns took early retirement from the Gangster Squad.

Without its hands-on protector, O'Mara and his team got a rough ride from the new boss, Chief of Police William H. Parker, who believed in policing your own harsher than you policed the city. No more vice cops pleasuring themselves with the best hookers in town and perhaps no more Gangster

Squad. Parker appointed his aide, Captain James Hamilton, in charge of the squad and prepared transfer orders for O'Mara. The tough cop kept on going – after Cohen. He planted an informant with the gangster's team and discovered that Cohen was flying to Dallas with Florabel Muir's newspaperman husband Denny Morrison.

It only took a quick phone call to the Texas Rangers for them to greet the two men as if they were a Soviet invasion. They were arrested and paraded for the Dallas newspapers. The publisher of the *Los Angeles Daily Mirror* was swamped with calls asking why his star columnist's husband was travelling with gangster Mickey Cohen. Florabel told her boss her husband was home in bed with her. He believed her and complained to Chief Parker. O'Mara was told: 'Your ass is in a sling.'

It wasn't.

When Cohen arrived back from his un-welcome in Texas, Florabel Muir's husband was on the flight with him. She dismissed the incident, but it gave O'Mara and his men high praise from the Texas Rangers, a reprieve from Chief Parker and a new name – the Intelligence Squad. It wasn't as much fun.

But as organised crime became corporate, the authorities had to combat it in kind. In Hollywood, the Mob's national consigliere Sidney Korshak had established an influential network along with his closest friend Lew Wasserman, arguably the most powerful show-business tycoon – and major presidential fixer – in America until his death in 2002. Their funny business was conducted in plush offices not at street corners.

Both sides were revealed in downtown Los Angeles in November 1951, when the Senator from Tennessee, Estes Kefauver, came to town. He was the head of a cumbersomely titled operation, the *Special Senate Committee on the Investigation of Syndicated Crime in Interstate Commerce* – it was no surprise it was known as the Kefauver Committee. Which is what it was when it became more popular on American television than Sam Giancana's favourite *The Red Skelton Show* and madcap Lucille Ball's *I Love Lucy*.

The ever polite, slow-spoken Kefauver was a womanising (Sidney Korshak would take advantage of that) and ambitious Senator, but he came from Davy Crockett's state and had an Abe Lincoln look and a folksy-frontiersman way about him as he peered through his big, horn-rimmed spectacles at the strange bunch of characters who appeared before him as he and his committee criss-crossed the country. Post-war, serenely smug America – Americans – had seen nothing like it. The Cold War and Communists seemed so distant. They could be chased away.

Now here on their doorstep was organised crime, something called 'the Mafia' in their front rooms: a parade of gamblers, thugs, hoodlums, crooked cops and sheriffs, caricature criminals, sweating and tapping their fingers nervously under the bright lights, every word recorded, every movement seized by the television cameras. These were guys talking in broken English, in 'Runyonesque'. Others, who couldn't count to five, were taking the Fifth Amendment. Even that magician with numbers, the Mob's important pay-out man, 'Greasy Thumb' Guzik followed suit, not wanting to 'criminate' himself.

Home viewers were mesmerised day after day, while in bars and cafés with televisions workers gathered voyeuristically. Shops and offices nationwide piped in day-long radio broadcasts. Although most didn't own their own sets, the American public were finding places to get this insight into crime, and specifically gambling, the other booming post-war economy in America. It was an exciting eye-opener into the dark secrets of a criminal organisation; a close-up of a deadly group, with Sicilian antecedents, that their FBI director J. Edgar Hoover had told them didn't exist. It did now in the public consciousness, as it always had in reality.

You can argue that this was the first public revelation of an underground way of life, of businesses with dubious legality, not just the Mafia in America and Europe but also groups worldwide, any sort of mafia, who pursued their own aims without thought to any rule of law or the decency expected by and imposed upon mainstream society. Under the bright

117

lights, for once, were people who bankrolled the kind of dirty tricks that brought down governments, even if it was just the middle management. These men stole politicians' power and replaced it with something more malleable. They would finance military coups and rebellions.

So often the entertainment value, to the delight of those in the shadowland, obscured the passion and the politics of it; it was neither left nor right – that didn't matter – the dark heart of it was profit at all and any cost. Glamour veiled the true depravity of gangsterism.

Kefauver had dished out subpoenas from New York and New Orleans to Detroit and Los Angeles. His lawyer-investigators went ahead to each of the 14 cities where the committee would hold hearings. Most often they were met with disdain by city controllers – elected and gangland appointed – who wanted to maintain the status quo, their way of running things, and their own power.

In New Orleans, the sheriffs said they did not exactly enforce the law when it came to gambling and prostitution in the parishes of Louisiana. 'Diamond Jim' Moran, the owner of La Louisiane restaurant in New Orleans, saw the television coverage as a marketing opportunity and while giving evidence said that his establishment, which had rows and rows of illegal slot machines, served 'food for kings'.

In Detroit, the Kefauver Committee was a hit, with nine out of ten television stations tuned in for what WWJ-TV described as 'a parade of hoodlums of every description: the most terrific television show Detroit has ever seen'. In St Louis, the city's unsettled police commissioner said he couldn't recall any details of his financial status before becoming a public official. The betting commissioner James J. Carroll refused to testify on television, stating that it was an invasion of privacy. The show was more popular than baseball's World Series broadcast a couple of months earlier. Kefauver calmly instructed him: 'This is a public hearing and anyone has a right to be here. Mr Carroll, I order you to testify.'

The jut-jawed Carroll shouted back: 'This whole proceeding

outrages my sense of propriety. I don't expect to be made an object of ridicule as long as television is on.'

Kefauver warned Carroll he'd be cited for contempt by the Senate, but still Carroll, walking jerkily around the courtroom, refused to answer any questions. Finally, he sat down. Did he know Frank Costello? Never met the man. Mickey Cohen? 'I have no recollection.'

It wasn't long before Hollywood's most notorious hoodlum got his chance to speak. The hearings on the West Coast drew the largest audiences recorded in daytime television. In a courtroom of the Federal Building in downtown Los Angeles, the Senator and his committee heard many mobsters insolently reply: 'I don't remember.'

Al Smiley, who'd been around with Benny Siegel and was there the night he got shot, refused to explain why, after Siegel's untimely death, a Houston man had asked him to come down to Texas and why Smiley had shuttled back and forth between Houston and the Beverly Club, the gambling casino near New Orleans controlled by New York's Frank Costello. Smiley's reward for these questionable services was 'a small piece of property'. What kind of property? 'Well, it may have had a few oil wells on it.'

Mickey Cohen was late for his show time. He was due at 9 a.m. at the Federal Building. He was still in bed. When he was alerted by committee investigators, he said he had to take his time dressing, as it was 'like going to a Hollywood premiere'. He was a star. As a witness. He wore a brown suit (first time out in that one), a cream shirt and brown tie. He wasn't bothered about his time keeping: 'All I got was a call to come down here, and I came down, and I'm here.'

And he lied. Dissembling was the duty of the day. He never muscled, bribed, pistol-whipped or strong-armed anyone. Prostitutes? Perish the thought. Corruption, bribes? What a dreadful suggestion. Where Cohen came unstuck was on his income. His lifestyle didn't match it. He'd borrowed the money. It wasn't much of an answer. The paradox was that there was a certain honesty about him – who expected the truth from a man who even in his Sunday best looked like a rolled-up carpet?

When the Kefauver Committee got to New York in March, the proceedings were broadcast to dozens of stations across the country. The city was obsessed with it: Broadway theatre and cinema audiences dwindled, as, for eight days, the Mob put on their show – a carnival of criminality, scandalous and wonderful all at the same time. It was theatre – tragedy and comedy, dark Jacobean and Shakespearean slapstick – featuring the likes of the 'Lemon Drop Kid' and gunsels such as 'Golf Bag' Hunt who were far more sinister than the comedy of their names.

The engaging Longy Zwillman had helped one governor of New Jersey get elected and had offered $300,000 to aid another; all he wanted in return was to choose the Attorney General, the state's lawmaker. The Mob wise man felt he was being generous. He could have asked to choose the legislature.

But the leading man was Frank Costello, the New York boss who, with his deputy Joe Adonis, ran casinos, slot machines and crap games. Costello refused (in his hoarse voice – the result of a botched childhood tonsils operation) to testify, as the microphones would prohibit him from privately consulting with his lawyer sitting next to him. Kefauver compromised: the TV cameras would not show his face but focus only on his hands (newsreel cameras captured Costello's entire face and body as he spoke). On live television, the cameras followed his meaty hands as he fingered the spectacles resting on the witness table, or moved to dab a handkerchief to his off-screen face as he dodged question after question. Mr Sinister in action. When asked to name one thing he'd done for his country, Costello growled: 'Paid my tax!'

Hollywood's home-town newspaper of record, the *Los Angeles Times*, called the testimony 'the greatest TV show television has ever aired'. The influential *Life* magazine reported on the New York testimony:

The week of March 12, 1951, will occupy a special place in history. People had suddenly gone indoors into living rooms, taverns, and clubrooms, auditoriums and back-offices. There, in eerie half-light, looking at millions of small frosty screens, people sat as if charmed. Never before had the attention of the nation been riveted so completely on a single matter.

This was *Hooray-for-Hollywood* time. The ratings were a historic high for the new medium of communication: television. It couldn't get any better. But oh yes, it could. When this particular pantomime opened in Washington DC.

Enter Virginia Hill, one-time paramour of Benjamin Siegel and gangster aristocracy, wearing a mink cape, silk gloves and a large hat, oozing Hollywood presence. She sashayed into the US Courthouse in Foley Square and told the guys in suits about other guys in suits, *fellas*, who gave her gifts and money. But as to how these men came into their money, she didn't know 'anything about anybody'. She admitted she and Siegel had fought after she'd punched out Wendy Barrie in the lobby of the Flamingo Hotel: 'He told me I wasn't a lady.' She said it in a way that questioned why anyone should think that about her. Like all her evidence, it was combative.

There was never a doubt the leading lady of the Kefauver Follies was Virginia Hill. Or, more accurately, Virginia Hill-Hauser. By the time of the hearings, she had married for the fifth time and, with Hans Hauser, an Austrian businessman, had a young son, Peter. The family were living in some luxury in Miami. Her new domestic arrangements did not inhibit her testimony. The Committee's Senator, Charley Tobey from New Hampshire, was mightily challenged as to how Miss Hill made, as it were, ends meet. Senator Tobey remained puzzled as to why so many men gave her money and presents: 'Why would they do it?' he asked.

Virginia Hill evaded the question.

The Senator kept repeating it. He was especially intrigued as to why an ageing bookmaker in Chicago, Joe Epstein, a man old enough to be her father, maintained regular payments. 'Why?' he persisted. 'Young lady, why?'

'You really want to know why?'

'I really want to know why.'

'Senator, I'm the best goddamned cocksucker in America.'

She had some renown, but for the executive mobsters her most gratifying skill was moving money around the world without detection. Outside the hearing, she was confronted by Miss Marjorie Farnsworth of the *New York Journal-American*, leading the newspaper corps into quotation action. Miss Farnsworth got thumped in the face, a vicious right hook. An intrepid man from the *New York Times* tried to intervene and was kicked in the shins. The woman the New York newspapers called 'the Queen of the Gangster Molls' marched out onto Foley Square and chucked one comment over her shoulder and back at the aghast press corps: 'I hope a fucking atom bomb falls on y'all . . .'

By then she had to leave town – quickly. The Internal Revenue Service (IRS) wanted a word about $161,343 in unpaid taxes. That the IRS knew about. Seems the 'fellas' had given her quite a bit of cash.

She had a strange effect on Walter Winchell, newspaper columnist, staccato broadcaster and friend and tipster of J. Edgar Hoover, who pondered on the effect of reality television: 'When the chic Virginia Hill unfolded her amazing life story, many a young girl must have wondered: who really knows best? Mother or Virginia Hill? After doing all the things called wrong, there she was on top of the world, with a beautiful home in Miami Beach and a handsome husband and baby!'

The one city where the hearings did not play too well was Chicago. There Sidney Korshak met privately with Kefauver and presented the Senator with photographs of himself in his Drake Hotel room, in bed with a couple of good-time girls. Kefauver had been honey-trapped by Korshak's team. Kefauver's dalliance wasn't illegal, but it gave the gangsters a little leverage and Korshak much kudos.

Such tactics didn't give the politician much anxiety, however. The hearings made him so popular he sought the Democratic Party's presidential nomination in 1952, defeating the incumbent, Harry S. Truman, in the New Hampshire primary, following which the President abandoned his campaign for renomination. Kefauver lost out to Adlai Stevenson, who himself lost to Eisenhower and his vice president, Richard Nixon.

Kefauver will always be remembered for confronting the mobsters. His committee produced an 11,000-page report, but their recommendations were ignored.

The major crime syndicates were soon back on track. In Hollywood, it was business as usual. But not quite. This was now the regime of Sidney Korshak's masters. The political connections were priceless. Korshak met and made presidents. Korshak's legitimate clients included half a dozen racetracks, major Hollywood studios, Chicago's O'Hare International Airport, the Grocery Owners' Association, the Thoroughbred Racing Association, Madison Square Garden, Gulf and Western, Las Vegas hotels, Max Factor Cosmetics, General Dynamics and Diners Club. And that was just a small percentage of his influential list.

What Sidney Korshak understood, as did Meyer Lansky with legalised gambling, was that honesty paid better. There weren't the overheads. And if you were honest in your crookery in a clever way, you didn't get caught. It worked liked this: the Mob would approach a movie studio or a union or any organisation and threaten disruption or other problems and extort money from them. It then became a negotiation, monitored by Sidney Korshak, for which he would receive a legal 'fee'; his offices in Chicago – where 'Joe Batters' Accardo's daughter Marie worked as a secretary – would process that payment, show it on their taxes as income and pay whatever was due to the United States government. The 'fee' would be the same amount as the extortion money but would now be laundered, be legal and be divided among those involved.

In January 2012, George Christy, the veteran *Hollywood Reporter* columnist, reminisced in Beverly Hills about Sidney Korshak. He'd known him for decades: 'His life was one of living in a minefield, but never stepping on anything. Sidney's cousin Leslie said that Sidney understood the power of anonymity – he wore power the way a regular guy wears a sweatsuit. He arranged multimillion-dollar loans from pension funds that financed the growth of Las Vegas's casino industry. Sidney had that envied touch in settling "impossible" labour relations between large corporations and management. He bragged that he paid off judges; a Chicago judge said Sidney had a hot line for "high-class girls" for his clients – "none of those $50 floozies!"

'Sidney represented Jimmy Hoffa of the Teamsters Union and gangster Frank Orsatti, who was MGM's Louis Mayer's best friend. It was Sidney who welded big labour to big business to big movies. It was Sidney who cleared Frank Sinatra and Joe DiMaggio of any rap when they busted into Marilyn Monroe's apartment to catch her in a sex act. If you weren't on Sidney's list for his New Year's Eve party, you feigned that you were called out of town. Or in the hospital. Sidney knew everybody.'

It's doubtful anyone, including his immediate family, really knew Sidney Korshak. In fact, it was probably better to know him only enough to say hello or accept a drink at his annual party at the Bistro on North Canon in Beverly Hills.

I saw Korshak there a few times but never at the Number One table, which was lusted over by the famous but insecure. It turned stars 'into barbarians', according to Kurt Niklas, the owner who began the business with $3,000 in investments from 60 fans of his cooking, including Sinatra, Jack Benny, George Burns, Billy Wilder, Tony Curtis and department store tycoon Alfred Bloomingdale. It was always jammed with names and fans of names, but Korshak always had his booth off to the right-hand corner, where he sat with his back to the wall and away from the window. For less public meetings, there was the private dining room upstairs, where you could hear the buzz going on down below but which worked as useful soundproofing for the more heated discussions.

Almost the whole room wore walnut tans from Miami or Palm Springs – a Hollywood tan is shades lighter – and their faces were lost against the similar dark wood of the walls and tables. They said he left a good tip but never a clean plate, but that's just waiters' gossip.

From the mid-1970s, I was friendly with Marvin Mitchelson, the Hollywood divorce lawyer, and we would lunch at Harry's Bar in Century City. It was there that he introduced me to Korshak, who was polite, unassuming and left shortly after Mitchelson told him I was a writer working on some of his more celebrated Hollywood divorces. Mitchelson confided titillating detail to me. It was information he'd received in sworn testimony and affadavits. He talked about almost all his cases involving high-profile clients or adversaries, including Mick Jagger, Joan Collins, Marlon Brando, Rod Stewart, David Bowie, Rock Hudson, Mike Tyson, Razor Ruddock, Martina Navratilova, Norman Mailer, Roseanne Barr, Sonny Bono, Alice Cooper, William Shatner, Sylvester Stallone, Neil Young and Hugh Hefner. It was often unprintable, as well as an obvious breach of lawyer–client confidentiality. He couldn't stop himself: he was a compulsive gossip.

Yet, Mitchelson said little about Korshak, who was known in town as 'the Myth' – which was apt, for he left no fingerprints: he was always careful. He used new $100 bills from the bank so that crime cash notes could never be traced and linked to him. When any client left a message for him, it was in a prearranged code, usually the names of famous authors. Early in her marriage, his wife Beatrice was impressed by his literary connections . . . Mr Hemingway was always on the phone. Her husband kept things quiet.

After the noise of the hearings, everything was going to be clean in the dirty businesses. Honesty was the new policy. And the best place for that was a neutral landscape like Hollywood, where politicians could mix with stars, gangsters with film people, the corporate with the corrupt. This change had been apparent, if not carefully noted, on 15 November 1950, when the Kefauver Committee arrived in Las Vegas, where Moe Dalitz was the man that counted. He was out of town. Kefauver and his committee interviewed only six witnesses and the *Las Vegas Review-Journal* reported:

> The United States Senate's crime investigating committee blew into town yesterday like a desert whirlwind, and after stirring up a lot of dust, it vanished, leaving only the rustling among prominent local citizens as evidence that it had paid its much publicised visit here.

What the investigators were experiencing was that the relationship between politicians, authorities and mobsters was not as clear as the Nevada sky. Syndicate members were often major donors to political campaigns. Many prominent politicians had intimate ties with Syndicate members. In fact, Kefauver committee member Herbert O'Conor was linked to the Mafia. In an attempt to keep out organised crime and any associates, Nevada legislated that any casino owner had to be licensed by the State Gaming Board (SGB).

You can see the problem right away. But even if the SGB could not be bought, the new law helped organised crime to move in. Any corporation would have to license its thousands of shareholder 'owners' – each one would have to be approved – whereas individuals could ride on into town. The mobsters and their partners had the front men who had the money. Organised crime concentrated in Las Vegas as criminals exposed in their home states hightailed it into Nevada.

They'd hit the jackpot. New laws had given them new dreams – beyond their wildest. The Mann Act, making it a federal crime to traffic women across state lines, had cut the profits in prostitution. Bootlegging booze and gang wars and carousels doubling as funerals were for yesterday. Organised gambling was the big pot of gold. It needed no trucks or bottling plants or secret garages or machine-gun battles with coastguard cutters and motorcycle cops. Gambling was a businessman's business. Slot machines, punchboards, policy and numbers games, casinos and bookmaking: the profit was staggering. In 1950, an average slot machine cleared $50 a week and the smallest joint would have at least a couple of hundred slots – that's $5,000 a week tax-free. *One* of the eight big wheels of chance in the policy numbers game in what the

Kefauver Committee called 'the Negro section of Chicago' netted $1 million a year. A gambling casino in New Jersey cleared $255,271; one in Florida, $205,000. Bookie Tony Gizmo in Kansas City said his little news-stand handbook netted him more than $100,000 a year.

While Hollywood was going Technicolor and the movies were making millions, the gamblers were having even better luck. Helping the boom was the dedicated change of image, grabbing gambling from the gutter and dressing it up with fancy accessories. The upmarket move was working. With America not much more than halfway through the twentieth century, the federal government estimated gambling as a 'conservative' $20 billion-a-year business.

The Mafia dons and the overlords from the Syndicate and the Outfit had now all become 'Corporate Man'. The swagger, the sequined, squealing half-dressed girls and the camel-hair coats had gone and, with them, the squads of dark-coated goons with bulges under their armpits. All was tasteful, expensive, often imported. Cars were Cadillacs, but in the wife's name. The kids were down for college. Charities and the arts were supported, politicians cultivated. There was the city home or apartment, New York and Chicago, Cleveland, but also the place on the West Coast and another in Miami. It took a little time, but they learned not to carry guns personally. But they did carry cash for *all* transactions.

'Joe Batters' Accardo, who'd earned his name wielding a baseball bat for Capone, lived in River Forest, an upmarket Chicago neighbourhood. He had 'board meetings' sitting at the head of a long table in a wide-open basement room lined with an antique gun collection. One year Accardo decorated a 40-foot Christmas tree on his lawn with electric-driven skaters who glided around on tracks as carols played. Tony wanted to be a good neighbour. He hid the dove tattoo on his right hand, his gun hand, from when he was Capone's main bodyguard. Jake Guzik conducted his bookkeeping and other business on an ivory-handled telephone from the steam room next door to Chicago's Crime Commission. Charlie Fischetti had his Miami estate and a Chicago duplex penthouse, and was a regular at Manhattan's Stork Club. He and his brother had security for their prized art collection. It was all kept quiet. Meyer Lansky and Joe Adonis had dice games in New Jersey and roulette in Miami; Lansky had Cuba in his back pocket, and London and Continental Europe in his plans.

Philadelphia's Dave Glass and Cleveland's Al Polizzi were partners in Miami Beach's Sands Hotel and had a few million in the Desert Inn in Vegas. But they were quiet; they were businessmen. They filed income tax records punctually, if not entirely accurately – acutely aware of what had happened to Big Al.

There were legitimate sources for their income. Mickey Cohen's old bosses in Cleveland, Morris Kleinman and Lou Rothkopf, each owned apartment houses. Anthony Milano in Chicago was in daily contact with Mickey Cohen in Hollywood; he had a loan company – where Cohen got some of this spending money – and an import firm. Moe Dalitz owned a substantial share of the Detroit Steel Corp. Other 'locals' of the Mob ran service industries involving drink distributors and vending-machine companies, and extra business could always be encouraged. Joe Adonis owned the conveying company that had a monopoly on the delivery of cars from the Ford assembly plant at Edgewater in New Jersey into the New York area. Frank Costello owned oil leases and many Wall Street buildings.

These all added up to the most powerful social and political weapon: money, money, money. Cash to pay their way out of trouble, to hire the great legal talents, such as Sidney Korshak, and to create more and more, an endless supply. They purchased immunity from the rule of law and corrupted those pledged to uphold it.

Yet you can't change everything about a business.

Especially the Mob one.

Some people have to die.

6

THE SANDS OF TIME

'A lot of holes in the desert, and a lot of problems are buried in those holes. But you gotta do it right. I mean, you gotta have the hole already dug before you show up with a package in the trunk. Otherwise, you're talking about a half-hour to forty-five minutes' worth of digging. And who knows who's gonna come in that time. Pretty soon, you gotta dig a few more holes. You could be there all fuckin' night.'

– Nicky Santoro (Joe Pesci), *Casino*, 1995

TIME DOESN'T HEAL EVERYTHING, ESPECIALLY A VENDETTA.
In the early 1950s, nearly a dozen years after he ratted on the Mob in the Hollywood extortion case, survivor Willie Bioff had a brand new life and name. He was now William Nelson (from his wife's maiden name) and lived a ride-through desert away in Scottsdale, Arizona, and he was great friends with gamblers and politicians. He was working at the Riveria Hotel-Casino in Las Vegas, trying to keep the costs down for the boss, Gus Greenbaum.

In 1955, 'Joe Batters' Accardo, owner of the newly opened Riviera in Las Vegas, which should have been a gold mine but had lost money for three months straight, knew there was more than bad luck involved. He had a clean out. The staff were given 15 minutes to leave. Or else.

Greenbaum, who'd retired from the Flamingo, which he'd operated successfully after the demise of Benny Siegel, was asked to take charge at the Riveria. Greenbaum was lotus eating in Scottsdale and politely turned down the job opportunity. Three nights later his sister-in-law was murdered in her bed. Greenbaum started work for Accardo that same day. Willie Bioff/Nelson went with him. They'd commute together from across state.

Willie was a close friend and fund-raiser of Senator Barry Goldwater. 'Mr Conservative' Goldwater had serious intentions of becoming President and an eclectic group of contacts to help. Willie, who first met Goldwater at a fund-raiser in November 1952, introduced him to a lot of people. Willie was a natural for politics: likeable – and rich. Goldwater, a Brigadier General in the Air Force Reserve, flew his man William Nelson all over Arizona on the campaign trail.

Senator Goldwater's brother Robert was connected to Moe Dalitz, who owned the Desert Inn with Meyer Lansky, who had encouraged the political connection. One of their former colleagues told me in February 2012: 'They had the fix in with Democrats for the White House, but Meyer liked to hedge the odds. He had Barry Goldwater as the runner for the Republicans, although he was an outsider. Meyer knew they could help him. Moe Dalitz was building hospitals and libraries and that kind of sweetness. Philanthropy's like flattery – it gets you everywhere. Meyer and Moe Dalitz never took chances. They'd buy the county sheriff and the chief of police, too – and neither would know about the other. Belts and braces – and your pants don't fall down. You don't get fucked.'

Yet the area was known for it. Downtown Vegas had begun at the start of the century as a railway hub, linking in Utah, home of the Mormons, Arizona and California. Like Hollywood, it was created by a curious mix of characters and an equally surprising combination of cash, this time from the Mob, the Mormons and the United States government. Pre-Pearl Harbor, the Nellis Air Force Base was established on 14,000 acres of desert wasteland to the north-east of the frontier town. That meant money and people – as had the construction of the Boulder (later Hoover) Dam in the Black

Canyon of the Colorado River. The arch-gravity dam also attracted another helpful economic ingredient: sightseers. The tourists began driving up from California, but they were only an hour or so out along the way from Barstow (where they chill the tableware) before they began to see the first signs for the gambling to come. The Mob started building resorts along Highway 61 from Los Angeles to catch visitors before they got downtown. And the casinos were conceived as self-contained resorts, places with everything you'd ever need – so you'd never have to leave, or stop gambling.

The Vegas entrepreneurs worked everything to bring the gamblers in. They promoted the testing of the atomic bomb near Nellis Air Base as a reason to stay at their hotel-casinos and constructed platforms with dozens of tables for 'atomic viewing breakfasts'. Radiation, possibly death, as a side effect was not mentioned. As Meyer Lansky always said, there is an element of risk in everything we do.

He and Moe Dalitz went way back to 1929 and the Atlantic City crime conference, when bootlegging booze was the business, plus all the other times the Mob had met to plan their future. The new plan was for some peace and quiet as they made money. The problem in that dream of silent larceny was that Willie Bioff had changed his name but not his appearance. He was spotted for what he was – a stoolie – and targeted.

On 4 November 1955, he wandered out to the driveway of his home and climbed into his white Cadillac. The key turn on the ignition set off a bomb that sent him and his car soaring in bits into the sky. It was a simple enough kill – dynamite wired to the starter, nothing too sophisticated. Four weeks before the assassination, he and his wife Laurie had been on holiday with Senator Goldwater and his family. Goldwater showed up for the funeral and denied, with a straight face, knowing who Willie Nelson really was. Later, when the pressure continued, he justified his relationship with the former Chicago pimp and Hollywood mobster by explaining he was compiling material on labour racketeering for a US government study. Such hot air went the way of his pal Willie – into the wide blue yonder.

The Admiral went the other way when time caught up with him. Tony Cornero, who'd been shot and bombed out of Beverly Hills and Hollywood gambling clubs by Mickey Cohen, had redeployed to Las Vegas to build the largest, classiest casino joint in the whole wide world. It was called the Stardust and it was a dream too far. Cornero, who'd made more than $25 million as a gambler, was down to $800 stake money by 31 July 1955, the day he died.

He spectacularly fell down dead on the floor of the casino of the Desert Inn, where he was playing craps. Moe Dalitz watched him collapse from seven tables away, having just refused to loan him more money to complete construction and preparations for the opening of the Stardust, which, with 1,032 rooms, was the desert's biggest.

The one-time Stetson-wearing buccaneer had borrowed $4.3 million from the Mob, yet now he didn't have the cash to pay the staff or supply gambling tables. He was a useless businessman who couldn't account for much of the spent funds. It had been agreed that the Mob would take control of the Stardust without forwarding another cent to Cornero, who was so dangerously red. Still, they went through formalities in the conference room at the Desert Inn over who would own what. When they adjourned for a pee break, the gambler went to the dice tables with his last $800 and did what he had done all his life – gambled. The $800 turned into minus $10,000 in markers in less than an hour. Who makes such bad luck? A cocktail waitress then appeared by his side, asking him to pay his bar tab: $25. The high-roller went ballistic. He was an honoured guest of the house, of Moe Dalitz himself. Yet Dalitz watched the embarrassing cabaret and did not intervene. Cornero had an epic tantrum, then he fell to the ground, holding a highball glass in one hand and his chest with the other.

He was certified dead on the casino floor. His glass of Seagram's Seven Crown whisky and 7-Up, his regular '7&7', which he'd been sipping before he dropped, was taken away and washed. There was no post-mortem.

Moe Dalitz said Cornero wanted to be buried in Los Angeles, so his body was shipped there for a quick funeral, with an organist from the Desert Inn, who played a rousing version and all the verses of the American folk classic 'The Wabash Cannonball'. Including travel time, at the point of the last two lines – 'I have rode those highball trains from coast to coast, that's all, But I have found no equal to the Wabash Cannonball' – Tony Cornero had been dead for all of eight hours.

Almost as fast, John Factor, an old-school English swindler known in the Mob as 'Jake the Barber', was brought in as the front man, the face of the Stardust. His half-brother (same father) Max Factor was the millionaire cosmetics tycoon and used the services of Sidney Korshak to control labour disputes. The lawyer also advised John Factor, who was the new owner of record of the Stardust Hotel, which now belonged to the Chicago Mob. They expanded with the partnership of Moe Dalitz into the Riviera, the Fremont and the Desert Inn. There was the Mob-packed Thunderbird, and the Hacienda and the Dunes on the Strip, and down at the junction of Glitter Gulch, a nickel-and-dime bonanza of a crossroads, were the sawdust-and-spittoon Golden Nugget and the Pioneer. The Teamsters Central States' Pension Fund provided financing. And looking after it all – aged 47, but still called 'the Hollywood Kid' by the gangsters – was Johnny Rosselli. He was in charge of the skimming, making sure that important winnings by the house were never counted as part of net income.

Rosselli was the perfect mobster – or rather, change a letter, *monster* – for Las Vegas and Hollywood. He could be anything anybody wanted him to be. He was attractive to women (by now lovers included Betty Hutton, Lana Turner and Donna *'It's a Wonderful Life'* Reed) and men found him fun, good company and a generous all-around guy. He was a facilitator. He could arrange the murder of 'Russian Louie' Strauss, who tried to blackmail his friend Benny Binion, the owner of the Horseshoe Casino, while getting a girl a date with Frank Sinatra or vice versa. He met with Howard Hughes and acted as his go-between with Lansky and Dalitz. They said George Raft was a great dancer, yet Rosselli could dance expertly to any tune.

And he certainly danced around the sudden death of his persecutor, Willie Bioff, who'd turned up in Las Vegas around the same time as he had. Funny, they hadn't even caught up on old times. Of course, old times had caught up with Willie Bioff. The cops, strangely, never did ask the connected Rosselli about the death of his old friend.

Rosselli was called 'the Henry Kissinger of the Mob', a compliment to his diplomatic skills; likewise, you could argue that by proxy Dr Kissinger had taken out a few people too, in his mission to save the world. Rosselli had contacts everywhere – he did favours for Howard Hughes through the mad tycoon's facilitator-of-choice, the former FBI agent Robert 'Bob' Maheu. The two men walked a tightrope together.

The people in Las Vegas whom I spoke to in the winter of 2011 often referred to a story that they said summed up Rosselli. A connected guy had warned him: 'If we have a problem, I'll make a call to Chicago.' In answer he was told: 'If we have a problem, you're dead.'

Beneath the smile and the suit and the civilised sheen, Rosselli was and remained an animal. It had made him a powerful figure. In Las Vegas, the skim was running into more than $10 million a year on top of real profits, which was shared out with the American dons, including Carlos Marcello of New Orleans.

Marcello was an expert in casinos. Since 1947, he'd been into upmarket carpet joints. His Beverly Club, with its crystal chandeliers – and, yes, showgirls did swing from them – in Jefferson Parish outside New Orleans was America's classiest illegal casino. Sophie Tucker and Tony Martin entertained there. That glitz was now appearing outside in neon on the Strip. Sinatra's Rat Pack of Dean Martin, Sammy Davis Jr, Peter Lawford and Joey Bishop, and unofficial best pals such as Rosselli, sparkled stardust around the desert. The Pack 'mascots' were Angie Dickinson, Juliet Prowse, Shirley

MacLaine and Marilyn Monroe, whom Rosselli adored.

After Tony Cornero sipped his last 7&7 at the Desert Inn craps tables, a conference was called in Chicago. Rosselli was to be at a meeting at Moe's Restaurant with Murray Humphreys and Jake Guzik to discuss the marketing formula for the Stardust. It had been a golden investment since opening night, when Texas Senator Lyndon B. Johnson and his political adviser, Bobby Baker, were guests of honour. The new plan was to make the Stardust even more attractive to both high- and low-rollers. Rosselli was told that Humphreys had arranged for a $1 million loan from the Teamsters Welfare Fund through Jimmy Hoffa to provide even more accommodation. Also it was made clear that they were going to extort, steal and take every cent they could for the casino and if there was ever a problem, Jake the Barber was there to take the consequences – he was the fall guy.

It was a fortune that they were making – nearly half a million dollars a month came from the Stardust casino and that was just the slot machines. Poker, blackjack, craps, roulette and Keno brought in three or maybe four times that.

Ralphie Thomas worked there: 'Everybody played with cash. You couldn't get the paddle into the slot at the craps table, there were so many hundred dollar bills crammed into the drop boxes.'

'Greasy Thumb' Guzik had teams of bookkeepers involved. Cash from the skims was paid out on a sliding scale in terms of the percentage of points you held in a casino; it would be a regular handful of thousands of dollars. The big payday was at the end of March each year, when the accountants completed their end-of-year calculations. That was the signal for party time. Outside 'investors' flew into Las Vegas and everything was free: the hotels, the women, the gambling – and their cash. No need to pay tax on those half-dozen suitcases of greenbacks. But, in turn, their cash payments had to be invested.

This was the empire of Irving 'Niggy' Devine, who, in the upper-world, was a part-owner of the Silver Slipper and Fremont casinos, and New York Meats and Provisions, which had an exclusive on the supply of meats to the hotels along the Las Vegas Strip and downtown. He was also a superior bagman for Meyer Lansky. It was his wife, Ida Devine, who'd taken over from Virginia Hill as the international courier for the Mob. She had a similar style; the FBI files (when they didn't know her identity) marked her out as 'the lady in mink'.

She carried so much cash she had to make the first stretch of every investment trip by train to Chicago, where she was met by a protection team at Union Station. Then, at the Ambassador East Hotel on Goethe Street, she'd supposedly rest but in fact shared out cash to other couriers for the Mob. Sam Giancana was getting $600,000 a month and, being a little paranoid guy, always thought Ida was ripping him off.

She wasn't. She was much, much smarter than that. She was putting her and her husband's and Lansky and company's share into European and Caribbean property developments. They had 'a portfolio'. She also carried a Derringer from the days when she and 'Niggy' Devine were gunrunners in the Deep South. As Vegas prospered, so did they, and the 'banking' became more and more sophisticated through Berne in Switzerland.

The mobsters then held a board meeting at the offices in Beverly Hills of Sidney Korshak. Present were 'Joe Batters' Accardo, Meyer Lansky, Longy Zwillman, Moe Dalitz, Morris Kleinman and Sam Giancana's new West Coast favourite Marshall Caifano, the sadistic killer of Estelle Carey. Accardo said that they were making at least $1 million *a day* out of Vegas and there had to be one man overseeing this fortune-making machine. And he and Giancana – he had taken to collecting his own cash from Vegas, which also allowed him to spend time with the girls, specifically Phyllis McGuire of the McGuire Sisters – had given the job to Marshall Caifano.

With Marshall Caifano, aka another 17 aliases, whose enforcement equipment of choice was a blow-torch, as the lethal 'Outside Man' looking after the Mob interest, there was more time for Rosselli to keep Hollywood and the entertainment side of the business in line. He'd become deeply ingrained in the Mob's Nevada business, ensuring those with different allegiances and interests were not edging out his masters of their full share of the profits. Now, he was to be a problem solver in Hollywood. He had a track record for that.

Despite Giancana keeping his career afloat, the ambitious and needy Frank Sinatra was drowning in his own misery. The Mob helped him out and Rosselli did the business. There was a precedent. When Sinatra had wanted to go solo in 1943, the Mob had helped him out of a long-term contract with the bandleader Tommy Dorsey. Frank Costello had been Sinatra's benefactor then – the barrel of a revolver was said to have been waved in Dorsey's face; he himself told *American Mercury* magazine in 1953: 'I got a visit from three men who told me to sign. Or else.'

Sinatra continued to get a helping hand in the management of his career, especially in the summer of 1952. The connection here was not purely Rosselli or Hollywood; 'Jimmy Blue Eyes' Alo was a loyal and lifetime lieutenant of Meyer Lansky, working with him and the gambling genius Dino Cellini.

Cellini was a boyhood friend of Dino Paul Crocetti, and they both were dealers and stickmen at Rex's Cigar Store in their hometown of Steubenville, Ohio. Now, with his nose fixed, Crocetti was known as Dean Martin. With his comic partner Jerry Lewis, he was one of the hottest acts in America on stage, radio and television. Also 'Martin and Lewis' played Las Vegas. Regularly.

They knew all about Sinatra's problems and ambitions. They also knew he was desperate to appear in the film of James Jones's bestselling wartime novel *From Here to Eternity*. Executives from the William Morris Agency – Jimmy Blue Eyes had a solid percentage stake – had suggested to Columbia Pictures, who were making the movie, that frail-framed Sinatra would be perfect for the beat-upon Private Maggio. It was a Capone-style *opportoonity*. Of course, Harry Cohn was a pig.

Sinatra had made exactly one dozen movies, but nothing on this scale. As Cohn noted: 'Who the hell wants to see that skinny asshole in a major movie?' His wife Joan did. So did lots of other movie people, but Harry Cohn wasn't 'White Fang' for nothing. He was adamant. He was certain. There was no way he'd change his mind. Sinatra was a bum. Who'd pay to see a bum? And Cohn was the head of the studio.

Rosselli called around to see his old friend, who was still wearing his ruby ring. It was pointed out that interested parties wanted Sinatra to play Private Maggio alongside Burt Lancaster, Montgomery Clift and Rosselli's one-time sweetheart Donna Reed. Otherwise that ring would be stuck up Harry Cohn's ass. And a .38 revolver after it.

'That was how Harry Cohn got the message,' one of Dino Cellini's old partners told me in 2012, rather redundantly pointing out: 'And that's how that Sinatra got the part. He was never truly grateful and he was even more of a pain in the ass after he got the award.'

That 'award' was the Academy Award and it was vital: Sinatra was named Best Supporting Actor and took his Oscar home from the RKO Pantages Theatre in Hollywood on 25 March 1954. It was one of eight won by director Fred Zinnemann's black-and-white triumph, depicting pre-Pearl Harbor turmoil in Hawaii. Rosselli's girl Donna Reed won Best Supporting Actress.

Hollywood knew Sinatra had chased the role – it was made for an Oscar – and gave him credit; *Newsweek* magazine in 1954 reported: 'Frank Sinatra, a crooner long since turned actor, knew what he was doing when he plugged for the role of Maggio.'

Rosselli was to get involved in another Hollywood horror in 1956, a distasteful business involving the equally distasteful Harry Cohn. It involved brutal threats to Sammy Davis Jr, whose career at that time was soaring: from Vegas to New York, he was a 'Standing-Room Only' entertainer.

Nearly 30 years later, I sat and talked to Davis about it at his home in Beverly Hills. After all the years, he remained cautious about that period. It was a vibrant memory. He sat at his piano and offered: 'I had a lot of bad times in my life, but that was the worst. I felt cornered, I *was* cornered.'

In 1954, Davis had been driving to Hollywood from San Bernardino when he lost his left eye in a car crash that almost cost him his 29-year-old life. During his long hospital stay, he discussed faith with his friend Eddie Cantor and in time converted from Catholicism to Judaism. He said: 'The Jews would not die. Three millennia of prophetic teaching had given them an unwavering spirit of resignation and had created in them a will to live which no disaster could crush.'

He had to call on that thinking when Harry Cohn got word of his affair with Kim Novak. Columbia Pictures had the actress under contract and regarded her as their answer to Marilyn Monroe. She was the hot property of the moment. Davis had first met the 23-year-old blonde ingénue when he was performing at the Chez Paree club in Chicago and later at a dinner at the home of Hollywood's 'golden couple', Janet Leigh and Tony Curtis. Their romance was genuine and by necessity furtive. In 1950s Hollywood, it wasn't easy to hide. They were stars. She was blonde. He was black.

Harry Cohn was adamant that the liaison with Davis would ruin Novak's career and his investment. Officially, he put private detectives on the couple. Unofficially, he had a word with Johnny Rosselli and Sidney Korshak. He also talked to Sam Giancana, who was close to Sammy Davis – the Mob owned a percentage of him, always did, always had. Just as they owned singer Vic Damone, who said on record that he only ever owned 20 per cent of his lifetime's earnings.

But this was young love.

Wil Haygood, who wrote *In Black and White*, a biography of Davis published in 2005, was told about Cohn's attitude by Davis's friend Cindy Bitterman, who worked for the publicity department of Columbia: 'At dinner, the names of Kim and Sammy came up. Cohn had no idea of my relationship with Sammy. He asked somebody at the table: "What's with this nigger? If he doesn't straighten up, he'll be minus another eye." My stomach started cramping. I went to the bathroom and threw up. I threw up out of fear and greed and Hollywood money-making.'

Davis was visited backstage by a gunman and told he'd be killed if he carried on the affair. Another 'friend' told him his other eye would be plucked out. But Sidney Korshak knew what the compulsive performer's true weakness was: amid all the threats of violence, he told Davis that unless he ended the affair he would never work *anywhere* again.

Cohn confronted Novak, but she was going places. She had the arrogance of success and youth. Sidney Korshak dealt with her, too. When he told her the affair must end, she protested it was her private life. Korshak countered her argument with films he had acquired from a camera Davis had set up in his bedroom to film his sexual encounters – with well-known, white actresses. He handed Novak a selection of the films, which she began to rip up. It was explained that the negatives were elsewhere. She was told again that the affair must stop. And it did. Photographic evidence was so often a clincher in many 'understandings'.

It was a compromise over the compromising. Which in Hollywood had become a lucrative business. The most useful word for it is blackmail, but the gangsters who did it, like Mickey Cohen, were always finding euphemisms for extortion. The most common phrase was 'making life a little easier for you'. It was doing the exact opposite and costing.

Like the gangsters, the movies were trying to publicly clean up their act. There were constant cover-ups of excessive drugging and drinking, of wanton behaviour and illegal abortions, the erasing of criminal records – and some embarrassing people. Many in the Nevada desert.

The Mob had created Murder, Inc. for a clear purpose; likewise Mickey Cohen had one thing in mind when he came up with the idea for his own enterprise: Ladykillers. Think of a male B-movie star from the 1950s and that's what Cohen believed was a woman's fantasy man. He found lots of them hanging around Hollywood, but one in particular, a shooter as well as a swordsman, Johnny Stompanato – aka John Holliday (after Doc Holliday of the O.K. Corral), John Steele, John Valentine and many other names that looked good on cheques

– had the determination. He could romance a fading star and delight a promising starlet. He'd seen war action in the Pacific and wilder stuff on the streets of Chicago, where he was born. He was a slab of beef with conversation. He was a gigolo who was also tough enough to be a gunsel alongside Mickey Cohen, who'd been around Hollywood long enough to have heard every female sob story. He could sense feminine vulnerability by osmosis. He could also see it in the behaviour of the stars in the Hollywood restaurants and clubs, and also in the gangland gossip, which itself was a valuable currency.

Even more valuable were the recordings, pictures and films of actresses doing things they really shouldn't with men and women they shouldn't be doing them with. Marilyn Monroe was set up when she lived at the Studio Club, a rental apartment block for movie people, but any record of it vanished or was never made.

Mickey Cohen liked Johnny Stompanato's style and trusted him; he made him a moneyman, a walking handbag. He was arrested twice carrying $50,000 in cash, money Cohen didn't want to be nabbed with during one of his regular roustings by the cops. But Johnny was always taking the money to the bank or paying this or that off; there was always a ready story. Indeed, he had enough wealthy women on his books to explain it away.

For Johnny Rosselli's former lover Lana Turner, the muscled Stompanato was an intrigue in a life that was not going to script in 1957.

She'd been spotted, aged 15, skipping school in Currie's Ice Cream Parlour on Sunset Strip by Billy Wilkerson and the *Hollywood Reporter* magazine owner had got her on the books of the Zeppo Marx Talent Agency. In turn, Zeppo had got her into Mervyn LeRoy's *They Won't Forget* – she was screen dynamite from her first two-minute stroll, bouncing along in a tight sweater.

And no one forgot Lana Turner. She was now 'the Sweater Girl'. She made three more films in 1937 and the following year worked steadily, moving her way up the screen credits and making herself well known around town. She shocked many, including herself, by eloping with bandleader Artie Shaw on her 20th birthday, 8 February 1940. They'd met when she made her starring role debut in *Every Other Inch a Lady* (1939), but the whirlwind marriage lasted 17 months before steadfast acrimony bitterly blew it apart.

Lana Turner didn't like to be lonely. She was dancing one evening at Mickey Cohen's favourite, the Mocambo, when the some-time actor, card-player, man-about-town and most affable Steve Crane kept her on the dance floor all evening. Crane was an easy man to like, a charmer, and Lana liked him a lot. They married in 1942, but when it was realised his first marriage had not been properly dissolved it was annulled and they married again, by which time she was pregnant with their daughter Cheryl. Their daughter was born on 25 July 1943, and the actress won a divorce action and custody. Lana Turner was an epic name on and off screen.

In 1946, she co-starred with John Garfield in the remarkable film version of James M. Cain's *The Postman Always Rings Twice*. When audiences watched her on screen, many were only thinking about one thing. The way her wayward wife Cora Smith smiled was sinful. The sexual tension was palpable. The undercurrent was electric. Some argued Lana/Cora shouldn't be allowed to smile and say 'hello' at the same time. It was scandalous.

She was involved with Frank Sinatra and Tyrone Power, whom she chased around Europe. One romance was with Howard Hughes; they flew from New York to Hollywood to marry but by the time the plane touched down he'd gone off the idea.

Her fourth marriage in her final total of eight ('my dream was to have one husband and seven children, but it went the other way around' – she married Crane twice) was to Lex Barker. He was famous for being a screen Tarzan, a husband of Lana Turner, and masturbating over and raping his step-daughter.

In 1957, after learning that Barker had been abusing Cheryl,

Turner kicked him out. Nevertheless, she still didn't like being lonely. Mickey Cohen told Johnny Stompanato to turn on the charm with Turner, a woman at a low ebb in her life, the ink fresh on her messy divorce papers.

Stompanato made the traditional approach, with flowers every day and all the right words, and it worked. John Steele, as he was calling himself, slipped into the life of Lana Turner and her daughter. Mickey Cohen gave him $900 to buy Cheryl a pony. He played the mature, caring man, giving his age as five years older than Turner – it was the other way about. He was always the gentleman, for he was always acting the part.

'My mother had no idea of what he did or who he was, other than he was attractive,' Cheryl Crane said in an interview in 2011.

The star herself wrote in her autobiography *The Lady, The Legend, The Truth*: 'That's how the blackest period of my life began. It started with flowers and an innocent invitation for a drink, and it was to end with screaming headlines, in tragedy and death.'

It also began with much passion. Previously, Turner had revealed: 'He was utterly considerate, and I began to warm toward him physically. His wooing was gentle, persistent and finally persuasive. By the time I found out his real name, we were already having an affair. I believed the lies a man told me, and by the time I learned they were lies it was too late. I was trapped, helpless because of my fear for my own life, for Cheryl's.'

She said she had mixed feelings about dating a man who was a known gangster: to her, he was dangerous, yet appealing. She appeared to want it all.

'Call it forbidden fruit or whatever. This attraction was very deep – maybe something sick within me – and my dangerous captivation went far beyond lovemaking,' she wrote.

At the time, taped recordings of her lovemaking with Stompanato were being circulated on Mickey Cohen's underground sex circuit for $50 a go.

George Schlatter, a Hollywood producer and friend of Sinatra, said in 2011: 'She really was crazy about Johnny

Stompanato. However, she did not really want to be seen with him that much.'

Stompanato lavished Lana and Cheryl with gifts, including jewellery Turner wore as Constance MacKenzie in her 1957 film *Peyton Place*, the first great screen 'soap', although a for-the-times sanitised version of Grace Metalious's 1956 novel.

It was at the time of that movie – and Turner's nomination for Best Actress at the Oscars – that her romance with the mobster finally spiralled out of all control. She was in England in the autumn of 1957 filming *Another Time, Another Place*, a small melodrama nonsense, with Sean Connery as her screen lover, when Stompanato burst in on her on the set in Borehamwood, Hertfordshire. There was reportedly another melodrama on the film set when Stompanato produced a gun and pointed it at Turner. Sean 'Big Tam' Connery was said to have disarmed the gangster. Whatever did happen, the lovers had a tremendous argument, which went viral, with Turner badly choked. She could hardly speak for some days afterwards. When her lover offered more trouble, she informed the police he was in the country on a false passport as John Steele. He was quickly deported.

Back in California, the snubbed Stompanato brooded.

Meanwhile Harry Cohn died, on 17 February 1958, from an unexpected but not surprising heart attack. He aggravated easily. He collapsed shortly after having dinner at the Arizona Biltmore Hotel in Phoenix, where so many of his Mob-related investors lived. He was interred in the Hollywood Forever cemetery in Hollywood. His funeral attracted an overflow of mourners of which Red Skelton remarked: 'It proves what Harry always said: "Give the public what they want and they'll come out for it."' Turner missed the event, as she was concluding filming in England.

Stompanato, with Johnny Rosselli's help through his studio contacts, established the filming dates of *Another Time, Another Place* and also, via the movie's production department, Turner's travel itinerary. In late February 1958, she was on her way to Acapulco, flying from London via Denmark. When she walked off the plane at Copenhagen, there waiting was her gangster lover. He flew with her to Mexico, to the Villa Vera Tennis and Racquet Club resort, which sits high on the hill directly above the town, overlooking the bay. Stompanato liked the view, too. He was stalking his lover. This added an even more sadistic element to the affair, though Turner seemed to like the rough with the smooth. And Mickey Cohen was paying the expenses.

It was romantic in Acapulco, with the waiters at the Villa Vera scuttling with room service back and forward to their suite, with its open-air showers, which they shared with a couple of iguanas. They had their own pool and never left their villa.

Harsh reality played out back in Hollywood, with Cheryl, 14, being a typical teenage girl. She had run away a couple of times from her Catholic boarding school and her behaviour had made the columns of Hearst's star gossip Louella Parsons and celebrated columnist Walter Winchell.

The uplifting news was that Turner had been nominated as Best Actress for *Peyton Place*. Stompanato was more delighted than her or her agent. It would give him 'juice' in Hollywood and with the Mob. He was with a *real* star. When they flew back to Los Angeles, at the airport to greet them were Cheryl and the photographers. Telegraphed worldwide, the caption with the image read: 'Lana Turner returns with Mob figure'.

She knew she couldn't be seen at the Oscars with Stompanato. But he had other ideas – such visibility gave him status and, at the age of 32, he had dreams of a sparkling and glamorous life as a leading man, even if off screen, in Hollywood. After superstar Lana Turner, there were plenty of others to be used and wooed and treated with what his conquests confirmed he was entitled to call his own 'special Oscar'. It had impressed Ava Gardner and Janet Leigh, Ann Miller and Kathryn Grayson.

The MGM studios had much rolling on *Peyton Place* and wanted as much positive publicity as possible. The film company's Eddie Mannix had covered up much involving Hollywood stars, including a murder, and, unaware that

Mickey Cohen had started the Turner–Stompanato affair in the first place, went to him for help. Reluctantly, Cohen agreed to put a ban on Stompanato's insisting on going to the Oscars.

That awards evening, 26 March 1958, when the Best Actress Award was won by Joanne Woodward for *The Three Faces of Eve*, pictures present Lana Turner as everything a star should be. And a Hollywood mother, which played well in Middle America. There she was in a tight, strapless white lace gown, a knowing smile, topped by platinum blonde hair. Next to her was the modestly dressed but grown-up looking Cheryl. What lifts the Hollywood image even more is that leaning between them and the Martini glasses is Cary Grant in white tie and tails.

Stompanato watched it all on television and believed the handsome guy in the middle should have been him. He had a few more drinks. When Turner returned home and Cheryl had gone to her room, the gangster quietly told the star that she would never leave him home alone again. Then he gave her a professional beating. The punches were all to the body, where the bruises could be covered up. The only visible mark was a scratch from an earring. Threats of more violence followed. She would be murdered and disfigured – a knife was produced for emphasis – and Cheryl would be hurt too.

In the story of her life, she reported: 'He cracked me a second time, this time knocking me down. I staggered back against the chaise and slid to the floor. He yanked me up and began hitting me with his fists. I went flying across the room into the bar, sending glasses shattering on the floor. "Now do you understand?" he asked me. "You will never leave me out of something like that again. Ever."

'Underlying everything was my shame. I was so ashamed. I didn't want anybody to know my predicament, how foolish I'd been, how I'd taken him at face value and been completely duped.'

She went to bed bruised and beaten. Johnny Stompanato slept beside her. Cary Grant was still at the Oscar parties.

The events that followed over the next few days show how

Hollywood lived, and lives, on a different planet, with different laws, values and morals. However much anyone pontificates about humanity and what we do to one another, the only important matter in this galaxy of stars is image and the ability to make money.

Lana Turner was a bona fide superstar when she and her family moved to a suitable address for that status, 730 North Bedford Drive in Beverly Hills, south of Sunset Boulevard, north of Wilshire, on 1 April 1958.

Turner herself felt stronger and more defiant in her attitude to her lover. The retired gambler I talked to in Nevada, who watched over a club on Santa Monica Boulevard at the time, said that Mickey Cohen had plans to exploit her even further. And she knew it. He said that was *her* motive to kill Stompanato. But the story of Hollywood history has Cheryl Crane stabbing Johnny Stompanato to death and being cleared in an inquest that declared the mobster's demise as justifiable homicide. If Lana Turner had been charged and convicted, she probably would have been given the death penalty, a place on San Quentin's Death Row. Many mobsters and Hollywood veterans don't believe the teenage Cheryl had the strength of will or the physical power to stab Stompanato to death. But that was her and her mother's story.

It was just after 9 p.m. on Good Friday when Cheryl heard a furious fight going on in her mother's first-floor bedroom, with Stompanato screaming that Turner was going to die. She ran to the kitchen, picked up a ten-inch carving knife (bought by her mother that day) and rushed off to help her mother. Stompanato then apparently ran into the knife, which cut into his aorta, and he collapsed, bleeding to death in front of her. As Lana Turner watched, his last words, she testified, were: 'Cheryl, what have you done?'

At that point only one thing was certain. There was a corpse at 730 North Bedford. Lana Turner said she found it difficult to find '0' on the telephone. Longer numbers were easier. She called her lawyer, Jerry Giesler (he'd looked after Marilyn Monroe in her divorce from Joe DiMaggio four years earlier) and then her press representative. Cheryl Crane called her father, who was at his Polynesian restaurant, The Lua, on Rodeo Drive.

No one called an ambulance. The Beverly Hills police found out two hours later, when they were officially informed by Jerry Giesler. When Police Chief Clinton Anderson, who spent his working life dealing with movie people, arrived, Stompanato's body was spread over the floor. There was little blood. The body had been moved. There were fingerprints on the knife but they were smudged and no good. Jerry Giesler helped Lana Turner and her daughter tell their story. Chief Anderson had the evidence and the confession and that was officially that.

The other version is that Lana Turner had taken enough and stabbed Stompanato in the bed they shared. The bedding had been removed and Giesler (some many years later) was quoted as saying that the bed 'looked like a hog had been butchered on it'. Many versions of this manifested (Stompanato had been caught in bed with Cheryl by her mother), but with Lana Turner's box-office potential (and no statute of limitations for murder) no definitive evidence was provided.

Hollywood, says the legend, protects itself. It was certainly doing that by the time Mickey Cohen arrived at North Bedford. Jerry Giesler knew him well from their Benny Siegel days and requested a favour: 'If Lana sees you, she's gonna fall out altogether. John's dead, the body's at the morgue. Don't blow your top about it. I want to talk with you, but I don't want to leave right now.'

Cohen went to the morgue alone and made a positive identification of the body for the authorities. He told John Nugent on the tapes what he thought: 'I don't believe Cheryl killed him. Johnny was an athlete. He could stand up for himself pretty well. They say she stabbed him while he was standing, but I can't believe that anybody could. I think he was in bed by himself, sleeping. Only way Cheryl or someone else could have done it is if he was asleep, understand what I mean? Of course, you hear a lot of bullshit with these Hollywood things.'

Which, even for Mickey Cohen, was an understatement.

He played down all the celebrity coverage of Stompanato's death, but he loved talking about it, being at the centre of all that sparkling bullshit. He spouted a lot of it himself. He loved Johnny, he loved Lana, he knew they were truly in love – and for a few bucks you can hear a tape of them fucking. There never was a truer Hollywood gangster.

He felt obliged to talk to the press, he said, for the sake of Johnny's family: 'I can't understand it. I thought she liked him very much. We were happy – Cheryl and Johnny and me. We used to go horseback riding together. I don't like the whole thing. There's lots of unanswered questions. I'm going to find some of those answers, no matter what happens.'

Johnny Stompanato had taken racy photographs of Lana Turner and they were on a roll of film of him having sex with other women. Clever editing would have compromised the actress, but the material was discovered and destroyed by Jerry Giesler, with the help of Johnny Rosselli, who was putting a marker down with Hollywood's top lawyer.

But Mickey Cohen had the love letters, which proved that Turner was smitten by the gangster, as she wrote of 'our love, our hopes, our dreams, our sex and longings'. He gave them to Hearst's *Los Angeles Herald Examiner*. Cohen said he wanted to show 'true love', explaining: 'I thought it was fair to show that Johnny wasn't exactly unwelcome company like Lana said.'

It was sensational stuff. The day after the killing Los Angeles County District Attorney William B. McKesson publicly made it clear the case would receive no special treatment because Lana Turner was involved. Cheryl, who had been held overnight in the Beverly Hills Prison (as nice as it sounds), was taken to Los Angeles County Juvenile Hall. There was still no talk of criminal charges, and Cheryl Crane was not being held as a suspect but as a material witness and adjudicated juvenile.

On Easter Monday morning, Jerry Giesler told a court hearing he could prove justifiable homicide and asked that Cheryl be released. Police Chief Anderson said he was satisfied that Stompanato was 'killed with a knife and we have the party who did it'. District Attorney McKesson wanted Cheryl held in custody – he was fearful she'd be got at by her mother or the Mob. He also ordered, against police opposition, a coroner's inquest, which would be televised from the Hall of Records in Beverly Hills. Jerry Giesler said Cheryl was too traumatised to testify and she was excused.

So, the star of the show was Lana Turner, who was the one witness to the killing other than her accused daughter. On her performance depended her daughter's future: whether Cheryl would walk out of court that day or be charged with first-degree murder, a capital offence. In *Peyton Place*, Turner's character, Constance MacKenzie, is quizzed in a courtroom scene about the actions of her daughter. Now, here was Hollywood playing Hollywood in Hollywood.

On 11 April 1958, on a blazing hot southern California morning without the benefit of a Pacific breeze, queues started gathering for the public seats at 6 a.m. There were 160 available and 120 went to the press. The CBS and ABC television networks broadcast live, as did radio outlets. To the constant pop of flashbulbs, the coroner's cast worked their way into the Hall of Records. When they walked in, the jury of ten men and two women was already seated.

Mickey Cohen was first up, as he'd identified the body. It was a startling cameo, as he told the court: 'I refuse to identify the body on the grounds I may be accused of this murder.' He was stood down.

Lana's close-up was on. She was impeccably tailored in a grey silk suit and white gloves, her platinum haircut neat and short. She sat at the witness table and slowly took off her gloves, then looked straight ahead to the back of the packed hall. She perfectly recounted, under Jerry Giesler's gentle questioning, the story of how Cheryl and the knife had collided with Stompanato's vital organs.

There was much evidence about blood and hairs and smudged fingerprints, but after Lana Turner's testimony not many people were paying much attention. The jury went off for 27 minutes and found John Stompanato's death was justifiable homicide. Acting out of fear for her life and for her mother's life, Cheryl Crane had justification. She was innocent of murder. The decision was not unanimous and didn't have to be. The inquest was not binding on District Attorney McKesson, but he let it go.

Mickey Cohen didn't: 'It's the first time in my life I've ever seen a dead man convicted of his own murder. So far as that jury's concerned, Johnny just walked too close to that knife.'

The mobster helped Stompanato's family bring a wrongful death lawsuit against Turner, Cheryl and Steve Crane. Cohen wanted Stompanato to be a victim of Hollywood, a man who loved the wrong woman and died for it. He never indicated his role as a blackmailing Cupid.

Of all the anomalies in the killing of Johnny Stompanato that hypocrisy captured the attitude of the Mob to Hollywood. And Hollywood to Hollywood. The civil lawsuit said Turner had herself killed Stompanato and asked for $752,250 in compensation. There was no new hard evidence, but the case was settled out of court for $20,000 – worth it to avoid more headlines. Or questions.

In 2011, Hollywood producer George Schlatter commented: 'Johnny Stompanato walked into the knife. Now if you believe that, I've got some real estate I'd like to sell you. The saying then was "Get me Giesler." Jerry Giesler was a brilliant criminal defence attorney. And he arrived and he said: "Everybody stay cool, stay calm, and shut the fuck up." I always thought it might have been Lana. Those of us who were on the periphery of this said, "OK, matter closed." But in many of our minds the matter was not closed.'

Eric Root, a self-described 'hairdresser to the stars', had known Lana Turner in the years before her death from throat cancer in June 1995. He'd met her when she'd appeared in the television soap opera *Falcon Crest*, which ran on the wings of *Dallas* and *Dynasty*. On 19 November 2011, he went on prime-time television in America and in a CBS broadcast said: 'Lana Turner told me that she killed Stompanato. [She said:] "If I die before you, I want you to tell the world."' Root most certainly has done that. In a book, he said she told him this in April 1985, specifically saying: 'I killed the son of a bitch and I'd do it again.' Cheryl Crane dismissed this claim in 2011.

Peyton Place hadn't done too well at the box office when it was released, but within days of the death of Turner's real-life lover it received a 32 per cent boost in tickets and became a blockbuster – after *The Bridge on the River Kwai*, the second-highest-grossing film of 1958. What career fears Lana Turner had were quashed when she was given the lead role in the 1959 weepie *Imitation of Life*. It was a remarkable remake of a 1934 picture revolving around an ambitious actress who ignores her daughter (Sandra Dee) and then finds that the girl is in love with the man she plans to marry. It was another box-office smash, critically regarded, in time, as magical CinemaScope, a masterwork by the director Douglas Sirk.

Veteran George Schlatter, who has produced a spectacular number of television specials since his days in charge of *Rowan and Martin's Laugh-In* (1968–73), has worked with almost all the great entertainers. He still believes the Lana Turner gangster affair is the perfect Tinseltown tale: 'I love this story. This story is about what Hollywood is about. It's about mystery. It's about sex. It's about fights, about arguing. And about love. It's what the town was built on. It's what the industry is built on. That's what Lana was. She represented the mystery, the love, the passion that is Hollywood . . .' He forgot money. And murder.

BOOK TWO

FATAL ATTRACTIONS

'Men of power and the criminals in our society are distinguished only by their situation, not by their morality.'

— Francis Ford Coppola, on the release of
The Godfather, 1972

7

BEAUTIFUL PEOPLE

'You know my story. I'm pretty.'
— Sheila Farr (Angie Dickinson) to Johnny North
(John Cassavetes), *The Killers*, 1964

IN HOLLYWOOD (WHERE THEY MADE A HUGE BOX-OFFICE movie about infidelity and called it *Fatal Attraction* (1987), *human error* is so often defined as being the wrong person at the wrong time in the wrong place, with that being anything from the casting couch to the boardroom. Emotional entanglements can last for the whole eight weeks of filming. In the early 1960s, much of this was still being covered up, as were the constant brief entanglements of President John F. Kennedy. Hollywood had the studios and press agents; he had the Secret Service, who held to their title.

The movie people got behind the push for JFK to become President of the United States just as much as his father's Mafia friends from his bootlegging days. While the Mob saw money and influence, the stars confused charisma with competence, which was — still is — their habit around town, where celebrity equates achievement.

Extraordinarily, the way America interprets politics, as it did in the 2012 presidential election campaigns, is still surrounded and somewhat shaped by the myths of JFK, of the Kennedy Clan, the malicious machinations of one-time movie mogul Joe Kennedy, of Jackie Onassis, the widow of opportunity, of Marilyn Monroe and Frank Sinatra and Sam

Giancana – and *Judith Exner*. Cash might be king, but a shiny, impenetrable veneer wins votes and the power follows.

I met Judith Exner in 1976 in Los Angeles when she'd first burst the bubble of high ideals and fine words, the rhetoric rather than results creation that had been worked up and given the name of that other myth, Camelot. She had kept her secrets for 16 years and they were astonishing. History making and changing. She'd been the lover of JFK and of Johnny Rosselli and Sam Giancana, who, by the by, had both been recruited by the CIA to assassinate Fidel Castro. Frank Sinatra had made some of the introductions.

She'd only been identified as a 'close friend of President Kennedy (who) had frequent contact with the President from the end of 1960 through mid-1962' in a report published on 20 November 1975 by the Senate Committee on Intelligence Operations. It had been enough for her to go public, especially with the report's zinger: 'FBI reports and testimony indicate that the President's friend was also a close friend of John Rosselli and Sam Giancana and saw them both during this same period.'

Sitting on a yacht in San Pedro Harbour in Los Angeles with her husband Dan Exner, this femme fatale didn't look at all femme fatale. She was conservatively dressed in a white shirt and tailored navy blue slacks and carried a jacket with an expensive Beverly Hills department store label showing. She was forthright and assured.

The purpose of our meeting was for her to elaborate on what she had written in *My Story*, her account of her time with President Kennedy and the Mafia. The interview followed weeks of investigation, during which I'd spoken with her former husband, the likeable and polite actor William Campbell, then at the Motion Picture and Television Fund's hospital in Woodland Hills, California; her one-time date, actor Robert 'R.J.' Wagner; and many others, reluctantly willing to be drawn into what was, following Watergate, more controversial revelations about the workings of the US presidency – and the government's close connections with the corporate and the criminal. Yet no matter how naive and unknowing she presented herself, her relationships belied her innocence.

In her late teens, as Judith Immoor, she belonged to what Bill Campbell told me was 'the young Hollywood set', one around which Johnny Rosselli prowled. By the time their six-year marriage began in 1952, she knew many more people. Her husband was a talented actor. He could turn himself to all manner of roles, from co-starring and singing in Elvis's first movie *Love Me Tender* (1956) to appearing as a Klingon warrior in *Star Trek* on television. Through him his wife met stars such as Elvis Presley and became friends with Angie Dickinson and Juliet Prowse; she liked to be part of show business, of Hollywood.

But for Bill Campbell, who died aged 87, in April 2011, there was always a mystery: 'How she ever met the President, I don't know.'

He was being kind. The meeting was orchestrated – it gave the Mob a contact within the immediate White House circle. And it gave the young Judith Exner more celebrity contact than she could have imagined. It wasn't as if JFK wasn't an easy lay. Exner was a bright, attractive young woman who easily mixed in powerful circles. She was a Californian 'party girl', a fine decoration in a glamorous world that she was excited to be in. Exner had a perfect pedigree in this particular game. She was the daughter of Irish-American parents and her father, Frederick Immoor, earned well as the chief draughtsman for an architectural firm. He liked to spend – champagne at the weekend – and his daughter was brought up living a high life (at Frank Sinatra's Palm Springs home, she commented what a 'small house' the singer owned). She had a tutor and there was much help around the house. She was used to the California good life.

Robert Wagner, like Judith Immoor, lived in the San Fernando Valley. He had dated her before she married Campbell; in fact, he was the one who introduced them. The actor told me: 'They didn't want her to get married to me because Mama was a very pushy Hollywood mother who wanted her daughters [older sisters Joan and Jacqueline] to be movie stars. There is no way that she could have done so with Judith because Judith just didn't have the talent. Or the interest. But Mama felt that I would get in the way.'

But Bill Campbell had a pass key to Hollywood and had the opposite effect. He and Exner mixed with the ambitious young Hollywood group of actors and actresses. She was more interested in actors than acting.

'She was a good-looking girl and there were plenty of guys paying attention to her,' Lloyd Bridges remembered when we talked about the 1950s, the decade during which he was blacklisted by the House Un-American Activities Committee, before achieving stardom with the television hit *Sea Hunt* (1958–63), in which his young sons Jeff and Beau Bridges appeared.

Bill Campbell said the marriage 'wasn't real' after two years, then Exner took up with the older and more worldly Tony Travis. 'The divorce was pretty amiable. Judy was not a demanding girl. She didn't try to mangle me in terms of money.' He told me he later paid her a lump sum of $5,000, adding: 'We were too immature for marriage. Judy's main concern was with her looks and her clothes. Nothing much beyond that interested her. I'm not saying she was dumb, but she was no great intellectual either.'

She had taste and elegance, but the thought of work never occurred to her. She had alimony and a small private income. She had a very expensive wardrobe to which she was always adding. Her mind never turned beyond her social life, which was dining and dancing every night and being seen in the right places with all the right people. She wanted to be admired, for her looks, her style and her taste. And she was. She was also a perfect identikit mistress for the President of the United States: presentable and acceptable like, say, Marlene Dietrich, but an adventure easier to disguise than dalliances with Marilyn Monroe. In terms of risk, Judith Exner was low for high returns. She could do no harm, she was discreet and she had no strong political views. Her policy belief was in having a good time.

Of course, the paranoid master of mischief J. Edgar Hoover saw her as yet another woman in his JFK file. The FBI director cross-linked her with Sam Giancana. His ever-watchful agents reported that little Judith would often leave President Kennedy's bed and trip off to Chicago to meet with the Mafia boss. Hoover was delighted. With his job under threat from Kennedy's Attorney General brother Robert Kennedy, this would give him wonderful leverage with these so-called knights of Camelot. He ordered a full-scale investigation of Judith Exner.

The Mafia–White House go-between for Judith Exner was Frank Sinatra. The FBI agents, several sent from out of town offices, were soon working out of the Federal Building in Los Angeles. They'd meet for coffee at a doughnut shop across the street in Gayley Avenue in Westwood for unofficial briefings. Sinatra was the key. His marriage-go-around with Ava Gardner, Johnny Stompanato's occasional lover, was over and *From Here to Eternity*, the movie the Mob had got him, had indeed truly boosted his career. The Beatles were still in Hamburg, the Rolling Stones in Fulham, London, and his record sales were in the many, many millions. The world, it appeared, loved the sound of his voice. When Humphrey Bogart died in January 1957, his 'pack' found its way into becoming Sinatra's Rat Pack, an entourage he liked around him like an Arab sheikh. One member was Peter Lawford, a wishy-washy, chinless English actor who won points by marrying JFK's sister Pat in 1954. They were friendly with another young married couple in town, Sidney and Bea Korshak, who also knew Sinatra. Lawford was a weak man and in the 1980s he would spend afternoons and evenings at table at the Café Rodeo bar in Beverly Hills pouring drinks and despair. None of it – Jack, Marilyn, Bobby – was his fault. By then, it was clear as you sat with him that he wouldn't know if it had been. Peter Lawford knew the secrets but not how they went together. It was never really a puzzle.

The Rat Pack often had more fun than their audiences. The comic Joey Bishop was at the top of his game, Sammy Davis was Mr Bojangles and Dean Martin had a bespoke brilliance. Around them were Angie Dickinson, Shirley MacLaine and Juliet Prowse, all of whom were contenders for the best legs in show business.

Judith Exner was with Sinatra when he holidayed in Hawaii with Peter and Pat Lawford. They simply assumed she was just another of 'Frank's girls'; but she was more than a casual plaything.

Joseph Kennedy had summoned Sinatra to the family's compound at Hyannis Port in Massachusetts in December 1959 and encouraged him to engage himself and his Hollywood friends in support of his son's bid for the presidency. Frank could be the US Ambassador in Rome: it was the *Mamma Mia!* moment for Sinatra, as the crafty Joe Kennedy knew it would be.

Kennedy had a good chance, but the Republican's Richard Nixon would have been the better bet at the start of 1960. He'd been Eisenhower's vice president. But Kennedy undoubtedly had the charisma – and a winning haircut.

'He is my friend and I know how to help my friends,' Sinatra used to say, according to Exner, before their affair ended. She said she walked out because of his unusual sexual demands, involving a black hooker. Perhaps he just got bored; he had the attention span of a five year old. They remained close and in the newspapers she was a 'regular date' of Sinatra, who by then was engrossed by Juliet Prowse.

Judith Exner was a personality by default. In early 1960, she was dating, dancing and dining virtually every night at the right party, a fully fledged member of the Sinatra 'clan'. In Las Vegas, the Rat Pack had turned themselves into an act and were making the original *Ocean's Eleven* on location there. Sinatra was Danny Ocean and Angie Dickinson was his wife Bea, named after a certain lawyer's spouse.

Dickinson is a class act of Hollywood. I talked to her at her LA home in Coldwater Canyon (driven there by her friend Richard Gully, one of the legendary Hollywood cognoscenti) and on location in Hawaii. She has always been gracious – and cautious. She's a one-of-the-guys kind of girl, but ever since her saloon girl 'Feathers' flirted outrageously with John Wayne in Howard Hawks's *Rio Bravo* (1959) she'd never be mistaken for one.

She'd always loved the movies: 'I remember a Humphrey Bogart movie where he was a reporter, so I wanted to be a reporter, and then he was a parachutist and I wanted to be a parachutist. Even a priest, when Gregory Peck was a priest in *Keys to the Kingdom* because the women didn't do anything! They were just wives or old maids. I wanted to look like Dietrich or Grable or Lana Turner, but I wanted to do what the men did.' Which was the perfect attitude for the Rat Pack movie.

She met Frank Sinatra when he was a guest star on US television's *The Jimmy Durante Show*. She was all legs as a showgirl: 'It was my first show, my first step onto a professional stage. I had not even seen one before. I had come from work in a fill-in job, and I stepped on the stage and there were Frank Sinatra and Jimmy Durante, working. I just walked in and thought: "Oh my God, this is what I want to be a part of."'

In turn, Sinatra became 'the most important man in my life. He was so important, because he was so powerful when I got to meet him.' Their affair went on over ten years.

With Sinatra and Dean Martin and the others, she played poker and told dirty stories between filming: 'Frank and I stayed friends for all those years, and it was just one of those great, comfortable things where you always desire somebody, but you can live without them. It was wonderful, it was kind of perfect, but I don't think he ever had a great passion for me, which is why I think it lasted as long as it did. And I for him. There's a difference between having to have something and wanting something.'

It was Sinatra who introduced her into the Kennedy political arena. The candidate's sister Pat, with her husband Peter Lawford, staged a fund-raising dinner at their oceanfront home in Santa Monica shortly before the Democratic Convention in Los Angeles in 1960.

'It was Frank who brought me in. The future president was there and Joe Kennedy, and Bobby and Eunice and Pat, of course – and Frank. We were feverish to work for him. I was Frank's wife in the movie, so I was already one of the boys.'

During filming of *Ocean's Eleven*, the cast's friends would fly or drive into Vegas at weekends, and Judith Exner was a regular at the downtime parties. On 7 February 1960, she successfully fought off Teddy Kennedy, 28, who was trying to seduce her in her Sands Hotel room; then she was introduced to his brother, whom she knew as 'Jack'.

Sinatra had promised the 42-year-old Democratic candidate for the presidency a good and relaxing time as a break from the campaign trail. For the Kennedys, the visit was for business and pleasure, and Sinatra would help with both.

Senator Kennedy addressed a meeting of nearly 600 people in the city's convention centre, and then he went to a select cocktail party where several dozen wealthy Democrats – casino and hotel people – met him and wrote big cheques. Then after the business, the dinner.

While Sinatra sang for his supper, the Kennedy brothers sat down with Peter and Pat Lawford and Judith Exner. Teddy mauled her, Jack Kennedy fascinated her. He made her feel she was the only person in the room. The next day, at noon, when she was still half-asleep, the telephone by her bed rang: 'Hi . . . this is Jack Kennedy. I'd very much like us to have lunch.'

Distraction had always been JFK's problem. He also believed his brain worked better after sex. His father was aware of his son's faults, but Jack had become the candidate only by default. Joe Kennedy had been planning forever – since his Hollywood mogul period and romance with Gloria Swanson, and his booze-smuggling empire building with Meyer Lansky – that a Kennedy would get into the White House. Joe Kennedy Junior was to have become America's first Irish-Catholic President, but when he was killed in the war his brother had to fill his shoes.

On the election trail, father could not monitor son, as Joe

Kennedy's overbearing presence would have been poor public relations. JFK had to be seen to be his own man. His sexual adventures were accepted, as long as the women involved could not damage him politically. He was also a show-off and liked an admiring audience. He wanted to impress Judith Exner and invited her to his press conference by the main swimming pool of the Sands Hotel. He was in mid-speech when she appeared; he stopped, looked at her and announced: 'Hi Judy, I'll be right with you when we finish.'

It was an audacious – but he believed safe – way of operating with these extra women in his life. There were often more women than men in his audience, and far more women than men in the groups of campaign workers pursuing his presidential dream for him. People and the press, respectful, reticent and not too enquiring, were used to seeing him with smart, attractive females and were never suspicious. He told his new sexual attraction he had borrowed the patio of Frank Sinatra's suite, which was much more intimate than the restaurant, and there they would be able to talk through lunch. He would persuade her to talk about herself, the Catholicism, the Irish blood which they shared. She whispered the Hollywood secrets: 'He could never get enough gossip.'

Or sex. But JFK was enamoured and as his relationship with Judith Exner developed she would become more than a casual fling. That evening in Las Vegas the presidential hopeful's supporters – many had flown in from Hollywood – staged a fanfare party for JFK. Gloria Cahn, the wife of songwriter Sammy Cahn, swooped on Kennedy like a mother hen. She gave Judith Exner the beady eye and led Kennedy away to meet and greet the Democratic Party faithful. When the event finished, Kennedy was back by the side of Judith Exner, but for them the evening ended there. The next day back in Beverly Hills a dozen red roses arrived from Kennedy. He telephoned in the evening. The calls began to be regular and from all over America, where he was chasing votes. She, it would seem, was a distraction for Kennedy from the constant campaign, this same speech, those same people and the rubber chicken dinners.

He was 36 when he married Jacqueline Bouvier and their relationship worked: she had her interests outside politics. Mrs Kennedy was not prepared to make an open issue of her husband's philandering. Judith Exner was flabbergasted and flattered to the point of exhilarating madness: in the middle of this great political battle, Kennedy would stop and telephone *her*. He told her how much he missed her. How much she interested him. He would say he was tired or elated depending on how that day's campaigning had gone. He told her how to find him any time of the night and day by routine calls through his secretary, Evelyn Lincoln.

Exactly one month after meeting in Las Vegas they became lovers, at the Plaza Hotel in New York.

It was an important evening in many lives.

It was also the eve of the New Hampshire Primary in which Kennedy triumphed, a win that vastly improved his chances of being the Democratic Party's presidential nominee.

Two weeks after that encounter, on 7 March 1960, Judith Exner went to Miami for the opening of the touring stage act of Sinatra's Rat Pack held at the Fontainebleau Hotel, where Meyer Lansky had regular meetings. She had a quiet drink with Sinatra and he introduced her to Joe 'Stingy' Fischetti, whose brothers Charlie and Rocco were heavyweight members of Al Capone's Outfit. Joe Fischetti was a Mafia 'minder' for Sinatra and reported to Frank Costello. An earlier Sinatra 'minder' had been Sam Giancana. Exner met him at the Fontainebleau Hotel four days later.

She was attending a party and was called over by Sinatra, who was sitting with Joe Fischetti and another man, to whom she was introduced, named Sam Flood.

'It's a great pleasure to meet you, Judy,' said Flood, taking her hand. 'A very real pleasure.'

Smiling, he looked into her eyes: 'Do you mind if I say something to you, Judy?'

She didn't think that she really minded at all.

'You're far too beautiful to be wearing junk – excuse me – I mean, costume jewellery. A beautiful girl like you should be wearing real pearls and diamonds and rubies.'

'A girl like me sometimes does,' she replied.

'No offence, please. Real pleasure meeting you. Hope to see you again soon.'

In that mock Sicilian courtesy, you can hear George Raft, or maybe even Cagney, or Bogart in dialogue with Jane Russell, or some another cantilevered star ... but Judith Exner reported that is how it went.

By then, Sam Giancana, who'd worked his way through the Mob from killer to kingpin, was one of the most powerful gangsters in the world. He had hoodlums, accountants, burglars, counterfeiters, hijackers, drug pushers, chemists, loan-sharks, pimps, prostitutes, union bosses, businessmen, theatre and nightclub workers, bookmakers, crooked judges and police – and Frank Sinatra – under his control. The President of the United States would make a full deck.

He was earning about $1 million a week, with his interests going all the way out to Hawaii and Japan, with the Yakuza there running at around $2 billion a year. His home patch stretched from Cleveland to Kansas City, from Hot Springs to New Orleans, and out of the area were the lucrative rackets in Florida, the West Indies, Arizona and the lively, money-making territories of Nevada and California. If diamonds are a girl's best friend, then Sam Giancana had plenty of them.

He quickly wooed and won Judith Exner. She said he fell in love with her, but when I asked her if there might have been another motivation, she nodded: 'At first, he may have just wanted to use me, but it became more than that.'

It certainly did. She became the conduit between the Mafia and Kennedy.

The narrative might be circumstantial, but she met Giancana very shortly after she slept with Kennedy. For Giancana, there was the prospect of sexual blackmail: whether Kennedy won or lost the race for the White House, he would remain a powerful person in American politics.

Giancana was a widower, but for sexual companionship he had as wide a choice as any man in America: in addition to drug trafficking, gambling and hijacking, he controlled a prostitution business that provided exquisite beauties for some of the most important men in America.

But the days of the gang molls were over. Giancana's respectability demanded a lady at his side, a 'classy dame' in old days patois. Judith Exner filled both roles.

Giancana was the opposite of the handsome Kennedy, but he had power. He got 'Royal' attention. If he went into a restaurant and wasn't pleased, the unfortunate owners knew that their business was doomed. Deliveries would halt, unions would strike, customers would fade away and vandals would finally work things over so that nothing of value was left. There was no one in the world whom Giancana didn't dominate, who did not fear his power. Even the powerful names of show business – they all toed the line, some more than others.

Judith Exner discovered Giancana was poisoned with racial prejudice. He'd fought the upsurge of the Black Power criminal gangs and regularly announced he 'hated all niggers'. He always snubbed Sammy Davis Jr when he was around the Rat Pack. And elsewhere, as was shown when Exner recounted her experience at a cabaret show in Chicago:

'Sammy directed his performance to our table and Sam ignored him. This time, however, Sammy came to our table after the show. He greeted us, a big smile on his face, and Sam turned away from him. Sammy caught the movement and quickly turned his attention to me, asking me when I got in, where I was staying, how did I like Chicago? It was polite conversation but with a nervous edge, as he kept glancing at Sam, who was impatiently drumming his fingers on the table. Sammy, turning his full attention to Sam, asked: "Would you good people join me and a few friends for a little soirée?"

'Sam abruptly stood up. "We don't have the time."

'"Well, I thought . . ."

'"Just forget it, OK? I told you, we don't have the time."

'Sammy gave me an anxious look and backed away. "Sure, OK, see you good people later."'

On the way back to their hotel, Exner remarked on Giancana's rudeness. Abruptly, he told her: 'Don't worry about that nigger. He can take it.'

That evening she received a phone call from a nervous and apparently frightened Sammy Davis Jr, who asked: 'Have I offended him?'

No one offended Sam Giancana.

In April 1960, Judith Exner was all but living full-time in the John Barrymore Suite of Chicago's Ambassador East Hotel. It was a vintage champagne lifestyle. Yet the criminal empire was run from the Armory Lounge, a small bar and spaghetti restaurant in Forest Park, a Chicago suburb. There was a long bar down the narrow room and booths on the opposite wall. It had a jukebox and a coin telephone. And in the back there was a dining area, covered with bright, checked tablecloths, and behind that the back room, where fundamental decisions were made. The Armory was run by Doris and Carmine Fanelli; they catered for regular customers out front while Giancana and his inner circle ate pasta in the back. On FBI tapes, you do hear Giancana ordering – just as they do in Hollywood movies – a killing between spoonfuls of spaghetti.

(In the years of Giancana's rule, between 1958 and 1963, Chicago police recorded 53 mob murders and 24 major bombing attacks. The majority, the FBI believe, were conceived and planned in the Armory.)

Sam Giancana took Judith Exner to lunch at the Armory on 7 April 1960. He introduced her to his friends, who, between her conversations with them, talked among themselves in a language she could not understand. It was, explained Giancana, Sicilian. When she joked that she would go to a Berlitz language school to learn, 'he just about fell over laughing' she said.

It is here that Judith Exner's version of their relationship clashes with credulity. She maintained that even then, in the heartland of the Mob, as it were, she still believed Giancana was 'Sam Flood'. It seemed Sam Giancana had the acting talent his lover lacked: for him to accept the role as the 'other man' – and play it to perfection – meant a devolving of all his savage instincts. Although sharing a woman with another man was totally alien to him, given his position and background, he accepted it – as long as she saw him when she wasn't with the man she loved, Jack Kennedy. Then, they talked. The excited Judith Exner liked to talk, especially with a man who was friendly, sympathetic, the perfect listener. It was quite an act for Giancana: some of those who met him who are still alive say he smelled of evil. The way they tell it he had a look of Dorian Gray's picture – all that badness knotted up inside him reflected in his face and demeanour. But for California dreamboat Judith Exner, he was like a therapist. She told him the details of her love affair.

One day, she left Kennedy's bed at his home in Georgetown, Washington, then joined Giancana in Chicago. She explained the risky liaison with Kennedy. Mrs Kennedy was away in New England at the time and after dinner with a political friend Kennedy had taken Exner on a tour of the house and eventually they had made love in the master bedroom. Afterwards, he offered to buy her a mink coat, or pay for the one she was wearing, which she had bought out of alimony payments. She refused (but later took $2,000 towards the price of the coat). Kennedy had made it plain that he wanted a long-term relationship. He couldn't wait to see her again and asked if she would come down to Miami, where he would be the following week.

Giancana listened and said he understood, so much so that he offered to fly her down to Miami: it just happened that he had to go there on business, so she could come with him. He took her to nightclubs and floor shows and to his summer home in Palm Beach, not too far from the Kennedy family's Florida base. He bought her presents, not all of which she accepted. So the days passed while she waited for her assignation with Kennedy. One present Giancana bought her while she was standing in the same jeweller's shop. It was a turquoise and diamond earring and ring set. Delighted with her surprise, he boasted: 'You never even saw me buy this and you were standing right beside me.' She smiled at that: 'It always delighted him to put something over on me.'

What the mobster had in play was the future of America. The Kennedy brothers had been campaigning on a law-and-order ticket and Bobby Kennedy had pledged to hound organised crime out of business. In answer, the Mob needed bargaining power. The connective tissue between them and the government was already well established – America's Central Intelligence Agency, the aggressive CIA, had helped out the Mafia, and in return wanted the Mob to kill Fidel Castro.

Howard Hughes's right-hand man and CIA part-timer Bob Maheu had been the perfect man to introduce the CIA to Johnny Rosselli, to whom they offered $150,000 to do the job. Rosselli brought in Giancana and Santo Trafficante Jr, the seriously powerful boss headquartered in Tampa, Florida. They'd lost their gambling bonanza in Havana to Castro's coup and when the dictator turned sharp left, pro-Moscow, anti-Washington, they saw it as their patriotic duty – and an opportunity to retrieve their Havana casinos – by launching what became Operation Mongoose.

It was not only the fruit, rum and sugar interests that were hit when Castro imposed his Caribbean-style socialism, but also the crime industry. Under the leadership of Santo Trafficante, father and son, in drug trafficking, and Meyer Lansky in gambling, for three decades the Syndicate had run an illicit paradise; you could buy anything. The Mob owned the hotels, the gambling saloons, the bars and brothels, the boys and girls. Now all that was gone. But they still had their underworld infrastructure in Cuba, which was stronger than the CIA's underground political network.

Someone had the idea that the Mafia were the way to make Castro disappear. For the thinkers in the Mafia, it was perhaps a way to legitimise more of their businesses and investments. It was positive to have cooperated with the government in an important overseas insurgency mission.

Giancana was sceptical about any hit being a success. He says on tape that the idea was 'crazy'. But a favour was always repayable with another favour and the CIA could be welcome insurance he could use against a change in administration in the White House. If they assassinated Castro, the CIA could help take federal heat off the Mafia. And he had his personal liaison with Jack Kennedy, who was looking an even better bet to get the job as the most powerful man in the world. Whether he would actually *be* the most powerful man in the world was something Giancana was working on.

Kennedy and Judith Exner were meeting as often as possible in private houses and hotel rooms, and they talked. After these meetings, there would be phone calls from Giancana: 'Judy, I'm in New York. Why don't you come up and see me? I miss you.' And she would, for she liked flitting around America. The tickets were always first class; she didn't know the company wasn't. When Sam called, she went. He was so undemanding and so understanding.

She explained to him about Jack Kennedy. Of course it was confidential, but she knew she could trust him. The absurdity of JFK's behaviour was that he didn't want others to cause upset.

In 1960, election year, Peter Falk appeared as the mad killer Abe 'Twist' Reles in *Murder, Inc.*, which also starred Swedish actress May Britt, who caused controversy when it was announced she was to marry Sammy Davis Jr: interracial marriage was illegal in 31 states. The Kennedy brothers, Jack and Bobby, told Sinatra to tell Sammy Davis to postpone his wedding until after the election. The prenuptial warnings were also issued by Sam Giancana. (JFK won on 8 November, and Davis and Britt married on 13 November 1960.)

The manipulators were supposedly covering every angle. Kennedy was mounting the most professional political drive for the White House that America had seen since the days of Franklin Delano Roosevelt. He was surrounded by a group of tough, hard young political organisers, a new breed in politics men who could never be outsmarted. These supreme professionals were all led by his brother, Bobby. Their reputations, their incomes, their futures depended on Kennedy winning. And to win, there must be no slip-up. They had a motto: 'No Risks'.

And yet, at this vital moment, Kennedy was totally vulnerable. Some of the men around him were aware of Judith Exner, but not one of the supreme professionals checked out her background and contacts or asked: 'Is she a risk?' And the reason for this was the unwritten law around JFK. He had to have his fun – his girls. Then he could get out of bed and into politics. It was an unwritten law that became tolerated, accepted, even admired. It built a false confidence, for not one person imagined such innocent, manly fun could harm JFK.

(During talks to establish the Nassau Treaty, which was signed on 22 December 1962, replacing Skybolt with Polaris as the basis of the UK nuclear deterrent programme, the 'spy' element of the Profumo Affair, Kennedy is said to have confided about his sex drive to Prime Minister Harold Macmillan. He told him he had to have plenty of sexual relationships with different women or he felt unwell. Macmillan, with elegant Edwardian diplomacy, apparently changed the subject to the weather to cover what he considered rather bad form.)

Yet Kennedy should never have been in the Bahamas – or President. Had anyone known before the Democratic Convention or the November election that his lover was traipsing between him and Giancana, that would have been it. He got away with it and, maybe, it was the luck of the Irish. He certainly pushed that luck: the longer he survived, the more open he was about the affair.

With the Los Angeles Convention in full play, the candidates stayed away until the choice had been made. During the seven days before the convention opened in Los Angeles, on 11 July 1960, there were two challenges to Kennedy: two-time nominee Adlai Stevenson and Senate Majority Leader Lyndon B. Johnson. The 'new face' won. In a surprising move, he asked Johnson to be his running mate. After Johnson accepted the offer, Robert Kennedy went across Pershing Square to

Johnson's downtown Biltmore Hotel suite to talk him out of the job. LBJ was offended. If anything, it made him more determined to stay on the ticket. It was the catalyst for a fierce feud between them.

During all this high political drama, the president-to-be playboy had been romancing Judith Exner. JFK had phoned her, suggesting a drink in his room at the Beverly Hills Hotel. When she got there, a wild drinking party was going on. She said Kennedy had tried to get her into bed with him and another woman, 'a tall, thin secretary type', who left when she'd stopped the advances. It was a hiccup and by morning they were friends again.

Her friendship with Frank Sinatra drifted away, although FBI records show they still talked – she telephoning him. (When the story of it all first emerged, Sinatra offered: 'Hell hath no greater fury than a hustler with a literary agent.')

Sinatra was central to the Giancana manoeuvre, planting Judith Exner on JFK on behalf of the Mafia. He was one of the few people who knew the astounding secret that the President's mistress was also sleeping with a Mafia chieftain – and he kept it.

Johnny Rosselli knew the secrets, too. He saw more of Judith Exner as Giancana focused his attention on what he saw as his genuine desire, the singer Phyllis McGuire of the McGuire Sisters. She was a popular star and his long-time girlfriend and travelling companion. His relationship with McGuire had carried on during his 'romance' with Judith Exner, which gave him an edge. As did the CIA–Mafia plot to knock off Castro.

The anti-Castro stronghold was Miami and down in 'little Havana' Cuban refugees were gathering. Giancana and Rosselli met there with CIA agents. A deal was done on the understanding that the authorities would 'look the other way' as events rolled out. Giancana was wary of Robert Kennedy ever leaving them alone following his anti-crime pledges. It all became, of course, a tragic comedy involving some of the more preposterous plots in the history of political murder.

They attempted to poison Castro, but the Mafia assassins could never get close enough to drop the CIA cyanide into his drinks. Or explode his cigars. One particular CIA scheme involved putting a powdered drug into Castro's boots, which would work through the bloodstream and make all his hair fall out. CIA psychiatrists reasoned that without his beard Castro would lose his political charisma: 'Defoliate the son of a bitch and he'll never give you any trouble again.'

Castro kept his beard – and power – despite the Mafia.

The ideas may have been weird, but the CIA's electronic equipment impressed Giancana. He could see how he could use it for his personal affairs: what with the time taken up with Judith Exner and the CIA in Miami, he was paranoid that his beloved Phyllis McGuire was lacking his attention – and getting someone else's. He had the tall, smug-smiled Dan Rowan, half of the 'Rowan and Martin' duo, in the frame as the other man.

Robert Maheu lived in Las Vegas and would have drinks with old connections. He died, aged 90, in 2008, but 'never lost his marbles', according to one of his younger drinking buddies. As the years got older, they often talked about their younger ones.

Apparently when one scheme went wrong, Maheu almost lost his life. Giancana, it seems, was 'a jealous bastard'.

Robert Maheu had arranged for a specialist detective to tap the phone in Rowan's room to see what his relationship with Phyllis McGuire was all about. The private eye installed the equipment but was caught by a maid suddenly returning to the room. He was arrested by the Las Vegas police, who informed the FBI, who were themselves watching Phyllis McGuire, hoping to get something on Giancana. They had the premiere mobster on the federal charge of phone hacking, but the CIA stepped in and made it go away: they blocked the charges rather than have their criminal partnership exposed. There were a lot of dirty tricks going on.

Cold War politics involved Meyer Lansky, who met with Tony Varona, the leader of an anti-Castro group in south

Florida, at Lansky's home in Miami in 1960, when the gangster offered the Mafia's continuing support against Castro. Shortly afterwards Varona and his group employed the services of Washington lawyer E. Kipper Moss for propaganda and fund-raising.

Kipper Moss had founded Moss International, Inc. in 1954 and through it represented the National Coffee Association and the Bank of America. More importantly, he advised 19 countries and helped the Democratic National Committee organise conventions. He was a hugely influential and politically connected operator. His mistress was Julia Cellini, sister of the Mafia's gambling genius, Dino Cellini, whose secretarial services business at 1025 Connecticut Avenue, Washington, DC was a front for Kipper Moss's activities. One of which was arranging for Dino Cellini to offer $2 million on behalf of the Syndicate to Varona to finance operations against the Castro regime – on the understanding that the Syndicate *would share in the Cuba of the future*. When the Kennedy administration came to power, they scuppered the plans by shutting down on Varona.

The British supplied intelligence to the White House and the CIA that the anti-Castro support was dismal, but this advice was ignored and they went for it on 17 April 1961. The ex-pat Cubans trained up by the CIA were no contest for Castro's men, who'd had years of revolutionary arms experience and up-to-date help from their Moscow friends. Dino Cellini was 'executive liaison' on the abortive Operation Mongoose.

The Mob blamed a dilatory President Kennedy. Lansky and company, especially Philadelphia's Angelo Bruno, decided JFK was just like his old man, a rat-bag double-dealing bastard. They felt betrayed and a good deal of that resentment was nothing to do with patriotism; it was simply business. They'd lost funds and opportunity in Havana. They truly hated the Kennedy family, for, as far as they were concerned, they'd put Jack in the White House.

This was a little in the future. By then, the JFK–Judith Exner affair was at full throttle, as it had been since he'd won the Democratic Party nomination and made a victory speech at the Los Angeles Coliseum on 13 July 1960.

There was then a moment of serendipity. On the same day Kennedy became the presidential candidate, it was made public that Frank Sinatra, Dean Martin, Hank Sincola, a Sinatra friend and business partner, and 'Skinny' D'Amato had applied for permission from the State of Nevada to take over the Cal Neva Lodge and Casino at Crystal Bay on the Nevada side of Lake Tahoe. A convicted white trader, Paulino 'Skinny' (which he was) D'Amato was important in the life of JFK.

With his lawyer Angelo D. Malandra, who represented 'Jersey Joe' Walcott, the oldest Heavyweight Champion of the World, D'Amato had helped Kennedy win the West Virginia Primary election. They'd taken suitcases of cash to distribute to the local West Virginia sheriffs, whose annual convention brought them to D'Amato's 500 Club in Atlantic City (which unexpectedly burned down in 1973). The 500 Club was an illegal gambling operation providing slot machines, baccarat, craps, roulette and blackjack. Entertainment to attract the gamblers included Frank Sinatra, Sammy Davis Jr, Dean Martin and Jerry Lewis. The Kennedy suitcases were a nice gesture and a vote-winner by the man who ran the Atlantic City rackets for the always ambitious Genovese family. That summer (1960) he was on loan out on the California–Nevada border.

Veteran gangster Elmer Renner, of San Francisco, owned the Cal Neva, but owed $800,000 in tax. When, on paper, hoodlum Bert Grober bought the place, the tax man went after him, too. Then Sinatra and his saviours rode into town. What wasn't announced was that Sam Giancana had a big silent percentage in the Cal Neva and that he had persuaded 'Wingy Grober' to sell the property at an extremely undervalued quarter of a million dollars. The casino itself was no great money-maker, but it gave Giancana another hook in Sinatra, whom he wanted tight with JFK. With hindsight, you can see the perils of such business. Dean Martin saw them on the day. With the Mob all over the deal, he pulled out fast.

For an often drunk depressive, Sinatra seemed to have a rose-tinted view of business. He was aware that Anthony 'Fat Tony' Salerno, the New York Mafia power-broker, retained 'an interest' in the property. Giancana was putting up the money. That was pressure, but Sinatra was certain that the seasonal resort could turn a healthy profit and that was how he'd 'sold' it to Giancana. Sinatra did have the contacts – on opening night, Joe Kennedy was there with his presidential candidate son Jack, along with Marilyn Monroe and, a little out of the spotlight, Johnny Rosselli and Sam Giancana. J. Edgar Hoover's agents were watching the Cal Neva from Tahoe's famously heavily wooded hills. It didn't provide much of a view.

If made public, what the FBI agents failed to see would have compromised the Kennedys and changed the future of America. But JFK became President John Fitzgerald Kennedy on a snow-blown day in Washington on 21 January 1961, giving an impassioned inaugural speech that is being quoted more than 50 years later.

The previous night a gala had been staged by Frank Sinatra at the National Guard Armory (with familiar names like Jimmy Durante, Gene Kelly, Shirley MacLaine, Ella Fitzgerald). The one sour note was the forced absence of Sammy Davis Jr, who had been banned from the proceedings on the orders of Ambassador Joseph P. Kennedy because of Davis's recent marriage to May Britt. The just about President went to Paul Young's restaurant for a late-night dinner hosted by his father. Among the guests was Paul 'Red' Fay Junior, a friend who'd served with JFK during the Second World War. In his memoir *The Pleasure of His Company*, Fay, who became Under Secretary of the Navy, said his task that night was to escort Angie Dickinson; he recalled her 'wrapped in fur, standing all alone'.

It's dusty gossip that Fay was there to cover Kennedy's romance with Dickinson. She's never said yes or no about it. She returned the advance on a book, having completed more than 100 pages; in American publishing, it was gossiped that she'd written about her presidential affair but then decided against it. More than 50 years on from the inauguration, she was quizzed about it and of Fay said: 'He shouldn't have written it. It was too personal.' She described the gossip of five decades as 'kind of like having a broken wrist. It's an annoyance, but I have to live with it. They wouldn't believe me if I said it never happened.'

With the Kennedys, it's also difficult to know exactly what to believe in their relationships with Marilyn Monroe. Judith Exner was the go-between, connecting the White House to the Mob. Peter Lawford played that role with Monroe, who was sad rather than purely the victim or the heroine she gets most play as. Of course, she'll always be a star in Hollywood.

She was worth so much more dead than alive.

Mobster Mickey Cohen in his trademark hat before a Hollywood court hearing in 1950. Sitting with him is his bodyguard and film-land stud, Lana Turner's lover Johnny Stompanato. (© PA)

(213) 474-4526

John Rosselli

STRATEGIST

1333 So. BEVERLY GLEN
LOS ANGELES, CALIF. 90024

The business card of the ultimate Hollywood 'strategist', one of the main corrupters of Tinseltown, John Rosselli.
(Author collection)

ABOVE: Marilyn Monroe with her image team: 'Whitey' Snyder and, in the background, his wife and Marilyn's wardrobe mistress Marjorie Lecher. (Author collection)

LEFT: The gold money-clip Marilyn Monroe personalised for her long-time make-up man Whitey Snyder. (Author collection)

Happy on location: Marilyn Monroe takes a filming break with Whitey Snyder. (Author collection)

Robert Evans in the garden of his French Regency estate in the Hollywood Hills – where Marlon Brando signed to be 'the Godfather'. (© Paul Harris)

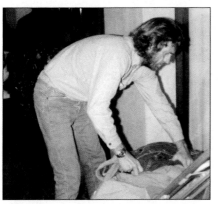

Steve McQueen: the man who got away with Robert Evans's third wife (of seven), Ali MacGraw, and felt the power of the Mafia. Douglas Thompson took the photograph, with McQueen's instruction to 'make it look casual', after they spoke in November 1978 at the Beverly Wilshire Hotel in Beverly Hills, two years before his death from cancer on 7 November 1980 in Ciudad Juárez, Mexico, where he was undergoing experimental treatment. It was one of the last photographs taken of him beyond a film set. (Author collection)

James Caan, the tough-guy star of many movies but most memorably as Sonny Corleone in *The Godfather*. (© Paul Harris)

Angie Dickinson, one of the grandes dames of Hollywood, poses at her home in the Hollywood Hills. Note the portrait of President John Kennedy on her wall. (© Paul Harris)

Deep Throat: Veteran star Lloyd Bridges spoke at length to Douglas Thompson on the beach and at his home in Malibu about movie moguls, the Mob and the young Hollywood set of his day, which included Judith Exner, the lover of JFK and Mafia kingpin Sam Giancana. (Author collection)

Douglas Thompson on location with Nicolas Cage, nephew of *Godfather* director Francis Ford Coppola and star of *The Cotton Club*. (Author collection)

Goodfellas: Robert De Niro talks the Mafia and the movies with Douglas Thompson. (Author collection)

John Travolta details the resurrection of his career with gangster movie *Pulp Fiction* to Douglas Thompson. (Author collection)

Love lawyer Marvin Mitchelson in a different sort of soap opera – with his wife Marcella at their home above the Sunset Strip in Hollywood. (Author collection)

Marvin Mitchelson escorts Joan Collins into Los Angeles Superior Court during her fourth divorce. (Author collection)

Vicki Morgan –
another Marvin
Mitchelson client – in
her favourite fur coat.
(© PA)

Firepower: Action star
Steven Seagal with his
then wife Kelly
LeBrock before his
name was dragged into
the ongoing
'Hollywood and the
Mob' scandal.
(© Paul Harris)

Super-casino: gambling entrepreneur Steve Wynn in Las Vegas, where he founded his business empire. (Author collection)

Neverland: Home to the late singer Michael Jackson, and the ultimate Hollywood fantasy – the place where time stops.
(© Paul Harris)

8

ROUGH EDGES

'Real diamonds! They must be worth their weight in gold!'

— Sugar Kane Kowalczyk (Marilyn Monroe),
Some Like It Hot, 1959

'MARILYN WAS FRIGHTENED ALL THE TIME. EVERY NIGHT SHE went to bed thinking she wasn't going to wake up. And one morning she didn't. It was sad and I was sad,' said Allan 'Whitey' Snyder, who was her make-up man (from her first screen test in 1947) throughout her time in the movies and at her death. We were talking at his home, way north of Seattle in the Pacific Northwest, overlooking the waters of Puget Sound. He and his wife Marjorie Lecher, a talented Hollywood wardrobe mistress (whose clients included Katharine Hepburn, Doris Day, Susan Hayward, Raquel Welch), had often sat up to the early hours with Marilyn, sipping a drink Whitey Snyder made with cranberry juice and over-servings of gin.

It was much less dangerous than her daily cocktail of uppers and downers, the amphetamines and barbiturates she used to get her working and then resting, but towards the end the drinking and the depression increased. 'Her terror was what I remember most. As the years went on, she had to be talked into everything. When we were doing *The Prince and the Showgirl* [1957] in England, Laurence Olivier would have his man feed me breakfast as we'd sit playing cards, waiting for Marilyn to show up. Sometimes his man fed me lunch, too.

She'd always been afraid of death – or rather what happened after. When she was about 27, we were making *Gentlemen Prefer Blondes* [1953] and she said to me: "Whitey, promise you won't let anyone touch my face." Something like that. It was morbid, I guess, but I said: "OK, honey, bring me the body when it's still warm and I'll be interested."'

And they did. At Westwood Memorial Park, the master make-up man and his wife went to look after Marilyn Monroe's appearance for the last time, but the Marilyn they found was not the Marilyn they remembered. Her face and breasts had dropped: 'Marilyn without a bust – she'd have freaked.'

With pieces of cushions and plastic bags, they recreated the famous figure. Whitey Snyder revived her face with his cosmetics skill. Mourners, unaware of his work, and who viewed her open casket, told him how beautiful she looked.

Yet her demise was a far from beautiful story. And it had begun to truly unravel at the Cal Neva Lodge up in the hills of Lake Tahoe.

What the FBI missed that night at the lodge was the honey trap of JFK by Sam Giancana. Expensive, specialist girls who worked for Skinny D'Amato on the Hollywood–Las Vegas circuit had been brought in to entertain the out-of-town VIPs. One unofficial report – not backed up by FBI files, but they themselves were manipulated by J. Edgar Hoover – claims that Teddy Kennedy was also present and that, according to Giancana, he and his brother Jack 'had sex with prostitutes – sometimes two or more at a time – in bathtubs, hallways, closets, on floors, almost everywhere but the bed'.

What Giancana wanted was a negotiable commodity: verified scandalous behaviour, not exposure. He wanted influence in the White House, not JFK and company out of the race.

He sensed a weak link in Frank Sinatra, whom he believed was getting star-struck by JFK, so he asked Johnny Rosselli to bring in a watcher at the Cal Neva. They agreed a hit man-turned-casino operator called Lewis McWillie was good for the assignment. McWillie had worked in Cuba with Rosselli when Meyer Lansky had first cut into the island's economy in the 1930s.

Before Castro's revolution ended the gambling bonanza of the 1950s, Lansky had been empire building. The Montmartre Club was close to the somewhat Moorish Hotel Nacional, which was owned by the Cuban government. When a casino complex with cabaret room – the Club Parisien – and a bar-restaurant was created within the walls of the Nacional, it was sublet to Lansky. Santo Trafficante's International Amusements Corporation (IAC) provided the entertainment and on opening night Eartha Kitt, at her feline prime as a sex kitten, was the star. The IAC fed talent to the casinos – the much-favoured Nat King Cole and Ella Fitzgerald, the premier names in jazz and cool – just as it did to the Hollywood studios. Every which way, the boys were earning. It was exquisite daiquiri diplomacy.

They had casinos attached to the Capri, the Sevilla-Biltmore, the Commodoro and the Deauville, and it was all mentored by Lansky's lieutenant Dino Cellini and his team, who kept these oceanfront money machines in around-the-clock working order. They also ran the gambling at the Tropicana, which was a Busby Berkeley cabaret all by itself in the jungle on the outskirts of town: the showgirls were startling and the best dancers, with endless legs and smiles. The high kicks invited vertigo. On offer was an escape into fantasy, a world where, for a price, all desires could be provided for. Lewis McWillie had run the gambling and called himself 'a key man' for the Mob in Havana. McWillie regularly flew up to Miami. He was visited by his friend Jack Ruby, who owned a nightclub in Dallas. Official records show they both spent a short time in prison following Castro's coup.

Lansky personally brought McWillie back to America and put him in the Tropicana in Las Vegas. FBI files describe McWillie as a killer, and a very good one. But on Rosselli's instructions, the always-stylish, silver-haired 'gentleman' became a blackjack dealer at Sinatra's Cal Neva Lodge to monitor the Mob's investment. And Sinatra's behaviour. McWillie moved in as a casino pit boss, his antennae alert.

It paid off, for a short time later there was a curious incident when back in Chicago the FBI's agents heard one of Giancana's hoods, 'Chuckie' English, claiming that if Bobby Kennedy wanted to know anything about Sam Giancana 'he should ask Sinatra'. When the nation's gangbuster, the new Attorney General, Robert Kennedy, was told about it, he instructed Hoover to 'prioritise' the FBI's surveillance on the entertainer and the Cal Neva. They already had a file on the prostitution ring Skinny D'Amato was operating from the front desk of the hotel. Women were being flown everywhere, including the Cal Neva, to provide room service.

With binoculars focused on the casino in the woods, there was a shooting at the hotel. Details have never been made public, but a man suffered a bullet wound, though he did not die. Shortly afterwards, on 30 June 1962, Deputy Sheriff Richard Anderson arrived to collect his new wife, who was a waitress there. She'd dated Sinatra before their marriage, and Anderson noticed the way Sinatra stared at his wife and heard about the rude and often suggestive remarks he made to her. A big man, Deputy Anderson warned the singer to stay away. Sinatra backed down – and then got all depressed and broody and angry about being closed down, humiliated by 'the big dumb cop'.

Another evening when Anderson arrived to pick up his wife, and he had stopped by the kitchen to talk with some of the staff, Sinatra had come in, seen Anderson and run up to him, screaming: 'What the fuck are you doing here?' Anderson said he was waiting for his wife, then, suddenly, while the cop was still mid-sentence, Sinatra grabbed him and tried to throw him out: there was pushing and shoving and finally Anderson socked Sinatra hard in the face, a bruising punch that damaged his features and his ego.

Several weeks later, on 17 July 1962, Anderson and his wife were driving down Highway 28, not far from the Cal Neva, when they were driven off the road by a late model maroon convertible with California plates. A silver-haired man was at the wheel. Anderson lost control of his car, skidded off the road and smashed into a tree. He was killed instantly. His wife was thrown from the car and suffered severe broken bones and fractures. The Cal Neva was Sinatra's lifetime albatross.

Arguably, so was the death of Marilyn Monroe.

She flew to the casino, where jazz genius Buddy Greco was the star attraction, on Sinatra's private plane, along with Peter and Pat Lawford. He'd told her he wanted to discuss a film project, yet she was reluctant to go until Pat Lawford explained that her brother Bobby Kennedy, who had replaced JFK as Monroe's lover, would be there, having concluded meetings in Los Angeles.

Monroe hadn't heard from the Kennedy Clan and felt snubbed – but she knew from the newspapers that the Attorney General was in California. While Judith Exner had been an important liaison for the Kennedys and the Mob, as well as an uncomplicated and always available sexual release for JFK, Marilyn was an indulgence. Now she was a nuisance. And could perhaps disturb the Mafia–Kennedy set-up.

That evening, according to witnesses and to FBI records, there was dinner with Sam Giancana, Peter and Pat Lawford, Sinatra and Monroe. Giancana was on the Nevada blacklist and banned from all gambling establishments. He didn't care – he was a Cal Neva regular . . . well, he owned most of the place. San Francisco's legendary and good-natured newspaper columnist Herb Caen wrote in 1979: 'I saw Sinatra at the Cal Neva when Sam Giancana was there. In fact, I met Giancana through Frank. He was a typical hood, didn't say much. He wore a hat at the lake, and sat in his little bungalow, receiving people.'

What happened next was vile – no matter which version of the story you accept.

It is clear that something bad happened to Marilyn Monroe. There is plenty of circumstantial evidence, but also testimony. Jimmy Blue Eyes told Dino Cellini that what went on that weekend was degrading and debauched – 'as bad as Havana'. Monroe got very, very drunk and told anyone listening at the table that the Kennedys simply used her as 'a piece of ass'.

Gone was the sexual sweetness, the easy swivel of her neck, the aliveness she had on screen, the pull of her shoulders and drop of her bottom beneath that long waist as she tottered along the train as Sugar in *Some Like It Hot*. The reality was awful. The exploitation much worse.

She was taken to her cabin and later, in her doped and drugged state, she was joined by Giancana and Sinatra and some of Skinny D'Amato's girls. It was a free-for-all, with Monroe as the central player. Photographs were taken of the men and women sexually playing with Monroe. The film was developed overnight by Hollywood photographer Billy Woodfield.

In the blur of the following morning, Peter Lawford was instructed to tell Monroe that Bobby Kennedy had remained in Los Angeles – and there was to be no contact with him or any of his family from then on. It was logical, but of course she had no grasp of reality, never mind logic. Robert Kennedy was the Attorney General, married with seven children, just named Father of the Year and a member of the Catholic First Family. And Marilyn believed he'd divorce and marry her. It didn't go.

After the yells of protest at being dumped, she was shown the photographs taken only a few hours earlier. That afternoon, she took an overdose of pills and had to have her stomach pumped. The following weekend, on Sunday, 5 August 1962, her body was found naked and face down on her bed at her home on Fifth Helena Drive, at the end of a quiet cul-de-sac in Brentwood, California. She was 36 years old. Given what had gone, it was a true reflection of the society in which she lived that the public were more shocked that she was found naked than found dead.

'The long-troubled star clutched a telephone in one hand. An empty bottle of sleeping pills was nearby,' reported the Associated Press that morning. Long before she was officially *dead* on the Sunday, neighbours had seen an ambulance parked outside her home – the ambulance of legend that took her away breathing and brought her back dead? The only person still alive in 2012 who was present that fateful weekend before her death is Buddy Greco, who was with Benny Goodman's Band but in 1961 made his breakthrough solo recording 'The Lady Is a Tramp'. In 2011, he spoke of what he saw that weekend at the Cal Neva. Also around the hotel were Dean Martin, Sammy Davis Jr, Juliet Prowse, who was engaged to Sinatra, and the hairdresser-playboy Jay Sebring.

Buddy Greco was sitting out by the lake with Sinatra when Monroe made her entrance: 'That day we were just sitting around, reading the paper, when suddenly a limousine pulled up and this gorgeous woman stepped out. It was Marilyn. I had no idea she was coming.

'I first met Marilyn when I was performing with Benny Goodman. She came to the clubs where I was working and we became friends. I adored her. She was very intelligent but also like one of the guys: she drank a lot, smoked a lot and partied a lot. She loved attention.'

She got it on her arrival.

'When she arrived that Saturday, you'd never believe that she had a care in the world. She [was] dressed all in green – everything green: coat, skirt and scarf. Before I realised who it was, I thought: "My God, what a beautiful woman. No taste in clothes, but what a beautiful woman." We said hello a few times . . . [then] when Frank introduced us, I said: "You won't remember me, but I was the piano player when you auditioned for the Benny Goodman Band in 1948." She got emotional at that and hugged me. She had such warmth – and I was moved. It was an unrepeatable moment, a time that would never happen again. It was magical.'

But brief. Buddy Greco had completed his first performance that evening and joined the Sinatra table in the lounge: 'Suddenly the room went silent and very still. It was surreal. As if somebody had turned the sound off. I looked at Frank. I could immediately tell he was furious. His eyes were like blue ice cubes. He was looking at the doorway where Marilyn stood, swaying ever so slightly. She was still in the same green outfit she'd worn all day. But the woman I'd met that afternoon – smart, funny, intelligent, fragile – had gone. Now she looked drunk and, well, defiant. She was clearly angry and I think I heard her say: "Who the fuck are they all staring at?" It was clear Sinatra was worried. She was in a state where she could have said anything.

'Sinatra motioned to his bodyguard – Coochie – to get her out of there. Coochie, a big guy, escorted her out. Actually, he picked her up and carried her out. It wasn't the star we were used to seeing.

'She was on my mind. I was worried about her. I went outside to find out whether she was OK. I knew that she had taken accidental overdoses in the past. I found her by the pool. There was nobody around. It was late and the pool was deserted. Maybe it was the moon, but she had a ghostly pallor. It still didn't occur to me that she might be a woman not long for this world.

'She was distressed, out of it, but that was all. Maybe her friends were used to seeing her like that, but it worried me. Anyway, we talked. I walked her back to her bungalow in the complex reserved for the guests of Frank and Giancana where we all stayed.'

Buddy Greco went off to perform his second show of the evening: 'I thought that the next morning I could put her with Pat Lawford, who was her companion, and make sure she got back to LA safely. But the next day when I called she had already left. That was the last time I saw her. After she had created that problem, Frank certainly wanted her out of there. He could be quite firm with her.'

On the point that Marilyn Monroe had been brought to the Cal Neva to be warned off the Kennedys, the entertainer, who was 84 in 2012, said: 'It's a possible scenario.'

The London film critic Tim Robey gave his intriguing reaction to a photograph of the initial arrival of Marilyn Monroe at the Cal Neva in an article he wrote for the *Daily Telegraph*. I think his perception is absolutely correct:

The world hardly wants for books about Marilyn Monroe and Frank Sinatra, and yet there are still mysteries to be cleared up, particularly during the brief period of their lives when they knew each other intimately. There's a photograph – not so much of the two of them, but one in which they both separately appear – taken at the Cal Neva lodge in Lake Tahoe, five days before Monroe died. In the foreground, she poses with the singer and pianist Buddy Greco, smiling, maybe a little drunk. In the background, Sinatra slouches in a pool chair, a newspaper on his lap.

He's gazing at them with an extraordinary, faintly chilling sidelong expression. It's hard to tell if he's jealous, concerned, wary or a mixture of all three. But there is something strange going on in that picture, and it's something no biography has adequately explained yet.

There was little for Monroe back home in Hollywood.

Fed up with her chronic absenteeism – in 35 days of filming, she had turned up a dozen times, and when she did arrive she was so heavily medicated she could not remember her lines – 20th Century Fox's studio boss Peter Levathes had fired her from *Something's Got to Give*, the film she was making with Dean Martin. He served a half-million-dollar breach-of-contract suit against her and replaced her with Lee Remick.

Whitey Snyder said that when he and his wife got the call about Marilyn Monroe they both thought it was a drug overdose of barbiturates. And despite all the theories that followed they always did. He showed me a gold money clip that Monroe had given him. It's inscribed: 'While I'm still warm, Marilyn.' The way he talked about her death, it was what I suppose in Hollywood you'd call 'natural causes'. It was tragic and sad and not necessary, but for Sinatra and the Kennedys and Sam Giancana it was convenient.

By the time Marilyn Monroe died, attempts had been going on for some months to sanitise the Kennedys' Hollywood connections. Attorney General Robert Kennedy, through committees and inquiries, was rousting organised crime and investigating Mob links with Jimmy Hoffa's Teamsters Union, which could halt a film mid-production and all but bankrupt studios at will. Sam Giancana's reaction was to stay close with the CIA, play one federal outfit against another. He was the user – and Sinatra believed he was his buddy – so much so, he and the Rat Pack performed on 9 November 1962 at the Villa Venice Supper Club in Wheeling, Illinois, without payment. It might have been Vegas that night.

The much-married singer Eddie Fisher (Elizabeth Taylor, Debbie Reynolds and company) was the opening act. Sammy Davis Jr was next, followed by Dean Martin and then Sinatra. The wow factor was when they all appeared on stage together.

The Villa Venice Supper Club, just outside Chicago, had opened in 1960. Most of its business came from private functions. In the summer of 1962, it underwent a major renovation, where canals were dug into the eight-acre property and stocked with gondolas, which you could hire with a gondolier and or girl. For those who didn't want sex in a gondola, there was the illegal casino situated close by. Buses and limousines shuttled customers back and forth between the club and the casino all night long. J. Edgar Hoover's men monitored it all. FBI agents interviewed the entertainers.

Eddie Fisher explained he appeared as a politeness to his close friend Frank Sinatra. Sinatra said that he'd put it all together as a favour to his old friend Leo Olsen, who worked for Giancana. Sammy Davis Jr, when asked why he had performed without pay, said: 'I have to say it's for my man Francis.' He was asked if he worked free for anyone else, like Sam Giancana perhaps? 'By all means,' was the reply. He was asked to elaborate, and on FBI tapes he did: 'Baby, let me say this. I got one eye, and that one eye sees a lot of things that my brain tells me I shouldn't talk about. Because my brain says that, if I do, my one eye might not be seeing anything after a while.'

There are also tapes of Peter Lawford – and remember, he's the President's brother-in-law – saying: 'I couldn't stand Giancana, but Frank idolised him because he was the Mafia's top gun. Frank loved to talk about "hits" and guys getting "rubbed out". And you better believe that when the word got out around Hollywood that Frank was a pal of Sam Giancana, nobody but nobody ever messed with Frank Sinatra. They were too scared.'

It worked the other way, too. Sinatra always hosted Giancana lavishly at his homes and hotels. Whenever he was in Nevada, the gangster, who knew he was under constant FBI surveillance, was always careful to stay away from casinos; at the Cal Neva Lodge, Sinatra made sure that Giancana was kept out of sight in luxury.

In July 1963, while Giancana was seeing Phyllis McGuire at the Cal Neva, he was pictured by the FBI playing golf with Sinatra and also having drinks with the McGuire Sisters. They also gained information about a bust-up between Giancana and Victor Collins, the road manager for the singing sisters, during a party in Phyllis's room. It all added up to bad news for them.

The row erupted after Collins became annoyed with Phyllis for continually walking by his seat and punching him on the arm. He told his story to FBI agents: 'I told her if she did it again I [was] going [to] knock her right on her butt. A half an hour later she punches me again and so I grabbed her by both arms and meant to sit her in the chair I got out of, but I swung around and missed the chair; she hit the floor. She didn't hurt herself, but Sam came charging across the room and threw a punch at me wearing a huge big diamond ring that gouged me in the left eye. I just saw red then and grabbed him, lifted him clean off the floor and I was going to throw him through the plate glass door but thought, why wreck the place? So I decided to take him outside and break his back on the hard metal railing on the patio.

'I got as far as the door and then got hit on the back of the head. I don't know who hit me from behind, but the back of my head was split open. It didn't knock me out, but I went down, with Sam underneath me. He had on a pearl grey silk suit and blood from my eye was running all over it. I had a hold of him by the testicles and the collar and he couldn't move; that's when

Sinatra came in with his valet George [Jacobs], the coloured boy – they were coming to join the party. The girls were screaming and running around like a bunch of chickens in every direction because nobody knew what was going to happen. George just stood there with the whites of his eyes rolling around and around in his black face because he knew who Sam was and nobody ever fought with Sam. Sinatra and George pulled me off of Sam, who ran out the door.'

Oh, my. The FBI report of it all went to the State of Nevada Gambling Control Board and the chairman, Ed Olson, called Sinatra at the Sands casino in Las Vegas and asked about the *persona non grata* Giancana being on the property. Sinatra said that he had seen a man who looked like Giancana and that they had just waved and nodded to each other and that was all. Sinatra was a casino owner, with substantial investments in the state, and he was also a major celebrity, responsible for drawing tens of thousands of tourists into Nevada.

When the pioneering *Las Vegas Sun* got the story, the game changed. Olson was forced to say his investigation would not be complete until 'certain discrepancies in the information provided by various people at Cal Neva could be resolved'. Sinatra invited Olson to the Cal Neva for dinner 'to talk about this – your statements'.

Olson replied that the arrangement was inappropriate, as Sinatra was under investigation by Olson's office; even if Sinatra weren't under investigation, Olson said, it would still be unacceptable for the gaming commissioner to be seen fraternising with a casino owner. Sinatra wasn't an easy turnaway, according to Olson's testimony: 'Frank kept insisting and I kept refusing, and the more I refused, the madder he got until he seemed almost hysterical. He used the foulest language I ever heard in my life. I agreed to meet him at my office, but he didn't show up. He called me later and said in a rage: "You listen to me, Ed – you're acting like a fucking cop. I just want to talk to you off the record."'

Olson grabbed some dignity. 'Who am I speaking to?' he replied.

'This is Frank Sinatra! You fucking asshole! F-R-A-N-K Sinatra.'

'Any meeting between us will have to be in the presence of witnesses,' Olson tried to explain, before Sinatra cut him off.

'Now, you listen, Ed! I don't have to take this kind of shit from anybody in the country and I'm not going to take it from you people . . . I'm Frank Sinatra.'

Olson said that Sinatra was required to explain to the Gambling Board what had gone on and would be subpoenaed if he did not appear voluntarily. Sinatra replied: 'You just try and find me. And if you do, you can look for a big fat surprise . . . a big fat fucking surprise. You remember that. Now, listen to me, Ed. Don't fuck with me. Don't fuck with me. Just don't fuck with me.'

'Are you threatening me?' Olson asked.

'No – just don't fuck with me. And you can tell that to your fucking board of directors and that fucking commission, too.'

Gambling Control Board investigators appeared in time for the official money count at the Cal Neva casino the next day. Sinatra shouted across the floor to Skinny D'Amato: 'Throw the dirty sons of bitches out of the house.' The count had started and the agents, having seen enough, left of their own accord.

When they returned 24 hours later, D'Amato offered them $100 each 'to cooperate'. The agents reported the bribe to Olson, who took moves to revoke Sinatra's licence. When the news was announced that Sinatra was under investigation and would probably lose his casino licence, politicians at the state capital in Reno felt that Sinatra needed to be taught a lesson. It was spelled out this way: his licence to operate a casino or hotel in Nevada was revoked. He had to sell his half of the Cal Neva and his 7 per cent interest, worth about $3.5 million, in the Sands in Las Vegas.

CIA agent Joe Shimon later revealed he had spoken with Giancana the day after Sinatra lost his place in Nevada: 'He told me that Sinatra had cost him over $465,000 on Cal Neva. He said: "That bastard and his big mouth. All he had to do was keep quiet, let the attorneys handle it, apologise and get a 30- to 60-day suspension. But no, Frank has to get on the phone with that damn big mouth of his and now we've lost the whole damn place." He never forgave him. He washed Frank right out of his life.'

Nevada's governor, Grant Sawyer, stood behind the Gambling Control Board's decision to revoke Sinatra's licence, but while the case was still pending President Kennedy attended a caravan parade through the streets of Las Vegas, sitting in the same car as Governor Sawyer. Kennedy turned to Sawyer and said: 'Aren't you people being a little hard on Frank out here?' The governor didn't reply but later repeated what Kennedy had said to Ed Olson, who told him: 'That's about the highest degree of political pressure you could ever put into the thing.'

The lost licence lost Sinatra much more. Peter Lawford said at the Café Rodeo in Beverly Hills: 'That packed up the Rat Pack. It was all over with the family and the boys.' If it had ever really been real.

Lawford explained: 'During one of our private dinners, the President brought up Sinatra and said, "I really should do something for Frank." Jack was always so grateful to him for all the work he'd done in the campaign, raising money. "Maybe," Jack used to say, "I'll ask him to the White House for dinner or lunch. There's only one problem. Jackie hates him and won't have him in the house, so I really don't know what to do." He was eventually invited for lunch, I think twice, but only when Jackie was out of the White House, and he was asked to use a side door.

'I don't think he wanted reporters to see Frank Sinatra going into the White House, that's why Frank never flew on Air Force One and was never invited to any of the Kennedy State dinners or taken to Camp David for any of the parties there.'

The Cal Neva debacle topped a string of concerns. Sinatra never saw it. He could survive a lot, but not his Mafia connections. He owned a percentage of the Villa Capri in Hollywood and the restaurant was also a Mob-investment meeting place. They let that slip, but then he put money into a racetrack in Rhode Island where his fellow investors included crime bosses Raymond Patriarca, Tommy Lucchese and New Jersey's gangster Angelo DeCarlo. All contact was stopped after that on the orders of the Mob's greatest enemy: Robert Kennedy.

Suddenly, one of Kennedy's investigators at the Justice Department 'discovered' Sinatra had ties to organised crime. The agent found this out by reading a Department of Justice report about extortion in Hollywood, which mentioned Sinatra. They had made the message loud and clear.

Peter Lawford, at John Kennedy's request, asked Sinatra if Kennedy could stay at his Palm Springs home while the President was on a West Coast fund-raiser. Sinatra went to work on his estate, building separate cottages for the Secret Service and installing communications with 25 extra phone lines and a helipad with a pole for the President's flag. When everything was set, and Sinatra had bragged and boasted to all of Hollywood that he would host the President, JFK called Peter Lawford and said: 'I can't stay at Frank's place while Bobby's handling the investigation of Giancana. See if you can't find me someplace else. You can handle it, Peter. We'll handle the Frank situation when we get to it.'

Lawford was scared of Sinatra, what he might do. He made up a story about security and the Secret Service wanting a different location. But Bing Crosby's house? That really hurt. Lawford recalled: 'Frank was livid. He called Bobby every name in the book and then he rang me up and reamed me out again. He was quite unreasonable, irrational really. George Jacobs told me later that when he got off the phone he went outside with a sledgehammer and started chopping up the concrete landing pad of his heliport. He was in a frenzy.

'When he heard about Bing, he telephoned Bobby Kennedy and called him every name and a few that weren't in the book. He told RFK what a hypocrite [he was], that the Mafia had helped Jack get elected but weren't allowed to sit with him in the front of the bus.'

The Mafia was even more upset with the Kennedys. Maybe if their bootlegging partner Joe Kennedy, always an ambitiously amoral wheeler and dealer, had been capable, the story would have been different, but on 19 December 1961, at the age of 73, he'd suffered a life-threatening stroke. He survived but lost all power of speech and was left paralysed on his right side. He couldn't pull the strings any more.

In turn, his sons had broken their deal with the Mob and were going after it. They'd agreed to let Mafia boss Joe Adonis back into America in return for the West Virginia presidential primary, all the suitcases of cash. Not only was that now not going to happen, they were also going to deport as many other mobsters as they could – from all across America, from New York to Hollywood, Miami to Cleveland to Chicago.

Sam Giancana was said by one of his bodyguards to have thrown a phone across the room at the bad news.

When it became clear that Sinatra wasn't going to get him what he wanted, the mobster had no use for him. He blamed Sinatra most of all. Maybe it was too many heavy helpings of the stuff that hits the fan. Things soon did with Giancana: 'Eat'n out of my hand! That's what Frank told me! Jack's eat'n out of the palm of my hand! Bullshit! That's what that is. Bullshit!'

Sinatra, the patsy, had failed. The gangster had to be talked out of having Sinatra 'cut up into little pieces'. He never did stop talking, with pleasure in his voice, about killing Sinatra.

There was other talk of violence. The voice of Santo Trafficante Junior, who'd been recruited for the wild plots against Castro, was also preserved on tape in August 1962 telling an FBI informer: 'Kennedy's not going to make it to the election – he's going to be hit.'

That same August, Carlos Marcello, the Mafia boss in New Orleans, explained why President John Kennedy, not Attorney General Robert Kennedy, would be killed: 'You know what they say in Sicily: if you want to kill a dog, you don't cut off the tail, you cut off the head.' For the Kennedys, the men who'd helped them to the White House were no longer quite so warm. What followed was a forever-in-rerun, made-for-TV drama. Kennedy was the first and, so far, only President to have been assassinated in the television age; he is also the only one of the four murdered (the others being Abraham Lincoln (1865), James Garfield (1881) and William McKinley (1901)) to be killed instantly. As a politician, he lived and died on television. It was the mass experience: what would grow in the following decades to become the 'sharing' of grief, with every aspect extravagantly enlarged by predacious cameras. The thinking – the theories – were equally exaggerated.

Whatever you believe about the assassination of JFK – 2013 marks the 50th anniversary of his death – there was a large cast of sinister characters entangled with the family before 22 November 1963, when you get to Lee Harvey Oswald and the grassy knoll of Dallas.

Or maybe something completely different.

9

CLOSE-UP

'The Warren Commission thought they had an open-and-shut case. Three bullets, one assassin. But two unpredictable things happened that day that made it virtually impossible. One, the eight-millimetre home movie taken by Abraham Zapruder while standing by the grassy knoll. Two, the third wounded man, James Tague, who was nicked by a fragment, standing near the triple underpass. The time frame, 5.6 seconds, determined by the Zapruder film, left no possibility of a fourth shot. So the shot or fragment that left a superficial wound on Tague's cheek had to come from the three shots fired from the sixth-floor depository. That leaves just two bullets. And we know one of them was the fatal headshot that killed Kennedy. So now a single bullet remains. A single bullet now has to account for the remaining seven wounds in Kennedy and Connally. But rather than admit to a conspiracy or investigate further, the Warren Commission chose to endorse the theory put forth by an ambitious junior counsellor, Arlen Spector, one of the grossest lies ever forced on the American people. We've come to know it as the "Magic Bullet Theory". This single-bullet explanation is the foundation of the Warren Commission's claim of a lone assassin. Once you conclude the magic bullet could not create all seven of those wounds, you'd have to conclude that there was a fourth shot and

> a second rifle. And if there was a second rifleman,
> then by definition there had to be a conspiracy.'
> — Jim Garrison (Kevin Costner), *JFK*, 1991

IN THE SUMMER OF 1963, JOHNNY ROSSELLI WAS STILL looking after Frank Sinatra, who'd never discovered that his Hollywood pal-about-town was more connected than he had ever been or would ever be. In his benevolent moments, Sinatra liked to do things for his friends, so he'd sponsored Rosselli's membership of the Friars Club, the celebrity fraternity in Los Angeles. It was an exclusive place, wall-to-wall money. Rosselli could smell the cash.

Then he saw it – Maury Friedman, a bagman for the Detroit Mob. He was a Friars Club member and had made his money skimming millions of dollars from the Frontier Hotel in Las Vegas. There had to be a scam, and of course there was. Handsome Johnny got in and got lucky with a clever card-cheating operation that took members, including Phil 'Sergeant Bilko' Silvers, Zeppo Marx (himself a spectacular card cheat), Debbie Reynolds's husband Harry Karl and the singer Tony Martin, for hundreds of thousands of dollars. The card caper involved spies in the attic, who peered through peepholes to read the cards of the players; they sent coded electronic signals to a member of the ring seated at the table, who picked up the messages on equipment he wore on a girdle beneath his clothes. Why not? It was there for the taking. Rosselli couldn't resist, even with all the muttering about killing the President of the United States. Money mattered. Money motivated.

'There is a price on the President's head. Somebody will kill Kennedy when he comes down South' was the quote from Carlos Marcello's friend, the New Orleans restaurateur Bernard Tregle, in April 1963. It's long established as something of an epigraph for the assassination/conspiracy theorists.

With the significant upcoming anniversary of 'the Death of a President' (William Manchester's reportage in his 1967 book of the same name remains a distinguished literary achievement and one of the greatest contributions to all discussions – Jackie Kennedy Onassis attempted to stop its being published), there is a revival in the long-running eclectic explanations of what may forever remain unexplainable: why Lee Harvey Oswald killed John F. Kennedy.

If we dismiss that he acted alone, the prevalent theory is that the Mob arranged the murder and the silencing of Oswald by Mob-connected Dallas club owner Jack Ruby. This does away with the Warren Commission's conclusion that Oswald was a twisted lone nutter and Lewis McWillie's friend Ruby a patriot who impetuously killed the assassin to spare Jacqueline Kennedy the ordeal of a trial. It also puts the twist on the lone-assassin conclusion that Oswald intended to kill Texas Governor John Connally rather than Kennedy.

The Warren Commission, set up to investigate everything about Kennedy's death, ignored that. Yet Oswald's wife, Marina, testified that Connally was the target. The commission relied on Texas prosecutor Henry Wade for evaluation of the alleged conversation between Oswald and Ruby, overheard at Ruby's Carousel Club by Dallas lawyer Carroll Jarnagin. Wade found Jarnagin sincere in thinking he had heard Oswald offer to kill Connally so that gangsters could open up Texas for their rackets, though he said the lawyer failed a lie-detector test on the subject.

Other theories persist: that Oswald, an avowed Marxist who had gone from service as a US Marine to spend more than two years in the Soviet Union, returned as a homicidal tool of the KGB; that when he tried to go back to the Soviet Union via Cuba in September 1963, Fidel Castro's Embassy in Mexico City encouraged him to kill Kennedy. The reason: Castro knew that the CIA had plotted with Sam Giancana and Johnny Rosselli to kill him. There is support for the Castro-hit theory in *Final Disclosure*, written by David W. Belin, a leading counsel for the Warren Commission. He wrote that 'it is possible'

CLOSE-UP

Oswald was part of a Cuban conspiracy that might have developed when Oswald visited Mexico City.

For us Mafia-conspiracy believers, the man who rode a bus to Mexico City before the assassination, talking to travellers about his plans to meet Fidel Castro and then causing a row at the Cuban Embassy, was not Oswald. He was a distraction sent by the Mafia, so that when the real Oswald killed the President, a Cuban–Soviet connection would be readily assumed. The existence of someone posing as Oswald would, of course, be proof in itself of a conspiracy.

The possibility of an Oswald double is shared by investigators and authors, including John H. Davis (*Mafia Kingfish: Carlos Marcello and the Assassination of John F. Kennedy*) and David E. Scheim (*Contract on America: The Mafia Murder of President John F. Kennedy*). G. Robert Blakey and Richard N. Billings also suggest anti-Castro elements and that the Mafia joined to use Oswald as a fall guy (*The Plot to Kill the President*). As evidence that someone was making sure that the real Oswald would be blamed for the murder, crime authors point to long-familiar sightings of Oswald in the Dallas area before the assassination: practice-shooting at a rifle range, acting rude while buying ammunition, test-driving a car and claiming he would soon have 'a lot of money' to buy it. (Marina insisted that he did not drive.)

Some readily accept this Oswald as an impostor. Others consider other alleged sightings of him as genuine: sitting in a New Orleans bar with a Marcello hoodlum and taking money under the table; travelling with another Marcello crony three months before the assassination.

But . . . but: almost all books agree that the Mafia had a strong motivation to cut down Kennedy and, in doing so, the Kennedy Clan. They had lied to them; they had betrayed them. Worse of all, the Kennedys had ratted on them.

Robert Kennedy's persecution of the Mafia went back to 1957, to Mickey Cohen and Carlos Marcello. When Robert Kennedy became Attorney General in 1961, the Justice Department waged war against organised crime. Despite the reluctance of J. Edgar Hoover, who had long claimed there was no Mafia, it indicted 116 members of the Mob. Kennedy also undertook a personal vendetta against Hoffa. His crusade against Marcello, whose territory covered Texas, was as intense.

Born in Tunisia of Sicilian parents, who moved to the US in 1910, Marcello later used a phoney Guatemalan birth registration to avoid deportation to Italy. Fully aware that Marcello was not a Guatemalan, in 1961 Kennedy had immigration agents hustle him aboard a 78-seater jet as its lone passenger and deposit him in Guatemala City. Marcello and his American lawyer were later flown to El Salvador, where soldiers dumped the two expensively dressed men in the mountains. Marcello claimed he fainted three times and broke several ribs before finding his way to a small airport. Slipping secretly back into New Orleans, he vowed revenge against the Kennedys.

The connections between Oswald and Ruby are endless. David E. Scheim, who was a manager of computerised information at the National Institute of Health, seems to have compiled every reference ever printed about the JFK assassination cast. They can be made to fit any theory, conjuring up the believable and the absurd. Still, it never feels like believing in UFOs.

Oswald's father Robert died of a heart attack in August 1939, two months before his son was born. Oswald spent much of his first three years with Lillian and Charles Murret, his aunt and uncle, in New Orleans. In April 1963, while looking for a job in New Orleans, he stayed with the Murrets again. Charles Murret was a bookmaker in a gambling operation run by Carlos Marcello and for a few months Oswald collected bets for his uncle. That summer, when Oswald passed out leaflets for his one-man chapter of the Fair Play for Cuba Committee, his literature listed 544 Camp Street as the chapter office. That building housed the offices of Guy Banister, a private investigator and former FBI agent. Banister had been hired by Marcello to help him fight court battles.

Working for Banister was David Ferrie, a former airline pilot who had publicly berated Kennedy for the failure of the Bay of Pigs invasion of Cuba. In 1955, Ferrie headed a New Orleans squadron of the Civil Air Patrol. One of his cadets was Oswald. Some witnesses thought they saw the two together in Clinton, Louisiana, in September 1963.

On the two weekends before the Kennedy assassination, Ferrie huddled with Marcello at a farmhouse on the mobster's delta property. Ferrie later told the FBI that he was helping Marcello map strategy for a perjury and conspiracy trial then under way. (Marcello was acquitted on the day of the assassination.) On the night of the assassination, Ferrie drove 350 miles through a rainstorm to Houston, arriving at about 4 a.m. He later insisted that this was a hunting trip, but he spent hours making calls from public phones at a skating rink.

Perhaps, the theory goes, this means that Marcello was using Ferrie to help plot the killing of Kennedy. The implication is that Ferrie's hasty trip was to make sure, from telephones beyond Marcello's haunts, that Ruby killed Oswald.

As the decades have gone by since Kennedy's killing, Ruby's role has become more and more linked to organised crime. It is supported by his hoodlum pedigree: he worked his way through the Capone Outfit – like Mickey Cohen and Johnny Rosselli – and in 1947 was assigned to the rackets in Dallas. It was a co-op with Marcello and the New Orleans organisation, where he worked in prostitution, narcotics and slot machines. Telephone records show that as the assassination date approached, Ruby made numerous calls to Mob figures in Chicago, New Orleans and Los Angeles, as well as to two associates of Jimmy Hoffa.

There is always another corner to turn. If Oswald was the fall guy, why did he shoot down officer J.D. Tippit, who was about to question him, after leaving the Texas school book depository building and picking up a revolver at his rooming house? Six witnesses identified Oswald as Tippit's killer, three watched him discard empty cartridges. The cartridges matched the gun he was carrying when police caught him.

Fragments of the bullets that hit the President were matched with the rifle found on the sixth floor of the depository. Oswald's fingerprints were on the rifle barrel. Fibres from the clothes he was wearing when arrested were caught on the rifle butt. That morning he had brought a long, thin package to work from the house in Irving where he spent weekends with Marina. He explained to the co-worker who gave him a ride that it contained curtain rods for his Dallas apartment, even though his flat had a full set.

Yet, but, yet . . . another gunman in Dealey Plaza, firing from a grassy knoll in front of the presidential motorcade. Numerous witnesses, including some officers, thought they heard shots from that direction.

An acoustics expert examined a police Dictabelt recording made of one of the two radio channels used during the motorcade. After tests in Dealey Plaza, the scientist concluded that sounds on the belt came from an escorting motorcycle with its microphone stuck open, that four shots could be detected on the belt and that there was a 50–50 probability that one of them came from the knoll. Two other experts raised the estimate to 95 per cent and the conclusion was of a 'probable' conspiracy.

When the National Academy of Sciences examined the same recording in 1982, its experts detected cross-talk from the other police channel on the belt, chatter that it identified as occurring one minute after the shooting: 'The acoustic analyses do not demonstrate that there was a grassy-knoll shot.' Three panels of independent experts examined the materials from Kennedy's autopsy and said he had been hit only by shots fired from behind him.

In his 1981 book *Best Evidence*, David Lifton argues that conspirators altered the President's body to conceal evidence of an entry wound from the front. Others note that Kennedy's brain has not been examined by anyone, except superficially by the autopsy doctors. Robert Kennedy did not turn it over to the National Archives with other autopsy evidence in 1966.

The timing of Ruby's shooting of Oswald tidies nothing. If

he had been stalking Oswald, why was he in a Western Union office wiring $25 to one of his strippers, Karen Carlin, at 11.17 a.m. that Sunday? No one knew for certain when the interrogation of Oswald would end and he'd be transferred to the county sheriff. A postal inspector had unexpectedly interrupted the questioning, which had held up the transfer by at least half an hour. Without the delay, Ruby would have been too late. His televised shooting of Oswald occurred at 11.21 a.m.

But there is a way around all anti-conspiracy thoughts.

Ruby visited police headquarters, where Oswald was being held, twice on the night of the assassination. He was at a press conference where Oswald was photographed. Ruby sat at the back of the room, allegedly carrying his handgun. He was spotted in a crowd outside the building around 3 p.m. on Saturday, when the transfer originally had been scheduled. On Sunday morning, three TV technicians reported seeing him near their van overlooking the transfer ramp well before 11 a.m. Ruby went off to Western Union at a crucial moment as part of a prearranged plan to make the killing look spontaneous. Someone signalled Ruby when Oswald's move began. The implication is that the signal came from law enforcement.

The members of the Warren Commission were informed of the CIA's scheming with the Mafia to assassinate Castro, even though Castro had warned publicly on 7 September 1963 that 'US leaders should think that if they are aiding terrorist plans to eliminate Cuban leaders, they themselves will not be safe.' Allen Dulles, a member of the commission who had been the CIA director when the plots were hatched, did not disclose this secret to the investigators. The CIA had told Robert Kennedy, but he too kept this information from the Warren Commission. If the Mafia link had been widely known, the conclusions might have changed.

Others claimed that a stripper – of course, a *blonde stripper* – who worked for Jack Ruby had driven Johnny Rosselli and Lewis McWillie to Dealey Plaza. There they met a sniper and supplied him with a weapon. Richard Gully, who worked as a personal assistant to Jack L. Warner before becoming an exclusive agent to stars like Angie Dickinson, was adamant that it was Rosselli who shot Kennedy. The question is whether he would have had such skill with a high-powered rifle. Rosselli's skill was people. He had the contacts. Especially in the Democratic Party. Why, the Texas Senator Lyndon B. Johnson had been with him at the opening night of the Mafia-controlled Stardust Hotel-Casino in Las Vegas. Along with Robert 'Bobby' Baker, who was known as 'Little Lyndon' in his years as secretary to the Senate Majority Leader. Harry McPherson, who also worked for Johnson, said Baker 'was very smart, very quick and indefatigable. Just worked all the time. He was always running someplace to make some kind of a deal.'

In the first half of the 1950s, when Meyer Lansky was planning his expansion from Cuba and courting the Caribbean for casino locations, Bobby Baker helped the Intercontinental Hotels Corporation to establish casinos in the Dominican Republic, which was the corrupted haven of dictator Rafael Trujillo. Baker was the go-between for Ed Levison, who fronted for Lansky and Sam Giancana.

Trujillo was evil, a twentieth-century Caligula. As an army officer, he had discovered a penchant for rape. When he took power in 1930 and became president, he ordered a constant supply of virgins for his bedchamber. He would humiliate his government officers by demanding they sacrifice the virginity of their daughters. When people attacked or mildly criticised his regime, they vanished. When he got angry at the President of Venezuela, he didn't bother with letters of protest in the diplomatic pouch. He tried to blow him up. He broke off with the Vatican and got a Dominican sorcerer to attempt to kill the Pope with the evil eye. Yet Trujillo ranted against the Communists and cleverly advertised which side he supported in the Cold War.

So, for America, he was politically acceptable, a degenerate but an anti-Communist degenerate, with a member of the diplomatic corps explaining to the *New York Times*: 'The fact that they murder their enemies or torture them doesn't usually come up over coffee cups.'

Eishenhower's vice president, Richard Nixon, toured the Caribbean in 1955. He trowelled it on: the Mafia-controlled Cuban leader Fulgenico Batista y Zaldivar was a reincarnation of Abraham Lincoln; Generalissimo Rafael Trujillo, the butcher who wept for the men he killed, was Nixon's best friend. In Haiti, the hapless Nixon tried to be a man of the people. He talked to a peasant woman who snapped: *Tell this coconut to get out of the way.* This was translated as: *Nice to meet you.* Which was all the encouragement America's vice president required: *What is the donkey called?* The reply: *He's crazy. It's called a donkey.*

For the Mob and Bobby Baker, it was called an *opportoonity*.

When Lyndon Johnson became vice president, Bobby Baker remained as his secretary and political adviser. He also continued to do business with Levison, Sam Giancana and Jimmy Hoffa's Mr Fixit Ben Siegelbaum, in the Dominican Republic. The man with the ear of the second-most-powerful man in the world argued the island was perfect for the Mafia to take over after the Cuban debacle. President Kennedy spoiled all that.

CIA intelligence, often an oxymoron at that time, indicated that Trujillo was so despised that a left-wing coup was likely. He had to go. But as with all things concerning the CIA's black operations – executive actions – it was not straightforward. A training camp was set up in Venezuela by Dominican exiles flown there by the CIA from the United States and Puerto Rica. They were recruited from the privileged sectors to avoid a Communist government replacing the fallen dictator. Rafael Trujillo was assassinated on 30 May 1961. His car was ambushed and sprayed with machine-gun fire. There wasn't much mourning.

Certainly not from Bobby Baker. Within months, he had another source of extra-curricular income, the Serve-U-Corporation, with his partners Ed Levenson and Benny

Siegelbaum. The company provided vending machines for companies working on federal government grants – which were manufactured by a Chicago company owned, behind a veil of paperwork, by Sam Giancana. The president of the company, Gene Hancock, was a business partner of Grant Stockdale, who was the US Ambassador to Ireland. JFK pressured him to quit Dublin in July 1962, when gossip of Baker's corruption emerged.

Baker was a rich man for a political aide. Robert Kennedy went after him and Baker was forced to resign six weeks before President Kennedy was shot. The president's secretary, Evelyn Lincoln, revealed (some years later) that JFK was going to drop Lyndon Johnson as his running mate in 1964 because of the investigations into Baker and also Johnson's involvement in dubious arms contracts in Texas. Of course, the Kennedys, both John and Robert – arguably because one of them was always trying to cover the shortcomings of the other – were a little late in trying to clean up the act, attempting to sweep so much dirt out of their history.

The Kennedys of Hollywood and Washington are best viewed, like so many of their associates, through a Doris Day lens: the gaudy and the misdemeanours disguised in a gauzy confection of their Camelot, their legacy transcribed by the diminishing faithful.

The wonder, always a question, is why any of these speed-lane loose-brained sociopaths were anywhere near the 35th President of the United States in his life and death. You can look at the evidence and find the answer, but still you wonder how it could happen.

There was no one to apply the brake, slow down the corporate merger of politics and gangsterism. Morality was put to one side and expediency replaced it. Marlon Brando, who would become the ultimate movie gangster, is good on that. The corrupt combination had been there long before 22 November 1963: all that happened prior to events, and in their lieu, is forever etched in history. Just like *Dracula* it can't be interred.

And there's always another Hollywood president ready to manifest.

Angie Dickinson had one of the screen's great femme fatale roles, as Sheila Farr, in her time out in *The Killers* (1964). Ava Gardner had the same part – different name, Kitty Collins – in *The Killers* (1946). Both films were based on Hemingway's story: the scheming of Sheila/Kitty is a masterclass in narcissistic malice. The Angie Dickinson version (with Lee Marvin and Clu Gulager as 'the Killers' and John Cassavetes replacing Burt Lancaster as the sad sap) was a significant parable for its time. The seductive Sheila Farr seduces Cassavetes's racing driver and involves him in a million-dollar heist. He's double-crossed and then double-crossed again by the mesmerising but conniving social monstrosity. When she pleads her innocence to Lee Marvin's business-like killer, he tells her: 'Lady, I don't have the time!' Angie Dickinson's Sheila Farr drops dead. The script couldn't let someone like her keep running around.

Earlier she'd been humiliated by B-movie actor Ronald Reagan in his last film role – and only one as a villain – by him slapping her face. He'd appeared as an organised-crime boss, Jack Browning, who evolved as a legitimate businessman in Los Angeles and hired 'the Killers' to eradicate anyone who might delve into his past. Reagan didn't like being the bad guy. Dickinson revealed: 'He was uncomfortable playing the villain and only did so to fulfil his contract.'

At that time he was auditioning to play the good guy; it was just a cameo before a starring political part – as the Governor of California. It was a role he discussed with friends, such as department store magnate and Diner's Club founder Alfred Bloomingdale (widows Betsy Bloomingdale and Nancy Reagan remained best friends in 2012), at a time when the Diner's Club credit card founder was paying off Mafia blackmailers. More counsel was given by Lew Wasserman, the chairman of MCA-Universal, Hollywood's huge entertainment conglomerate, who weighed it up with his lifetime close pal Sidney Korshak.

Reagan was filming with Angie Dickinson on 22 November 1963 when they got the news from Dallas. It was a phone call from his friend and Angie Dickinson's former lover Frank Sinatra.

BOOK THREE

FULL MOON

'I can't tell till I've seen you over a distance of ground.
You've got a touch of class, but I don't know how, how
far you can go.'
'A lot depends on who's in the saddle.'
— Philip Marlowe (Humphrey Bogart) to Vivian
Rutledge (Lauren Bacall), *The Big Sleep*, 1946

10

CHANDLERTOWN

'In the middle of a drought and the Water Commissioner drowns. Only in LA.'

— Morty (Charles Knapp) to J.J. Gittes (Jack Nicholson), *Chinatown*, 1974

EVERYWHERE YOU TURN IN THE WORLD, THERE'S HOLLYWOOD – and there's the Mafia. The crossover is inescapable. The assassination of JFK stopped nothing; it simply saw a reshuffle.

The relationship between Hollywood and the Mafia began in the days of *Hollywood Babylon* and silent movies, when much that went on was unspeakable, too. The Mob followed the money. From the start, they sought to control prominent 'legitimate' politicians and union and corporate leaders, at the same time establishing an image at the movies. The Mob leveraged giant screen names such as Valentino, for influence and control. It was, as we've seen, rather like stumbling into Dorian Gray's attic. After the shock, there's the terrible fascination.

It was this fascination that gripped the noir author most identified with Hollywood, Englishman Raymond Chandler. The loner's laureate, he believed style was the best investment a writer could make for posterity. He elevated himself from pulp fiction to use the genre for his own artistic ends. His work, just seven novels and a handful of short stories and screenplays, was placed in a voice-over world of cool blondes and stiff whisky, and vice versa. The spiritual and emotional questions of his times he tackled on the streets. To walk them, he created his tarnished knight Philip Marlowe, who used wisecracks as a shield to – among other 'weaknesses' – disguise his soft spot for making other people's troubles his own.

Marlowe was first named Mallory – a nod to *Le Morte d'Arthur* – and Chandler saw him as sensitive and strong:

> He is slightly over six feet tall and weighs about 13 stone eight. He has dark brown hair, brown eyes and the expression 'passably good looking' would not satisfy him in the least. He can be tough.
>
> Almost any sort of cigarette will satisfy him. He will drink practically anything that is not sweet. Certain drinks, such as Pink Ladies, Honolulu cocktails and Creme de Menthe highballs, he would regard as an insult. He is a late riser by inclination, but occasionally an early riser by necessity. He has not, and never has had, a secretary. He started out with a German Luger automatic pistol. He seems to have had Colt automatics of various calibres but not larger than a .38 and when I last heard he had a Smith and Wesson .38 special.

Here we had the private eye and public conscience. Chandler thought Cary Grant would be perfect to play his 'shop-soiled Galahad' in the movies. It seems everybody but Grant thought so too – 'I'm not sure if it would have been my métier,' Grant told me with a smile. It was Bogart in *The Big Sleep* who pulled that trench-coat belt tight and put a patent on the image.

The bespectacled, pipe-smoking Chandler – meek, shy and uncertain – provided the poetry with five o'clock shadow, the arsenic idealism. His was unique material, which he also developed in screenplays for Billy Wilder (*Double Indemnity*) and Hitchcock (*Strangers on a Train*, 1951), but under financial duress. His view of Hollywood was this: 'The making of motion pictures is an endless contention of tawdry egos, almost none of them capable of anything more creative than credit stealing and self promotion.'

Chandler was no self-publicist. He was reluctant even to release photographs of himself, afraid that readers expecting a macho-man author might be put off by his owlish look. He made no public appearances. Cinema's infant, television, held no attraction for him (*Philip Marlowe* ran one season in 1959, the year of his creator's death) and he stayed at home. He spent his time drinking. And writing. But letters, as well as detective novels. The price of a stamp could entice a few thousand words from Chandler in reply. His letters make as fascinating reading as his 'work'. The fiction was Marlowe or men like him.

When he was stuck, Chandler said, his way out was always to have a man come through a door with a gun in his hand. Or, of course, a dame: 'There was a small knocking on wood. It was a blonde. A blonde to make a bishop kick a hole in a stained-glass window.'

What makes Chandler so useful on crime and Hollywood is that he lived and wrote through a classic era. He injected a little poetry into the nastiness: California and the money and excess he'd witnessed, the complications and compulsions wealth can bring even, or maybe especially, in the sunshine. To Hollywood, he imported foreign substances with him from Europe – irony and morality. He used the simile like a sword. Nothing was itself. Everything was like something else. 'She smelled the way the Taj Mahal looked by midnight.'

Strangely, his decades-ago world of Los Angeles doesn't seem, to me, that different from what followed. The cosmetic cover-up, the veneer, like the make-up, is thicker because of the super-inquisitive high-tech cameras. Still, the place is populated by missing persons, runaways, gigolos, snoops, remote-control punks, gold diggers and 'the kind of lawyers you hope the other fellow has'.

Chandler wrote about abortionists, Dr Feelgoods, gurus and porn merchants before other writers – in fact, most people, including the police – knew or wanted to know they existed. He put Marlowe on similar 'mean streets' to Thelma Todd and all the others. Chandler's insight provided a university of writing on Hollywood, which he plugged with lethal .38

epigrams: 'She gave me a smile I could feel in my hip pocket.' All over town, from the mountains to the sea, they still do.

And around almost every corner, in a snakes-and-ladders of society, are all-American mafiosi. It's only their past that's a foreign country. Today, they often take on a remarkable metamorphosis. The vital wiseguys are as comfortable in the board room as the bar room, at home getting Oscars or favours at San Quentin Penitentiary, wielding a spreadsheet or a ball-bearing weighted baseball bat ('always knees first'). At times, you'd think it compulsory that every brand business has one.

In time, the Chicago Mob led their associates across America into the sunshine and corridors of power in California. By the time the movies began to talk, the gangsters knew how to count up to the Fifth Amendment and stayed silent. No matter how many committee inquiries were heard during the '50s and '60s, those 'helped' into political and business positions were not directly implicated: gossip could be dismissed as sour grapes, not the truth most of it was.

Empires were established on the foundations of the past. None was to be more powerful than the Music Corporation of America (MCA), created in Chicago in 1924 by Hollywood's true godfather, Dr Jules Stein, who died in 1981. With this crowd, nothing was ever as it seemed. There had to be veneer. When Jules Stein retired, MCA, as a special tribute, gave him the title of Honorary Founder, even though he really was *the founder*.

Onward to his own death in 2002 and throughout Stein's reign, the controller of all was Lew Wasserman. Forget noisy Sinatra. He was but a toy compared to Wasserman, the true *Chairman of the Board*. He was boss of the greatest entertainment company in the world, which included the biggest film studio and the company supplying television shows globally. This was the true genesis of twenty-first-century Hollywood. The players were much the same, but, like the accounts, even better dressed.

The movie-makers of the 1930s and 1940s had feuded with the unions. Studio chiefs, including powerhouses like Louis B.

Mayer and Jack Warner, had vainly tried to battle off organised labour, like the Teamsters Union. Wasserman bought them, particularly the evil-doing and evil-smelling bulldog Jimmy Hoffa, who delivered his bad news with carbon copies until he had to die.

Stein and Wasserman were secretive men who believed the stars should be glittering and highly visible, while they, their manipulators, remained all but invisible to everything but their percentages. They, in turn, had their own invisibility cloak, the velvet presence of Sidney Korshak. He was their lifetime consigliere, the Mr Fixit who dealt in billions of dollars and lethal control.

Wasserman and Korshak were both out of Chicago and both close to Meyer Lansky's partner Morris 'Moe' Dalitz, the under-reported gangster and amusing philanthropist. ('He thinks he's fucking Robin Hood,' Frank Sinatra once said.) Dalitz, in his work with half-daft megalomaniac Howard Hughes, boosted the film careers of a chorus line of actresses – Cyd Charisse, Jane Russell, Bette Davis, Juliet Prowse, Marilyn Monroe, Mitzi Gaynor, Martha Hyer – and, with Bob Hope, had an intriguing relationship with Jayne Mansfield. Bing Crosby was always too drunk to get involved in the sexual shenanigans that involved double mirrors.

Playtime didn't distract from the business of making money and wielding influence. The Mafia were there as the movies grew, as the entertainment business diversified into a vast range of media and associated products. Hollywood was a global brand; the Mob went with it. It always had. It was a terrifying combination of the new and the old: digital, high-tech enterprises patrolled by intimidation and murder.

Wasserman had witnessed the US government intrude on his territory in 1948, when the film studios were forced to sell their cinema chains, and in 1962, when MCA was hit with anti-trust lawsuits. It was better if the others ran everything. They'd had Jack Kennedy in the White House, although they believed he had more concern for his haircut than promises made. They kept it that way with President

Lyndon Johnson – Wasserman was as close to President LBJ as he was to elected officials across America. That was, of course, because Mafia money and Teamsters Union pension funds bought votes.

Outside money – 'the Kitchen Cabinet' – helped put Ronald Reagan in the White House; it also sat in with the Clinton administrations and returned, as it had his father before him, Jerry Brown, at age 73, for the second time to the California governor's mansion in 2011.

Jerry Brown had hair and the singer Linda Ronstadt as a girlfriend when he first became Governor of California in 1975. That was after Sidney Korshak had helped and advised Governor Pat Brown with the ambitions of his son. The black-and-white vampire soap opera *Dark Shadows* was in TV syndication, *Marcus Welby, M.D.* and Jack Lord's *Hawaii Five-O* entertained in the evening and the airwaves were full of Glen Campbell and Herb Alpert. Time was running out on the counter-culture. Jerry Brown – Governor Moonbeam to the Malibu Beach crowd – was eclipsed in his presidential aspirations by Ronald Reagan.

For so many of the Hollywood political cast, the only motivation is power. In their parallel world, the Mafia's only mandate is profit. Both, separate and entwined, wanted control of people, businesses and, most of all, events. They wanted plans to be made and kept. Order was what led to success. Anything off-message was unthinkable and intolerable. Like Charles Manson.

As much as anyone, Manson changed the life and attitude of Hollywood: those who live and work there, and the way the movies and organised crime operated. From Manson onwards, a superior effort was made to keep any 'ultimate sanction' out of the headlines.

Manson and his 'Family' made society's nightmare come true with their still disquieting and unforgettable killing spree, which began in the Hollywood Hills as the moon glowed shortly after midnight on 9 August 1969. When it was over,

Roman Polanski's pregnant actress wife Sharon Tate and six others had been horrifyingly butchered.

Lawyer Stephen Kay prosecuted Manson and his followers, and since 1971 he has stayed with the case, attending parole hearings and constantly opposing freedom for Manson, whom he believes continues to wield a chilling influence and impact on society. He told me that Manson had been caught in prison with a makeshift weapon and three mobile phones in early 2012: 'He gets letters every day. Many are from teenagers who want to join his Family. Other inmates act as his correspondence secretaries. His influence is enormous. Do I believe he could get someone killed? Definitely.'

In this he is supported by Manson, who with total unpredictability will sometimes grant interviews, which range from rantings to intimidation, with him saying things like: 'I get letters. I write people all over the country. There is no question I still run my Family . . . I plant the seed of thought.'

Kay has turned down major political appointments so that he is always available to argue against parole for any of the convicted killers. It has been his crusade, his mission, and, against the odds in fervently politically correct California, has not proved an impossible one. He is certain Manson will never be intentionally freed – the killer will be 92 at his next chance for parole – but added: 'There are always people who believe prisoners must be paroled. I'm not one of them.' He says he's not a right-wing zealot. He contrasts his law-and-order attitude with the bestiality of Manson and his Family, which comprised mainly middle-class girls, their minds and bodies scarred by the man they regarded as a combination of Jesus and Satan; the man who involved them in Helter Skelter, the title given to the killings after it was revealed that Manson had prophesied a black–white race war based on his cruelly conceived interpretation of the Book of Revelation and the Beatles' 'Helter Skelter'. Kay says there is still much to learn from the tragedy brought on by Manson.

Author Joan Didion, a true Californian and a chronicler of her home state like no other, quietly believes that the Manson-led horror 'was the end of the '60s for a lot of people in Los Angeles'. She wrote: 'On 9 August, I was sitting in the shallow end of my sister-in-law's swimming pool in Beverly Hills when she received a telephone call from a friend who had just heard of the murders at Sharon Tate Polanski's home . . . I also remember this, and I wish I did not: I remember that no one was surprised.'

Didion, who has so often pinpointed the psychopathic psyche and the resulting sick society, says that in Los Angeles in 1969 there was a mystical flirtation with 'sin', a sense that it was possible to go too far and that many people were doing it.

'I recall a time when the dogs barked every night and the moon was always full.'

It wasn't just the dogs that were barking.

But Kay insists Manson's acts were political, not satanic. They were not hippies. 'Manson and his family liked to call themselves "Slippies" – they would slip underneath the fabric of society, incite a race war, Helter Skelter, and then take over. If Manson walked into this room right now, you wouldn't be able to take your eyes off him. Manson can cast a spell – that's how he got other people to do his bidding and killing. He had these girls from nice families willing to kill for him. He had such evil control – and he still has it today.'

At the trial, his followers took all the blame; they were willing to die for their maniacal messiah in the California gas chamber.

Vincent Bugliosi prosecuted Manson and his Family and later, in 1974, would write *Helter Skelter*, his account of the crime and trial. Bugliosi continues to practise law and remains a best-selling author. When you ask him about the Manson myth, he offers: 'Here's this little goon, 5 ft 2 in. tall, though he gives the sense of being taller . . . Here's this little guy and his followers – ultimately killers – and they were kids from average American families.

'Manson sat back, pulling the strings and getting other people to go and kill strangers without asking questions. When people ask me about Manson, they don't ask me how many times someone was stabbed, they ask how did he control all these people? When I was first assigned to the case, it was called the "Tate Murders". Then Manson comes on the scene and he's so bizarre, so charismatic, that he upstaged the victims. It became the "Charles Manson Case". He's still pulling strings and the effect he had on society you can see every day.'

The Manson Family tree spread – kept on growing. Hollywood still lives under the shadow of what became Los Angeles Medical Examiner's Case No: 69–8796.

It's a lonely road that curves up a Bel Air hill to take you to 10050 Cielo Drive. In the summer of 1969, there was a redwood house there, a rolling lawn, swimming pool and guest house. Hollywood business manager Rudolph Altobelli had bought the property in 1963, but six years later was using it as a rental property.

Before the killings, the most recent tenants had been Terry Melcher, the son of Doris Day, friend of the Beach Boys and the then boyfriend of actress Candice Bergen. He and Bergen had been sharing the house at a time when Melcher was being pestered by a difficult man, Charles Manson, for a recording contract. Melcher had snubbed Manson's musical ambitions.

Phil Kaufman produced the original Manson version of 'Look at Your Game, Girl' after serving time with Manson at the Terminal Island Penitentiary at Long Beach, California, in 1965. Kaufman explained: 'That was the song Charlie used to entice girls into the Family. The song meant: *Look at your game, girl – see the head game you're playing when you could be free and be with me*. I'd listen to him sing it to these new girls and it worked.'

Manson meant nothing to Terry Melcher. He sublet 10050 Cielo Drive to film director Roman Polanski, who moved in with his wife Sharon Tate, who was then twenty-six, and eight and a half months pregnant. In 1968, the cinema owners of America had voted her runner-up to Lynn Redgrave as 'Star of Tomorrow'. Tragically, that never happened.

Polanski, who had suffered the commercial flop of *The*

Fearless Vampire Killers (1967), was enjoying the success of *Rosemary's Baby* (1968) in which Frank Sinatra's young wife Mia Farrow gives birth to the Devil's child. When the Manson Family cruised up Cielo Drive, the Polish-born director was in London discussing another film project. He was an absentee host. Staying at the house with his wife were coffee heiress Abigail Folger, 25, and her boyfriend, a mysteriously wealthy jet-setter and friend and financier of Polanski, Voyteck Frykowski.

Also staying there was star hairdresser Jay Sebring, who was present during the wicked weekend Marilyn Monroe spent at Sinatra's Cal Neva Lodge. He'd once been engaged to Sharon Tate and remained a close friend of hers and Polanski. (Part of Sebring's supposed 'charm' within the group were his unconventional sexual habits. He liked to tie up women with a short, red sash cord and then whip them.)

Just after midnight, as 9 August 1969 began, Sharon Tate was in bed wearing a flower-patterned bra and panties. Sebring was at the end of the bed, talking to her. Abigail Folger, in a white nightgown, was in the bedroom across the hall, reading a book. Frykowski, 32, her lover, was asleep on a couch in the room.

Then the coven of killers, told by Manson that the world was soon to end, arrived.

Susan Atkins, Patricia Krenwinkel and Linda Kasabian carried knives, while Tex Watson had a long, red-handled wire cutter. With it, he sliced the telephone wires to the house. Then he drove the car down the road, out of sight of 10050 Cielo Drive. It was 12.18 a.m. when the Family returned. The girls were barefoot, wearing jeans and T-shirts. They carried dark clothes and their weapons. After climbing over the fence, they were forced to suddenly hurl themselves flat on the lawn as a car drove up. Steven Parent had arrived to buy a stereo from caretaker William Garretson. As Parent drove up, Tex Watson stepped into the headlights of his Rambler car. The young man had time to shout: 'Please, don't hurt me, I won't say anything' before Watson pumped four bullets into his chest.

No one inside the house heard the shots, the first thunder of Helter Skelter. Half an hour later, they would also all be dead.

Frykowski was confronted by Watson, who told him: 'I am the Devil, come to do the Devil's work.' Frykowski was stabbed 51 times, clubbed with a blunt object 13 times and shot twice. He had been stabbed repeatedly after he was dead. Abigail Folger, who, with her lover, was a serious drug user, had multiple stab wounds. Jay Sebring had been shot and stabbed all over his body and a bloody towel was wrapped around his head as a hood and a rope was knotted around his throat. Sharon Tate had been stabbed to death. She was found lying with her legs tucked towards her stomach, as if to protect her unborn child. The rope tied to Sebring's throat was also wrapped around her. It had been thrown over a beam, apparently to 'hang' the two victims.

The butchery done, Susan Atkins dipped a towel into Sharon Tate's blood and with it wrote 'PIG' in idiot letters on the front door. She meant to write 'PIGS' but Sharon Tate's blood on the towel dried.

At 1 a.m. on 10 August 1969, it was the suburban home of supermarket owner Leno LaBianca and his wife Rosemary, 3301 Waverley Drive, Los Feliz, that was invaded by the Manson Family and by Manson himself. The four killers who had massacred at the Tate home the previous night were joined by Leslie Van Houten and Manson himself. Clean-shaven and wiry, he went into the house and tied up Leno, 44, and his 38-year-old second wife. He told them no one would hurt them. They were carved up with knives and forks from their own kitchen. It was mindless. The LaBiancas were a middle-aged, middle-class couple – their demise appeared demonic.

When Hollywood's celebrated and controversial Coroner Thomas Noguchi arrived, he found Leon LaBianca dead from 26 knife wounds. He had been symbolically hanged, with a blood-stained pillowcase used as a hood over his head. A cord knotted around his throat was attached to a heavy lamp and his hands were tied behind his back with a leather thong. An ivory-handled carving fork, which was one of the weapons used to stab him, was sticking out of his stomach, where the word 'WAR' had been cut into his skin. A knife was sticking out of his throat. His wife's nightdress had been pushed over her head by the killers.

Her back and buttocks were covered in stab wounds. She too was hooded by a pillowcase and had been 'hanged' by a wire attached to a lamp.

On the walls, written in blood, were the words 'Death to Pigs' and 'Rise'. On the fridge were words from a warped world, the misspelled 'Healter Skelter'.

'Helter Skelter' was a track from the Beatles' *White Album*. The theories began. And so did the paranoia.

Polanski hired a psychic. Peter Sellers, Warren Beatty and Yul Brynner offered rewards of $25,000 for information. The police were swamped with ideas: Manson saw some demented message in 'Helter Skelter'; Manson wanted to bring down society; or maybe he just wanted to kill Terry Melcher for not giving him a recording contract. Manson had let it be known he was 'looking for Melcher'.

Candice Bergen, in 2012 the widow of French film director Louis Malle, screamed at Melcher: 'But it could have been me! I could have been killed.'

Melcher asked her: 'Why don't you say we?'

Such questions still haunt Los Angeles. At the time, there was talk of drug and sex orgies, black magic, assassins on the loose. As the Manson murders became an international sensation, the sales of guns and the hiring of security firms boomed. You could sense the fear, the extraordinary paranoia. *Chinatown* screenwriter Robert Towne (Jay Sebring had cut his and Warren Beatty's hair), who had an isolated home nearby, moved away. There was talk in every office and home that Manson held a 'celebrity hit list' that included Steve McQueen and Elizabeth Taylor. Many thought like Candice Bergen, including Robert Evans, who had been invited to the party.

There was, of course, some wicked humour. Supposedly, Barbra Streisand screamed at her agent: 'They're killing people in the business.' She was reassured with: 'Don't worry, doll, they're not going after stars – just featured players.'

Within hours of the killings becoming worldwide news, Rudolph Altobelli, who was the business agent for Katharine Hepburn and Henry Fonda, had 33 offers to sell 10050 Cielo Drive. He didn't.

There were other victims of Manson and the Family. Donald 'Shorty' Shea vanished from the Spahn Ranch, a one-time movie set where silent westerns were filmed on the outskirts of Los Angeles. His body has never been found. Gary Hinman, a musician who got to know Manson during the killer's vain attempts to become a rock star ('bigger than the Beatles'), was found tortured to death in his hillside home in Topanga Canyon, the hippy capital of Los Angeles in the 1960s.

'The Tate–LaBianca case had all the good things and the bad things of the 1960s,' says poet and author Ed Sanders, who wrote a landmark book on the Manson killings. 'It had sex and murder, lifestyles, counter-culture, Hollywood, rock 'n' roll stars like Dennis Wilson of the Beach Boys – everything that makes for a circus. The trial was a combination of fascination and revulsion, like a snake with its tail in its mouth. It just kept rolling along, this revulsive snake. It's still rolling along . . .'

Manson's daily mail includes letters from youngsters wanting not just to join his 'Family' but also to kill for him. In the 1960s, there were just as many willing to do his bidding. He picked up the girls in the drug-culture capital of San Francisco, Haight-Ashbury, and on the freeways or in seedy apartments and usually had sex with them before running them around California in his battered VW van.

As the Family grew, they graduated to a school bus for their travels. At the time of the killings, there were 35 Family members but only a few were ever proved to have killed for Manson. One of them was the daughter of actress Angela *Murder, She Wrote* Lansbury. Her daughter Deirdre travelled around California in the Family's big black bus on their 'Magical Mystery Tour'.

Ed Sanders says: 'Deirdre was one of the jewels in Charlie's pack, although she was only about 13 at the time.'

'Malibu was a hotbed of youthful drug abuse in the 1960s,' admitted Angela Lansbury. 'Both my children, Didi and Anthony, became involved, which really shocked me because I didn't think it could happen to my own.'

Lansbury and her husband, the late theatrical agent Peter Shaw, moved their family to Ireland to escape the perils of 1960s California. It was a success. Anthony worked on his mother's tremendously successful television series and Deirdre became a successful restaurateur in Santa Monica. Her step-brother David Shaw recalled: 'It was a really scary time. Kids all around them were dying. And, of course, there was Manson. We all met him, a lot of people in Malibu did. He used to come around to our house looking for Deirdre.'

He was always looking for girls. Susan Atkins was a high-school dropout, a teenage runaway who had worked as a topless dancer and flirted with crime before she met Manson. Patricia Krenwinkel was the daughter of a middle-class insurance salesman. Leslie Van Houten was another middle-class girl; she fell under the spell of singer and actor Bobby Beausoleil before he took his harem and joined up with the Family. Tex Watson was a clean-cut Texas boy who, on arriving in Los Angeles, found he had a penchant for drug-dealing. Linda Kasabian, who drove the car on both murder nights – and would later be the star prosecution witness – had left a comfortable Midwest home to 'look for God'. She took lots of drugs to help her quest.

During the Manson trial (it took 38 weeks, costing $1.25 million, and resulted in 31,176 pages of transcript), the Manson girls, like one-time homecoming princess Leslie Van Houten, were dubbed 'witchlets'.

'I looked at them, just looked at them, and "witchlets" was the only word,' said the New York writer Theo Wilson, who sat through every day of the trial and first used that description. 'They looked like little girls. And had witch's eyes.'

'Witchlet' Susan Atkins warned the jury that convicted her:

'Better lock your doors and watch your own kids.'

Sharon Tate's mother Doris, until her death in 1992, aged 68, from a brain tumour, campaigned alongside Stephen Kay to keep Manson and his followers in jail. Sharon Tate's sister Patti, who was 11 years old when her sister was murdered, then took over. She herself died in 2000 from breast cancer but had spoken about her work to keep the killers behind bars: 'Life was perfect for Sharon. For me, she was an idol, someone who made me feel really proud. I was excited about the baby, too. Sharon was such a good person, an authentic person without an iota of evil in her body. If I look at a magazine or watch television, it's always there for me. Anything related to evil always makes me think of Charles Manson. And whenever they mention his name they always mention Sharon's, too. Her beautiful name is now synonymous with evil. I hate that.'

Manson brought fear to Hollywood more than anything or anyone ever had before. He was like an earthquake. You never know when the big one might arrive.

He and his followers were almost executed in the California gas chamber, but in 1972 their sentences were commuted when the state invalidated the death penalty. Manson is restless, always tapping on something, his own crazy energy force. Mad. Barking mad. But with the evil energy: 'I just live in a different time zone. You call it insanity. You call it psychotic, you call it all kinds of different things because you don't function in it.'

In turn, Stephen Kay remarked: 'Charles Manson is the greatest advertisement for the death penalty in the world today.'

Manson was 77 years old on 11 April 2012, when he was refused parole by the California Department of Corrections, who said it would be 15 years before the next opportunity for release was assessed. Manson was not present, but Sharon and Patti Tate's sister Debra was. The hearing was told that Manson had got hold of mobile phones in the California State Prison in Corcoran, but they would not reveal how. On the phones, Manson had placed calls and text messaged people in California, New Jersey, Florida and British Columbia.

Debra Tate heard recent remarks made by Manson to his psychologist, as part of the determination of his eligibility for parole: 'I'm special. I'm not like the average inmate. I have spent my life in prison. I have put five people in the grave. I am a very dangerous man.'

He wasn't alone.

Some on the fringes of the Mafia had offered to 'deal' with Manson, but the hierarchy, for once, wanted the law to take its course, which it did, at first ineptly and then slowly. But it got there in the end. Meanwhile organised crime used the distraction to organise themselves in Hollywood.

And Hollywood, for once, made profits out of them.

11

THE FIXER

'Senators don't have people killed.'
'Don't be naive.'
— Kay (Diane Keaton) and Michael Corleone
(Al Pacino), *The Godfather*, 1972

MARIO PUZO WAS BROKE. AND HE WAS FED UP BEING BROKE:
tired of being an *artiste* author and not a commercial one. He
had a big family and a bigger gambling habit. With $20,000
owing, he decided *to grow up and sell out*. His literary aspirations
would succumb to his tabloid instincts. He began a novel about
the Mafia in 1965, but his publishers, Atheneum, rejected his
proposal. Putnam's accepted it on a ten-page outline with an
advance against royalties of $5,000, which, for a hungry man
like Puzo, was just a starter.

He talked to gamblers he knew – 'I never met an honest-to-
God gangster' – and for his Hollywood sections looked up a
biography of Columbia's Harry Cohn; he had the correct scent
there. By the time he had written the first 100 pages, he'd got
that terrible need for more cash. It was an ongoing affliction.

By then, Sidney Korshak was arguably the most connected,
in every sense, guy in town, with an amazing network of
connections to union leaders, politicians, Hollywood and Las
Vegas moguls and key members of the Mafia. His circle seemed
to be producing, directing or starring in every blockbuster
movie or popular television series being made. He was a star.
But a shy one. At a Bel Air party another guest took a

photograph of him. He quietly and very politely asked if the film could be destroyed and discarded. While he watched.

One convenient client connection the lawyer had was with 'the Mad Austrian of Wall Street', the treacle-thick-accented business dynamo Charlie Bluhdorn. He went from making car bumpers to being chairman of Gulf & Western Industries, owners from 1966 of Paramount Pictures, with the help of Korshak. The wonderful thing about Bluhdorn for Hollywood, and those he delegated power to, was that he had no interest in the movies. He only got involved if they *lost* money. He just wanted to have as much sex as possible, with as many beautiful women as were available. He might as well have asked for a cheese sandwich. If anything, it was even easier to provide. A telephone call would do it.

Bluhdorn needed 'people to make movies' at Paramount Studios and his lawyer suggested Robert Evans. Evans was brought in to run the European division out of London, but in an executive shake-up found himself, vastly inexperienced, as the boss in Hollywood. But Evans took showers in confidence, he was soaking in the stuff, and he played a blinder. He was about to readjust the perception worldwide of the Mafia and Hollywood forever. With a great deal of help from Sidney Korshak. Who, as Robert Evans phrased it, became the godfather of *The Godfather*.

Evans is, he admits, no angel. He is a tarnished fable and, if you like characters on the racy side, a naughty delight. He has no illusions; his life has been punctuated with gunsels and dames, a Damon Runyon confection of guys and dolls, but mostly the dolls. A valley of them. The pills, the cocaine lines and the girls. Lots and lots of girls. And wives. The snag was he rather got confused with the girls and the wives.

Evans was Hollywood's great lover boy. Walking out of a Beverly Hills restaurant the day I spoke with him, a young woman spots him. He's wearing his trademark yellow cashmere sweater over an open-necked white evening dress shirt and is clearly age-challenged. This long-legged California antelope of a girl admires his straw hat and so he gives it to her.

'Keep it,' he says, with his winning grin. She scribbles down her phone number. 'What can I say? I like to be friendly.'

His home is a 1910 French Regency estate that once belonged to Greta Garbo, only a moment's drive from the centre of Beverly Hills and the world he has been gambling in for most of his life. Like the lawns around here, Evans has always been a perfect-looking specimen. The demons have been hidden, kept under the ground. He is the pretty boy who proved terrific as a Hollywood mogul, only to be professionally mugged by cocaine and personally sabotaged by an overcharged lust for life. Most of the time I spoke to him he was humming and buzzing around in that yellow sweater, like a bee hurriedly skipping from one moment to another. He had a certain panache. There was an English butler to greet me with an icy drink on a hot afternoon before a wander around the swimming pool, with its 27 separate jets of water that make a fountain out of the centrepiece. The garden is overlooked by a Wimbledon-modelled tennis court – Evans is a tennis fanatic – and the house itself. Waving his arm in the air, he declared: 'This was the table where Marlon Brando signed to be the Godfather.'

The black cast-iron table doesn't look grand enough. But dragging Brando to that place *and* getting him to sign was a grand achievement, the story of which goes back to down-on-his-luck Mario Puzo – and the wonder boy that Evans was in the late 1960s at Paramount. He produced some of the landmark films of the time, including *Rosemary's Baby*, *The Italian Job* (1969), *True Grit* (1969), *Love Story* (1970), *The Odd Couple* (1968) and *The Detective* (1968), and he was on a roll. Which was more than Puzo was when he entered Evans's office in the spring of 1968. Evans had never heard of Mario Puzo; the meeting was a favour to a friend in New York.

As Evans tells it, Puzo turned up with 50 or 60 pages of typed manuscript, which he didn't look at. It was titled 'The Mafia' – a name the Mob had been trying to eradicate since the Kefauver Committee hearings. He told the author: 'I'll give you ten Gs for it as an option against $75,000 [Puzo said it was $50,000] if it becomes a book.'

'[Puzo] looked at me and said: "Could you make it fifteen?"'

'And I said: "How about twelve-five?"'

Puzo's agents confirmed that figure. They say they tried to overrule their client, who insisted on accepting the offer. Paramount's business department issued a $12,500 cheque. Evans forgot about it until he got a call from Mario Puzo, asking: 'Would I be in breach of contract if I change the name of the book? I want to call it *The Godfather*.'

Evans had forgotten he was writing the book. It would be the last time. He would never again forget the cigar-chomping, overweight Mario Puzo, who completed his novel in July 1968. Before Putnam's hardback had reached the New York Times Top Ten best-sellers list (where it spent 67 weeks), Fawcett paid $410,000 for the paperback rights.

Such overwhelming publishing success was no guarantee for the Paramount executives that it would be repeated at the movies. They'd taken a bath with Mob pictures, most recently with (the interesting) *The Brotherhood* (1968), starring Sidney Korshak's friend Kirk Douglas and Alex Cord as vendetta-set Sicilian brothers.

The once-uninterested Evans buzzed. He lobbied for *The Godfather*. He argued that WASPs and Jewish producers had made the movies previously. To be 'able to smell the spaghetti', the project had to be in the control of Italian-Americans. He turned turtle on that instantly by hiring Albert 'Al' Ruddy, a non-Italian, to produce.

Ruddy, a gruff but likeable man, was known to be an on-budget worker and was the mastermind of the profitable *Hogan's Heroes*, which in itself was a first – a Nazi prisoner-of-war comedy, a POW TV sitcom. He had a $2.5 million budget that increased the longer *The Godfather* remained in the best-sellers list. As did the aspirations of Paramount. They understood they had a gigantic success to cash in on. They contacted all the 'name' directors of the moment: Costa-Gavras (*Z*, 1969), Peter Yates (*Bullitt*, 1968) and Franklin J. Schaffner (*Patton*, 1970). They were wary of being involved in a project that glorified the Mafia. Sam Peckinpah wasn't, but he didn't work out, his idea being akin to 'The Wild Bunch in the Mafia'. Peckinpah, in one of life's little ways and by proxy, got his revenge on Evans.

Francis Ford Coppola's accomplishment was he was an Italian-American. At 31, he was making movies, but they found only small audiences. The producers thought he would work cheap and do a good job, cover all asses. The young film-maker had only got to page 50 of the book, and passed on it and the offer. But he had more in common with Mario Puzo than *The Godfather*. He was broke. His production partner George Lucas, who was toiling on a sci-fi project – *Star Wars* – urged him to accept. They really needed the money. And what could he lose?

It was at this point that the game plan changed. Coppola began reading non-fiction books and articles about the Mafia in America. Suddenly, he envisaged *The Godfather* as a family saga and a reflection – a twisted mirror image, if you like – of capitalism.

Unknown to Coppola, that was exactly the ethos of the Mafia at that time, as the 1960s turned into the '70s: they were to play the stocks-and-shares corporate game, manipulate the market, dress for Wall Street, not the Armory in Chicago.

Robert Evans was not convinced, but he was under pressure. The bean counters at Paramount wanted to sell on the Puzo material for more than $1 million to Burt Lancaster, who planned to star as the central character, Don Corleone.

Coppola won the day and began work on the script with Mario Puzo. There are delights in how they got where they got. Coppola put a line in about pasta sauce and 'browning the garlic'. Puzo corrected: 'First you fry some garlic. Gangsters don't brown.'

While they were writing, Coppola would take time to test actors for roles, but Don Corleone, the title character, was clearly the most vital. He is involved in half of the story but dominates it all. Laurence Olivier was mentioned; Ernest Borgnine, Richard Conte, Anthony Quinn and George C. Scott were talked about. But Puzo was convinced Marlon

Brando was perfect. Following a run of ten duds at the box office, he wasn't a popular name along Hollywood's corporate corridors.

Puzo had sent Brando galley proofs of his book. Brando didn't read it but had the courtesy to telephone Puzo about the movie; he didn't think Paramount would hire him. Neither did Al Ruddy, who bet Coppola $200 to that effect.

The two of them approached Brando, who told them: 'I don't want to play an Italian gangster.' But Brando – tarred by all his ruinous relationships with directors and producers – again was polite. He'd read the novel before making a final decision. The question of whether art or life comes first appeared. Brando would play Don Corleone. He saw strong elements of social commentary in Puzo's work. Organised crime was allowed to prosper in America – because it was a business. It was acceptable to most of the population of the United States because it was a business, albeit a special type of enterprise.

Given the business styles and the corporate and banking upheavals of the twenty-first century, the prescience of Coppola and Brando's interpretation of *The Godfather* is a marvel. Later, Brando gave a rare (in his case, the correct word) interview to *Life* magazine. He didn't make it easy. He wanted to be interviewed by Shana Alexander, whom he trusted. She was the editor of the rival *McCall's*. It was Brando and it was done. He told her the film was 'a useful commentary on the corporate thinking of this country . . . I mean, if Cosa Nostra had been black or a socialist, Corleone would have been dead or in jail. But because the Mafia patterned itself so closely on the corporation and dealt in a hard-nosed way with money and with politics, it prospered. The Mafia is so . . . *American*.

'To me, a key phrase in the story is that whenever they want to kill somebody it was always a matter of policy. Just before pulling the trigger, they told him: "Just business. Nothing personal." When I read that, [Robert] McNamara, [Lyndon] Johnson and [Dean] Rusk flashed before my eyes.'

Brando's view of President Johnson and his two aides, who

were enmeshed in the Vietnam War, was echoed by this: 'The Mafia is the best example of capitalists we have. Don Corleone is just an ordinary American business magnate who is trying to do the best he can for the group he represents and for his family. He is a man of deep principle and the natural question arises as to how such a man can countenance the killing of people. But the American government does much the same thing for reasons that are not so much different from those of the Mafia.'

With the anti-business Brando ready to star as Don Corleone, it was a question of selling him to big business, to Charlie Bluhdorn. Brando was acknowledged as a pain in the ass, with his over-the-top demands, being fat and often fatuous. Coppola set the scene: 'You have to remember that they were very seriously considering if they had the right director, and I brought up Marlon Brando. I was told by one of the executives: "Francis, Marlon Brando will never appear in this picture, and I instruct you never to bring him up again." At which point, I fainted onto the floor as a gag and they got the point. Finally, they recanted and told me that I could consider Brando if I could meet three criteria: one was that he would do the film for nothing, that he would personally post a bond to insure them against any of his shenanigans causing overage [delaying production], and the third was that he would agree to a screen test. And I agreed, even though I didn't even know Brando.'

Here was a chance.

The tales are part of movie-Mafia lore, but from Coppola, the horse's mouth, shall we say, in *Godfather* context, it goes like this: the director casually told Brando he wanted to call round and shoot some footage and arrived at his home at the top of Mulholland Drive in the hills with bits and pieces of props. Brando emerged from his bedroom in a kimono, with his long blond hair in a ponytail. Coppola put the camera on him and Brando began a remarkable metamorphosis, which he had worked out earlier in front of a mirror. Coppola said of the footage: 'You see him roll up his hair in a bun and blacken it with shoe polish, talking all the time about what he's doing.

You see him rolling up Kleenex and stuffing it into his mouth. He'd decided that the godfather had been shot in the throat at one time, so he starts to speak funny. Then he takes a jacket and rolls back the collar the way these Mafia guys do. Brando told me: "It's the face of a bulldog: mean-looking but warm underneath." When Bluhdorn saw it was Brando, he backed away, but then he watched Brando become another person and he was sold on the idea. All of the other executives went along.'

There were lots of other mobsters to cast. Coppola admired Al Pacino: 'When I read *The Godfather*, I saw Al in the part of Michael. I remember when the shepherds are walking across Sicily, I saw his face, and when that happens it's very hard to get out of your head. So right at the front I said "Al Pacino" – and of course that was not viewed as a possibility. [Pacino was primarily a New York stage actor, having made only one major movie, *Panic in Needle Park* (1971); screenplay by Joan Didion.]

'They had me do lots and lots of screen tests. And I tested every talented American actor – Jimmy Caan tested for Michael, Dean Stockwell tested for Michael, Frederic Forrest, everybody. I kept coming back to Pacino, and kept hearing he was a "runt".

'I think Bob Evans was a handsome guy, a tall guy, so he tended to see Michael as someone more like himself. He was suggesting Ryan O'Neal or Bob Redford, and I was suggesting Pacino. I wanted someone more like me.

'Pacino's then girlfriend, Jill Clayburgh, had taken to berating me for stringing Al along. I'd call up and ask, "Please, could Al come back one more time?" and she'd get on the phone crying, "What are you doing to him? You're torturing him. You're never going to give him the part!"'

Of course, Al Pacino became, and for filmgoers will always be, Michael Corleone. But it only happened because of the intervention of Sidney Korshak.

Coppola was in London for meetings with Brando, who was in England co-starring with Stephanie Beacham and being directed by Michael Winner in *The Nightcomers* (1971).

When Coppola returned to Hollywood, he learned that Pacino was on as Michael, and James Caan, who was being pushed to play Michael, would play Sonny instead. Coppola was delighted: 'They'd seen a little footage of *The Panic in Needle Park* and I think they also decided that if they weren't going to fire me, they at least would go along with some of my recommendations.'

Enter a problem, and the problem solver, Sidney Korshak.

Pacino wanted to work and had contracted with MGM to make *The Gang That Couldn't Shoot Straight* (1971), a Mafia comedy based on Jimmy Breslin's book. He had to get out of that deal to become Michael Corleone. Robert Evans telephoned MGM boss Jim Aubrey, who took the opportunity to dump on Evans.

As he buzzed around his home while we chatted many years later, Evans picked up his autobiography, *The Kid Stays in the Picture*, and flipped to the pages that describe his conversation with Korshak, who was at his 'office' in the Carlyle Hotel in New York:

> 'There's an actor I want for the lead in *The Godfather*.'
> 'Yeah.'
> 'I can't get him.'
> 'Yeah.'
> 'If I lose him, Coppola's gonna have my ass.'
> 'Yeah.'
> 'Is there anything you can do about it?'
> 'Yeah.'
> 'Really!'
> 'What's the actor's name?'
> 'Pacino . . . Al Pacino.'
> 'Who?'
> 'Al Pacino.'
> 'Hold it, will ya? Let me get a pencil. Spell it.'
> 'Capital A, little l – that's his first name. Capital P, little a-c-i-n-o.'
> 'Who the fuck is he?'

232

'Don't rub it in, will ya, Sidney. That's who the motherfucker wants.'

With glee, Evans points to the transcription of his call from Jim Aubrey 20 minutes after he hangs up on Sidney Korshak.

'You no-good motherfucker cocksucker. I'll get you for this.'

'What are you talking about?'

'You know fucking well what I'm talking about.'

'Honestly, I don't.'

'The midget's yours. You got him.'

Evans took my copy of *The Kid Stays in the Picture* and signed it with: '*Dear Doug: Fuck 'em. Fuck 'em all, Robert Evans.*' Which was fine until he did it to himself.

With *The Godfather*, he had captured control with his charisma and contacts. And having operators such as Al Ruddy around. There were many dinner-table stories, including early makeshift screen tests of the younger male leads Coppola did at his home near San Francisco: 'My wife, Ellie, helped cut their hair, although later, when the studio felt Al Pacino was too scruffy, we brought him to a real barber and told him to give him a haircut like a college student. When the barber heard it was for the guy who might play Michael in *The Godfather*, he had a heart attack and they had to carry him to the hospital. He survived.'

It looked at times as though some would not. Sidney Korshak had many troubles, including taking care of Coppola's wish to film on location around New York. 'We looked high and low; somebody would follow us; we'd strike a deal for a location and suddenly it would unravel,' said production designer Dean Tavoularis. And the problem was the Mob.

Or, more specifically, a real life don, Joe Colombo, head of one of New York's Five Families. He was a modern Mafia man and was concerned for his and his Family's image. He was also a survivor, who'd found power by double-crossing several fellow mobsters. Now, he would attract a little too much attention. He took exception to the FBI's interest in his affairs – loan-sharking, income-tax evasion, a multimillion-dollar-a-year gambling operation – and charged them with harassment, not only of him and his family but also of *all* Italian-Americans.

And in New York, that's a headline. He then co-created the Italian-American Civil Rights League. Top of their agenda was to remove 'Mafia' from the English language. It was a smear, he told the New York reporters in a bold way: 'Mafia? What is Mafia? There is not a Mafia. Am I the head of a family? Yes. My wife, and four sons and a daughter. That's my family.'

But so are we, believed the other four Mafia Families. The Italian-American Civil Rights League began picketing the New York FBI offices on 30 March 1970. Around 250,000 turned out at the league's inaugural rally in New York City, with Colombo yelling through his megaphone: 'Those who go against the league will feel God's sting.'

The Godfather and the filming of it was an easy target. 'It became clear very quickly that the Mafia – and they did not call themselves the Mafia – did not want our film made and we started getting threats,' is how Al Ruddy's assistant, Bettye McCartt, recalled the time. The LAPD warned Al Ruddy that he was being followed. He began swapping cars with his staff and one night traded his for McCartt's company car. That night she heard gunfire outside her house on Mulholland Drive: 'The kids were hysterical. All the windows had been shot out of the sports car. It was a warning – to Al. On the dashboard was a note, which essentially said shut down the movie – or else.'

The Paramount Studio gates, an iconic Hollywood sight, were blown off their hinges. The Italian-American Civil Rights League threatened to shut down the Teamsters, the truckers, drivers, and crew members essential to making the film; the offices of Paramount's parent company, Gulf & Western were evacuated twice because of bomb threats; Robert Evans was staying at the Sherry-Netherland Hotel and received a warning involving his and his wife Ali MacGraw's newborn son, Josh: 'If you want your son to live longer than two weeks, get out of town.'

In his book, Evans relates a voice on the phone as he was in the room with his wife and son: 'Take some advice. We don't want to break your pretty face, hurt your newborn. Get the fuck outta town. Don't shoot no movie about the Family here. Got it?'

Al Ruddy says there was 'a slight hint of hysteria' in Evans's voice when he called him, saying: 'I just got a call from this guy, Joe Colombo, saying if this movie gets made there is going to be trouble.'

'So Bob says: "I'm not producing it. Al Ruddy is." And Joe Colombo says: "When we kill a snake, we chop its fucking head off."'

Evans asked Al Ruddy to meet with Joe Colombo. He met him at the Park Sheraton Hotel, where Mafia high executioner Albert Anastasia was himself executed for getting in the way of Meyer Lansky's gambling empire-building. Ruddy remembers telling the mobster: '"Look, Joe, this movie will not demean the Italian-American community. It's an equal-opportunity organisation. We have a corrupt Irish cop, a corrupt Jewish producer. No one's singling the Italians out for anything. You come to my office tomorrow and I'll let you look at the script. You read it, and we'll see if we can make a deal."

'The next day Joe shows up with two other guys. Joe sits opposite me, one guy's on the couch, and one guy's sitting in the window. I gave him the [155-page] script. He puts on his little Ben Franklin glasses, looks at it for about two minutes. "What does this mean – fade in?" he asked. And I realised there was no way Joe was going to turn to page two. "Oh, these fucking glasses. I can't read with them," Colombo said, throwing the script to his lieutenant. "Here, you read it."

'"Why me?" said the guy.

'Colombo grabbed the script and slammed it on the table. "Wait a minute! Do we trust this guy?" he asked his men. They said yes and he looked at them: "So what the fuck do we have to read this script for? Let's make a deal."'

235

Joe Colombo wanted the word 'Mafia' deleted from the script. Ruddy knew that there was only a single mention in the screenplay and instantly agreed. Two days later, Colombo called Ruddy and invited him to a press conference: 'To get the word out to our people that we're now behind the movie.'

Ruddy thought it was a good idea. He believed they'd get little coverage, but the world dropped by: there followed front pages on the *New York Times* and *Wall Street Journal*, and stories about Paramount making deals with the Italian-American Civil Rights League. Charlie Bluhdorn went ape. Ruddy had held a major press conference with mobsters without Bluhdorn's consent; he had made promises and cut deals with the Mob. Bluhdorn was determined to fire Ruddy, if he didn't kill him first.

'I ran to the Gulf & Western Building, to Mr Bluhdorn's floor, and there's a board-of-directors crisis meeting going on. Gulf & Western's stock had dropped two and a half points that morning. I walk in, and it was the most solemn group I'd ever seen in my life. Charlie Bluhdorn said: "You wrecked my company." Ruddy was fired. Bluhdorn shut down the set to advise Coppola and Evans to find another producer. Coppola fought him by saying: 'Al Ruddy's the only guy who can keep this movie going.'

Al Ruddy was back at work – and the Mafia men wanted work on his movie. He remembered: 'It was like one happy family. All these guys loved the underworld characters, and obviously the underworld guys loved Hollywood.'

Lenny Montana certainly did. And you wouldn't want to disagree with him. A towering 6 ft 6 in. tall, and 21 stone of muscled brawn, the former wrestler was the bodyguard to one of the young mafiosi who visited the movie set. Coppola cast him as Luca Brasi, the don's giant enforcer.

Ruddy said: 'He used to tell us all these things, like he was an arsonist. He'd tie tampons on the tail of a mouse, dip it in kerosene, light it and let the mouse run through a building.' But Montana/Brasi had a soft side. When Bettye McCartt broke her watch, a cheap red one, Montana noticed. 'He said:

"What kind of watch would you like?" and I said: "I'd like an antique watch with diamonds on it, but I'll get another $15 one." A week passes and Lenny comes, and he's got a Kleenex in his hand wadded up, and he's looking over his shoulder every step of the way. He placed the wad of Kleenex on the desk and there was an antique diamond watch inside. He says: "The boys sent you this. But don't wear it in Florida." The Mob were certainly paying respects to *The Godfather*.'

Robert Evans said: 'New York finally opened up like a World's Fair – on our side were the garbagemen, the longshoremen, the Teamsters – and security was in place for the locations. All it took was a call or two from Sidney Korshak. *The Godfather* would not have been made without Korshak. He saved Pacino, the locations and, possibly, my son. With Al Pacino, that problem went away with one phone call from Sidney. Not two phone calls – one phone call. Let's just say that a nod from Korshak and the Teamsters change management. A nod from Korshak and Santa Anita racetrack closes. A nod from Korshak and Vegas shuts down. A nod from Korshak and the Dodgers can suddenly play night baseball.'

It was the truth of it about a man who could call Henry Kissinger or Meyer Lansky within moments of each other. And be put straight through. And get things settled.

Earlier in 1971 Sidney Korshak's friend and regular Bistro lunch companion Albert 'Cubby' Broccoli was preparing his seventh James Bond film, *Diamonds Are Forever*. Sean Connery was to be 007 and Charles Gray, in a Howard Hughes take-off, was bad guy Blofeld. The glamour was to be provided by Lana Wood as Tiffany Case. A smaller role was to be filled out by Jill St John as Plenty O'Toole. Sidney Korshak, who was the legal adviser on the Las Vegas-shot Bond film, was seeing Jill St John, who had also dated Henry Kissinger. Natalie Wood's sister Lana and Jill St John switched roles. (In the intimate carousel of Hollywood, following Natalie Wood's death in 1981 Robert Wagner, first boyfriend of Judith Exner, found happiness and a long marriage with Jill St John.)

There were gangland links to the past for Cubby Broccoli,

whose close cousin was Pat DiCicco, the one-time husband of Thelma Todd. DiCicco had helped his cousin in Hollywood, taking him to meet Howard Hughes and stars like Cary Grant, who told me 'Cubby has an interesting story.' He was correct.

Ted Healy, an original member of 'The Three Stooges', had been involved with Thelma Todd after her divorce from DiCicco. Healy died in the car park of the Trocadero Club on Sunset Strip following a fight with Cubby Broccoli and the actor Wallace Beery. The death was never solved.

However, the death of Joe Colombo was clear-cut. On 28 June 1971, he was hosting the Unity Day rally of the Italian-American Civil Rights League in New York's Columbus Circle. Al Ruddy had been invited to sit on the dais beside Colombo, but he had then been advised not to. Carlo Gambino, head of the most powerful of the Five Families, had ordered Colombo to be sent away for drawing too much attention to the Mob. Joey Gallo and his boys were given the job. They knew they would never get close enough to waste Colombo. Gallo had good contacts with black gangsters in Harlem and recruited Jerome A. Johnson. He was told to blast Joe Colombo and, in a distraction created by Gallo's guys, to escape.

Wearing press photographers' badges, Johnson got within a step of Joe Colombo, drew a pistol and fired three shots into the Mafia chief's head. There was no distraction; it had not been intended. Colombo's bodyguards filled Johnson with bullets and he was dead instantly. Colombo was brain damaged and survived seven years in a vegetative state.

Carlo Gambino had thought it through: the Italian-American Civil Rights League was now tainted by bloody violence and simply drifted away. Colombo's death was also personal. When Colombo was causing so much trouble and getting attention, complaining about *The Godfather*, the two Mob bosses had met. Gambino had told his rival to back off. The upstart Colombo, believing his own publicity, spat in Gambino's face, demeaning the real-life godfather. It was five weeks to the day when he was shot.

On 29 June, at the St Regis Hotel in New York, Coppola

filmed a scene in which Richard Castellano blows away a group of Michael Corleone's enemies with a shotgun. 'Would you believe it? Before we started working on the film, we kept saying, "But these Mafia guys don't go around shooting each other any more."'

The film's premiere was held in five cinemas in New York. Evans managed to get Henry Kissinger to show up at his side for the film's grand opening, although he was flying off the next morning for secret peace talks to end the Vietnam War.

Evans said: 'Henry was a most unusual person. He enjoyed making fun of himself, of his own ego. He was brilliant, but he was naive in so many ways. He'd call me up from the State Department and say: "Are Raquel Welch's tits for real?"'

Al Ruddy tells another premiere story: 'Henry Kissinger, Teddy Kennedy – the whole world was going to show up, and I got a call from the Mob: "Hey, they won't sell us no tickets to this thing."

'"To be honest, I don't think they want you there."

'"That's very unfair, don't you think?"

'"What do you mean?"

'"When they do a movie about the army, the generals are guests of honour, right? If they do a movie about the navy, who's sitting up front? The admirals. You'd think we'd be guests of honour at this thing."

'So I snuck out a print that Paramount never knew about and I gave them a screening. There must have been a hundred limousines out front. The projectionist called me and said: "Mr Ruddy, I've been a projectionist my whole life. No one ever gave me a thousand-dollar tip." That's how much the guys loved the movie.'

As with their huge profits did Gulf & Western and Paramount and Charlie Bluhdorn. Mario Puzo became a star author. Shortly before his death in 1999, he appeared at yet another conference, from which this remark leapt out: 'I think the movie business is far more crooked than Vegas, and than the Mafia.'

Puzo, who had written *The Godfather* on the back of research and street-corner gossip, by then had proper inside knowledge. The clue to one of the best-kept Mafia–Hollywood collaborations is in the credit at the conclusion of *The Godfather: Part III* (1990) to Charlie Bluhdorn, who died, aged 58, in 1983 from natural causes, a heart attack: '*Dedicated to Charlie Bluhdorn, who inspired it.*' The final film of the Mafia trilogy only uses tiny touches to disguise the true-life story of how the Mob were about to take over Paramount Studios – and Mary Poppins. Or more precisely that film's star Julie Andrews, who became an unwitting asset of the Mafia.

Bluhdorn was a corporate raider, a fast-lane-living pirate of business. Shortly after taking over Paramount in 1966, he greenlighted *Darling Lili* (1970), a First World War musical-drama, starring Andrews and Rock Hudson, which was as bad as it sounds. When Paramount executives first viewed it, they were appalled. It was awful. But Bluhdorn only smiled and told the studio's Peter Bart: 'Don't worry, *Darling Lili* has disappeared from the face of the earth.'

Bart, the editor in 2012 of *Hollywood Variety* magazine, said: 'It was magic. Here was this horrendously awful movie and Charlie had made it vanish into thin air, so that its losses would be erased from the Paramount books.'

Bluhdorn had done a deal in Rome with a Sicilian banker named Michele Sindona: the Hollywood company got 6 per cent of shares in a conglomerate called Societa Generale Immobiliare; in return, a company was created for Sindona, Marathon Pictures. The assets of the company, which in 2012 was long gone, were the land on which Paramount Studios stood on Marathon Street in Hollywood and the rights to *Darling Lili*. Michele Sindona was a close friend of producer Dino De Laurentiis, who produced landmark movies such as Charlie Bronson's *Death Wish* (1974) and *The White Buffalo* (1977), and introduced Hannibal Lecter (played by Brian Cox) to film audiences in *Manhunter* (1986). De Laurentiis, who died in November 2010, was branded with Mafia connections, in that he dealt with extravagant amounts of capital that appeared and vanished. Quickly.

Italian government prosecutor Armando Spataro, an anti-Mafia crusader, explained to me in Milan in January 2012 that at the time the Mafia were invading America with heroin. They were flying it in. The movies were a convenient way to launder the massive profits.

While the head of one of Hollywood's big five studios was doing business with one of last century's shadiest mafiosi, huge consignments of heroin and cocaine were coming into Milan from Morocco and Turkey en route to New York, Miami and Los Angeles. The American market commanded double the European tariff. As it does in 2012, the smuggling organisation operated out of central Milan. There and in surrounding garages the cellophane-wrapped individual kilos of heroin would be subdivided into packets of double-sided tape and plastic, which would fit in empty bottles of shampoo, hair conditioner and body lotion – any toiletries you'd find in airline passengers' luggage. When the pack was in place, Sellotaped to the inside of the container, the shampoo or conditioner or whatever would be poured back in. They used any beauty products, which recruits would carry five or six at a time. It was very straightforward. And successful. Couriers got no money, but a free flight to America carrying £100,000 worth of drugs in their bags. In America, it was cut and worth much more. There were scores of 'drug tourists'. They were almost always women: mothers with babies, grandmas off to visit family, single girls off to America to find or make their fortune. What they all shared, along with their prepared stories, was their extra-strong perfume to confuse drug-sniffing dogs at customs.

Often they'd wear body belts, which were custom made to take half-kilo and three-quarter-kilo bags of heroin. The heroin was inside the thinnest of plastic film. The belt was cloth to absorb body sweat, so the belts wouldn't slip down at the wrong moment – a belt stuffed with heroin around their ankles at American customs. The body-belt tourists went return. On the flights back to Italy, the made-to-measure plastic packets were packed with US dollars.

In her 1994 book *Le Donne, La Mafia*, the Italian scholar Renate Siebert describes how it could go wrong:

> The business of packaging isn't always done with the necessary precision. Thus it was that Annamaria Cordovino nearly had to be flayed alive when she came back from America stuffed with dollars. Flesh and adhesive tape had all become one and it was a devil of a job: smeared with creams and lotions and put under a scalding hot shower, poor Annamaria ended up literally skinned.

For the businessmen of the Mafia, there was no way that Annamaria Cordovino could keep the money, which had been cleaned up for reinvestment in projects also financially interesting to the Vatican Bank in Rome.

Michele Sindona was a man of mystery: a money-launderer and adviser to the Gambino Family and the Vatican Bank, another partner of Società Generale Immobiliare. Sindona had the power to administer church funds. They were all people interested in money, lots of it.

Bluhdorn gradually learned what his corporate raiding had got him and Hollywood into. As it always had been, the film industry was a dream legitimate business for the Mob, affording massive opportunities for washing tainted money. And along the corridors of Paramount walked some of the keenest financial brains in the world – all working for the Mafia.

Bluhdorn was paranoid that Sindona wanted to become a film producer and in time take over the majority holding in Paramount. That was indeed the intention. The Mob wanted to *wag the tail*.

Events – violent, as they so often are with organised crime – bailed out Charlie Bluhdorn. Michele Sindona never got Marathon Pictures going; his financial escapades in America got him jailed for 25 years in 1980 for a string of offences, including fraud and perjury. Four years later, he was extradited to Rome, where he was jailed for a further 25 years for ordering the murder of a Milan lawyer. In 1986, at the age of 66, he died in his prison cell in Voghera in Lombardy. From a heavy dose of cyanide in his coffee.

While *The Godfather* broke many box-office and book-selling records, there was one man who was never a fan: Frank Sinatra. He made himself heard before filming began, giving his allegiance to Joe Colombo about the manner in which Italian-Americans were being depicted. It was purely personal: the character of Johnny Fontane – the drunken, womanising, Mob-owned singer who, with the help of a delicately placed horse's head, becomes a movie star – was generally believed to be him. He hated Puzo and threatened him in Chasen's, Ronald Reagan's favourite restaurant, which sat not far off Sunset Strip: 'I ought to break your legs. Did the FBI help you with your book?' Sinatra had endured humiliation from Ava Gardner – she was never going to give any man a quiet old age – and felt more of it when Johnny Fontane staggers into Puzo's novel on an early page 'sloppy drunk and fantasising about murdering his trampy wife when she got home'.

Johnny Fontane also had elements of Al Martino. He had become a star with 'Here in My Heart', a number-one hit song in America and the first ever in that same spot in the UK Singles Chart, published by the *New Musical Express* on 14 November 1952. (He remains in the *Guinness Book of World Records* for that.) Capitol Records made him a deal – but so did the Mob. They bought out his management contract and ordered him to pay $75,000 as a safeguard for their investment. He paid a little and then moved to Britain. Half a dozen successful years later a deal was done with the Mob and he felt safe to return home. From then on, he appeared in many, many Mafia-owned clubs and theatres in Hollywood, Vegas, New York and Miami, performing until not long before his death, aged 81, in 2009. Sam Giancana's girlfriend Phyllis McGuire saw a lot of him on that entertainment circuit.

Al Martino told people in Las Vegas that Phyllis McGuire had, for rather obvious reasons, devoured Mario Puzo's novel, telling him: 'I just read a book, *The Godfather*, Al. Johnny

Fontane is you, and I know you can play it in the movie.' Her friend thought so, too. But the 'suits' at Paramount were not so sure. Yet, he *did* play Johnny Fontane in the three films.

He had his own godfather. Al Martino had simply made one call. Not two. One call. That's all that was required.

12

CALL ME *MISTER* EVANS

'What are you, a monk?'

'I have a woman.'

'What do you tell her?'

'I tell her I'm a salesman.'

'So then, if you spot me coming around that corner . . . you just gonna walk out on this woman? Not say goodbye?'

'That's the discipline.'

'That's pretty vacant, you know.'

'Yeah, it is what it is. It's that or we both better go do something else, pal.'

'I don't know how to do anything else.'

'Neither do I.'

'I don't much want to either.'

'Neither do I.'

> – LAPD detective Vincent Hanna (Al Pacino) in conversation with armed bank-robber Neil McCauley (Robert De Niro), *Heat*, 1995

AL PACINO IS NOT THE EASIEST MAN TO GET TO, TO GET SOME recollections about *The Godfather* – about Hollywood and the Mafia and the movies. I've tried many times. To my utter amazement, Robert De Niro was more forthcoming on the times I sat with him in New York. The film made Pacino a star and *The Godfather: Part II* (1974) did the same for De Niro (and won him a Best Supporting Actor Oscar), who speaks

Italian throughout his appearances. Of *The Godfather*, Pacino offers: 'It was a very good story, about a family, told unusually well.'

Scholars have for decades attempted to analyse the links between real and screen violence, just as sociologists have tried to fathom why girls like the actress in Dory Previn's song 'jumped off the Hollywood sign because she couldn't become a star'. There's a story in it all and, as Pacino says, if it's a good story and well told it will be interesting. Maybe fascinating. Which is why actors like Pacino and De Niro and directors like Martin Scorsese have invested so many of their years in making gangland-related films. I met mobbed-up casino boss Frank Rosenthal, whom De Niro plays as Ace Rothstein in *Casino* (1995), and you couldn't meet a friendlier guy, even when he knew my limit at poker. It was a shock when I flew to Vegas the day the Mob exploded a bomb under his car. He survived and was still around, but never seemed to be as friendly.

Tony Spilotro, whom Joe Pesci portrays in the film as a terrifying monster, a true son-of-a-bitch psycho, was the far more dangerous and nasty character but, arguably, the more intriguing. His eyes cut into you like he was stabbing you.

Spilotro had been evil from the start. In 1962, young hoods Billy McCarthy and Jimmy Miraglia killed two Chicago Mob-connected brothers without permission. Spilotro caught McCarthy and tortured him for information on the whereabouts of his friend. Spilotro stuck McCarthy in the groin with an ice pick and put his head in a vice. Each time McCarthy refused to give information, Spilotro tightened the vice – until one of McCarthy's eyeballs popped out. McCarthy talked and both men's bodies were found in the trunk of an abandoned car.

A 'made man', his first job was running bookmaking in the north-west of Chicago. He was sent to Miami in 1964 to work with the gambling guru Rosenthal and in 1971 the demented Spilotro arrived in Vegas, along with his wife Nancy and their adopted son Vincent, in the tradition of Johnny Rosselli – to guarantee a continuing flow of cash from the casinos. He quickly became the 'King of the Strip'.

He opened a jewellery and gift shop at the Circus Circus Hotel-Casino, using his wife's maiden name, operating as Anthony Stuart Ltd. In August 1972, he was indicted for another 1963 murder but was acquitted in 1973. The following year, the *Los Angeles Times* revealed that in the three years Spilotro had been in Las Vegas, more gangland-style murders had been committed there than in the previous twenty-five years combined. If you look in the *Las Vegas Sun* files for that same year, you'll see Spilotro was indicted by a federal grand jury in Chicago with defrauding the Central States Teamsters pension fund of $1.4 million. Another defendant was Allen Dorfman, the convicted go-between of the Teamsters pension fund and organised crime. They were acquitted. The chief witness died of a shotgun blast before a trial could begin.

In 1978, Spilotro's name, like Sam Giancana's and all the others before him, was entered into the Black Book, forbidding him to enter Nevada casinos. A year later the FBI pursued a racketeering charge, but a Las Vegas judge said agents had overstepped their authority. Spilotro's attorney was Oscar Goodman, who adamantly argued: 'I think it's un-American. These are really Gestapo-like tactics. It literally has become a police state in this community.'

In 2011, after 12 consecutive years as mayor and running the Las Vegas community, the always ebullient Goodman stepped down and his wife Carolyn took over. On 14 February 2012, he opened the Mob Museum with a televised fanfare. The $42 million trophy to organised crime was called a waste of taxpayers' money, but Goodman found that his critics were no more than 'monkeys' following its unveiling on the 89th anniversary of the Saint Valentine's Day Massacre, the wall from which is on display.

Frank Cullotta was one of the many invited guests at the VIP event. His contribution to the evening and the Mob Museum is that he was deputy to Tony Spilotro – before he turned state's witness and testified against his boss, then happily joined the federal witness-protection programme. Cullotta is one of the Mob characters whose video interviews comprise the walking tour. He and Goodman do an Abbot and Costello number: Cullotta complains that the most valuable advice Goodman ever offered as legal counsel was how to properly do his tie, while Goodman counters that he did not tie Cullotta's tie tight enough. When I wondered about the taste of the event, while admitting my fascination, the answer was: 'This is the story of Las Vegas.' Which is a point.

In 1984, Spilotro was finally indicted for the 1962 torture killings of Miraglia and McCarthy in a case quickly named 'the M&M Murders'. Oscar Goodman got him out of jail and out of the charge twice.

There was more trouble with the law and a lot of attention on the Mafia's business in Las Vegas. On 14 June 1986, two days before yet another trial, Tony Spilotro and his brother Michael went off to a meeting together. They were never seen alive again. Their battered bodies were found buried in an Indiana cornfield four days later. The medical examinations suggested they'd both been buried alive.

It's easy to see the attraction of stories based around such characters for actors like Pacino and De Niro.

It's weekend brunch time in uptown New York and De Niro is dressed for a baseball game. Wearing jeans, a brown leather jacket and a wary look for ruminating on the past decade, he's talkative (for him) when we meet in a New York hotel. This shy man is playing nervously with his fingers and looks as though he would be intimidated if asked to carry a spear in the school play. But he made all these movies with Scorsese – Johnny Boy in *Mean Streets*, Travis Bickle in *Taxi Driver*, Jimmy Doyle in *New York, New York*, Jake LaMotta in *Raging Bull*, Jimmy 'the Gent' Conway in *GoodFellas*. These movies, says De Niro, took him back to the streets, back to his beginnings, back to the melting pot. He's part Italian, Irish, French and Dutch, which makes him all-American. If Brando and James Dean were rebels, then De Niro has been our screen identity seeker since 1973 and *Mean Streets*, which was his first collaboration with Martin Scorsese. They've grown up together. Still, some years later, he turned down Scorsese's offer of the title role in *The Last Temptation of Christ* (1988), explaining in what is a memorable only-in-Hollywood line: 'I couldn't relate to it.'

A nondescript face away from the camera – he's an athletic, 5 ft 10 1/2 in. tall man you really wouldn't glance twice at – De Niro will change his look through gestures or physically, as he did by swelling as Jake LaMotta and to play Al Capone in his larger-than-life turn in *The Untouchables* (1987). To play arguably the best-known name in Mafia history, he shaved his hairline and, on- and off-set, wore only Capone's preferred and imported brand of French silk underpants: 'The preparation is personal. That's secret – what you do and how you do it is a secret, as long as you arrive at whatever you need to arrive at. That, to me, is a rule. When you feel something is simple, you think there must be more to it, but the less the better. That's really the strongest way to go, the most powerful. Just having to do nothing. It's very hard for actors when they feel they're not doing enough.

'The people I love still live in Little Italy and I love to see them. My parents divorced when I was two, but they stayed friends. Their friends were other artists, poets, art critics, writers – people who expressed themselves in their work. My father used to take me to a lot of movies. Around the age of ten, I knew I wanted to be an actor. Later, at one of the acting schools I went to, the director asked me why I wanted to be an actor. I told him I didn't know. He said: "You want to be an actor to express yourself." And later on, when I got into acting seriously, I remembered this and said that is the reason I want to be an actor – to express myself. I believe the only way anybody will become anything is to become fully what he is and do what he wants to do.'

After her marriage broke up, his mother started a typing service to support herself and her son in an apartment on West 14th Street. De Niro – 'Bobby Milk' to the Kenmare Street

Gang because he was so pale and strange – got his entertainment watching the action in the neighbourhood bars and pool halls. All the Mafia movies – to some epic poetry like 'Le Morte d'Arthur' – are part New York anthropology and the city has been a major player in De Niro's life. He has a computer bank of gestures, walks and accents from memory.

His best work has involved playing characters with edge: 'As a kid, I didn't root for the bad guys. I certainly know the difference between right and wrong, but I think in our American tradition the bad guys get a lot of attention and you see it in the movies. There is a certain amount of glamour, a certain allure that they have, but we always have to remember to put it in the right perspective of what they represent. Like a Robin Hood thing in reverse, but you always have to be aware of what the real world is too.

'I think *The Godfather* started it, popularised it in a very grand sense. It was a movie about the most traditionally reactionary type of people set in a time where so much was going on, the anti-war movement and everything else at the time. But there was more loyalty going on – in a romantic sense, this isn't the truth – in the Family of *The Godfather* and the lines were drawn more clearly about what was what. That attracted a lot of people.

'Look at today. Who can you trust? Then, in those *Godfather* times, you couldn't have faith in the government; you could have faith in the Family government.

'The bad guys are always more interesting than the good guys. The antagonist is more interesting than the protagonist. Because we're human beings. There's good and evil in all of us, and villains act out the worst part of ourselves, the things we always feel. We kind of like to live through that vicariously. Anybody who knows anything about acting knows it's much more fun. There is more room to do more interesting sorts of characters and show the contradictions in people.'

And people can prove problems.

In 2012, the Mafia are running a prostitution ring that circles the world. The information moves on the internet, the girls in private jets, the hubs of the traffic in Hollywood, New York, London, Paris, Geneva, Tokyo and Beijing. It becomes more sophisticated by the day.

De Niro was drawn into an earlier version of it in 1998, when he was filming the high-minded but rip-roaring *French Connection*-style thriller *Ronin* on location. De Niro's name appeared in an address book seized by authorities. He was quizzed for nine hours by detectives investigating a prostitution ring serving celebrity and wealthy clients in world capitals. The high-cost hookers, often 'model-actresses' from Britain and France, were said to charge $7,500 a night. Some of the girls were aged only 16. A Lebanese man who said he supplied hookers to the ring claimed he had once 'dealt' Sylvester Stallone's former wife, the statuesque Brigitte Nielsen, to a Saudi sheik for $1 million. Nielsen has vehemently denied this.

Just as Wojtek Fibak, the Pope's former tennis coach, laughed off his alleged involvement in the scandal. Like De Niro, he was questioned by French detectives.

De Niro will admit that he was involved at one time – in a non-paying capacity – with a soft-porn British model who herself was part of the Paris-based investigation. But as far as the prostitution ring is concerned he says he was simply a 'minor witness to provide testimony in a case that had nothing to do with [him]'. It was a 'non-story'.

Al Pacino is not easy. He can frustrate you. It's slow to get him to commit to a film and, when he does, he always wants just one more rehearsal or one more take or one more test. I am with him in the lobby of a grand hotel in Beverly Hills, deciding where to go for lunch. His associates hang around aimlessly. The automatic doors open and close, swish-swish, by the dozen, back and forth and back again, in the time it takes one of the most important stars of his generation to make up his mind where to have pasta. A few hours before he began debating lunch, he was having a little difficulty with breakfast in a downstairs suite of the hotel. It was the coffee. You know, regular or decaffeinated? Decisions, decisions, decisions.

The actor is short but surely not 'too Italian-looking' (as Charlie Bluhdorn decried) to be Michael Corleone, the role that will always be by his shoulder. He says of Coppola: 'Francis is the visionary.' Yet, it was some surprise that he never saw the original *Godfather* on the big screen until a 25th anniversary party in San Francisco. ('I went, but I didn't stay. I was too nervous. It's like looking at an old photograph of yourself. You just wonder. You say: "I can't quite relate."') It brought back memories of a young actor so overwhelmed that he was expecting to be fired: 'I thought the role was impossible to do. I didn't know how I was going to go from being a nonentity to this guy who runs the whole show. Where was that? I remember staying really close to the story in my mind and heart and feeling that somehow I would chart out this character. I spent a lot of time doing that, and I spent a lot of time praying. Literally, I went and sat in churches and prayed.'

On another occasion, I meet him in a hotel suite across from New York's Central Park. He leans back deep into a stuffed leather armchair. He's dressed in standard Manhattan artistic chic – black shirt, black pants, black leather overcoat. Only a casually knotted red tie indicates he might like to get noticed.

He has never lost certain professional insecurities: 'I always think, the next thing I do had better be good – it just never changed for me.' Pacino takes several attempts to explain that while ambition is not a bad thing, just wanting to work is his motivation: 'My grandfather was a plasterer, and the thing about him, because he raised me, was his love of what he did. And he went away and did that for eight hours every day, and you felt he really wanted to go back and do that again.

'What is fame? It can be a pain. Once in Paris I was hounded endlessly. When you're in a public-enterprise thing, that's what you have to expect. But it's the persistence that causes you to react. But the good stuff outweighs most of that. I remember in East Berlin before the Wall came down, they knew me at Checkpoint Charlie. That was great.

'My first language was shy. It's only by having been thrust into the limelight that I have learned to cope with my shyness.

I once glued on a beard to go to a baseball game, but that just got me noticed. I was with Beverly D'Angelo [then his steady date]. So that beard is in the museum of mistakes now.'

Then there is an unusual sound. Al Pacino is giggling.

'It takes me half an hour to answer a question. I'm becoming verbose. There's a lot I'd like to do. No one ever asked me to play Hamlet. I don't think I'm right for the part, but it would have been nice to be asked.'

When director Michael Mann got Pacino and De Niro to appear together in the Mob-land heist thriller *Heat* (1995), someone said it was like getting Ben Hur to sit down with Spartacus. Or Warren Beatty just to sit down.

Beatty relishes his own mystique. He seems to have been with us forever and been famous most of that time. He was 75 in 2012 and had most certainly witnessed much of Hollywood history and made some of it himself. Gangsters made him a multimillionaire before he was 30 years old. He produced and starred with Faye Dunaway in *Bonnie and Clyde* (1967) and was able to write his own cheques and Hollywood story from then on.

The bloody but romantic saga of Bonnie Parker and Clyde Barrow's violent armed robbery spree through Depression-era Midwest America was cutting edge but poorly regarded by Warner Brothers Studios, who had made so much from the Cagney–Bogart–Raft black-and-white shoot-'em-ups. Instead of a producing fee, they gave Beatty a share of the profits. Decades on, he still recalls with great glee: 'They gave me 40 per cent of the gross.' In 1960s money, the movie made $53 million.

Beatty arrived in Hollywood as a 'star is born', with his first leading role in Elia Kazan's *Splendour in the Grass* (1961), a story of small-town sexual hypocrisy. He romanced the ageing Vivien Leigh in *The Roman Spring of Mrs. Stone* (1961), as our old friend the enigma wrapped in a mystery. The gossip columns began counting up the women Beatty kept company with. He was called 'Rabbit' Warren because of his bedhopping. He kept a suite on the seventh floor of the Beverly Wilshire Hotel and 'entertained' there. One lady journalist I know went to visit him there and emerged three days later. Happy. During decades of womanising, he has been involved with hundreds of women – many of them leading ladies. One love, Leslie Caron, scratched: 'Warren has an interesting psychology. He has always fallen in love with girls who have just won or just been nominated for an Oscar . . .'

He was engaged to Joan Collins in 1960 but broke it off following an affair with Natalie Wood during their filming of *Splendour in the Grass*; it ended Natalie's first marriage, to Robert Wagner. Joan Collins testified: 'He was insatiable. Three, four, five times a day was not unusual for him, and he was able to accept phone calls at the same time . . .'

Before, during and after his long romance with Julie Christie he was involved with Brigitte Bardot, Candice Bergen, Cher, Catherine Deneuve, Britt Ekland, Chris Evert, Carrie Fisher, Susan George, Goldie Hawn, Mary Tyler Moore, Soviet ballerina Maya Plisetskaya, Vanessa Redgrave, Jean Seberg, Barbra Streisand, Dewi Sukarno, Liv Ullmann, Michelle Phillips (shared with Jack Nicholson and Dennis Hopper), Joni Mitchell, Diana Ross, Dinah Shore, Carly Simon ('You're So Vain' was for him), Diane Keaton (shared with Al Pacino), Joyce Hyser, Isabelle Adjani and Madonna. The men of Hollywood, who respect such things, had already noticed. (His catch phone-phrase to women, 'What's new, Pussycat?', became a 1965 movie and Tom Jones hit. Woody Allen, who wrote the film, vowed: 'I want to be reincarnated as Warren Beatty's fingertips.') Even Sinatra, the Hollywood ruling swinger, acknowledged him – he was 'a whole Rat Pack rolled into one'.

Then Benjamin Siegel did what he had done for so many – changed his life. Beatty became set on making *Bugsy* (1991), depicting the life and Hollywood times of Siegel. The other big lead role was for Virginia Hill.

Beatty had been distinctly impressed by Annette Bening in *The Grifters* (1990), which includes a scene where, as a con artist, she lies naked on a bed and offers her body or cash to her landlord. The landlord didn't seem to have a choice.

Neither did Beatty. Was it love at first sight? 'Corny question – it took all of 30 seconds.'

It was just like the movies. In *Bugsy*, he starred as Siegel and was besotted by Virginia Hill. Beatty – at times it does seem he lives in parallel zones – explained: 'The thing about Bugsy . . . he was very promiscuous throughout his life until he met Virginia Hill. That's what makes the story so vital. When they got together, he never went after another woman. He found someone who accepted him for what he was.'

In the movie, Jack Dragna is seen being humiliated by Bugsy using the sheer force of his psychopathic personality, finally compelling him to crawl on the floor, bark like a dog and oink like a pig. When Dragna is allowed to leave, alive, he is grateful. On the point of tears, he tells Siegel: 'Thank you, Ben. You can count on me for anything.' Siegel replies: 'Yeah? We'll see. Everybody needs a fresh start once in a while.'

Beatty saw much of Hollywood in the Mob and vice versa: 'I think it was [Siegel's] relationship to Hollywood that interested me the most. He was infatuated with Hollywood to a degree unlike any gangster before or since. I think he really would rather have been a movie actor than anything else. Gangsters tried to copy Hollywood as much as Hollywood tried to copy the gangsters. Film-makers were very impressed by gangsters and the other way around. They were all part of the romantic swirl of American drama.' As he most certainly was.

He and Annette Bening married on 3 March 1992 and remain so, with four children: 'I've known a lot of incredible women in my time but never anyone like Annette.'

And he's known incredible times. He attended the funeral of Manson Family victim Jay Sebring, the model for George in *Shampoo*. Steve McQueen and his first wife Neile were sitting next to Beatty at the funeral: 'There was a strange guy came up the aisle talking loud. I saw Steve put his hand into his jacket, where he was carrying a .45. Everyone was edgy then.'

Few were more on edge than Robert Evans, as his cocaine habit increased and his fortunes fell. He admits he made one glaring mistake during his hard times – not asking Sidney Korshak for help. Without it, Evans was publicly demeaned. Korshak believed that reflected on his talents, his magic at making bad things go away and good things happen.

Sam Peckinpah, who'd been rejected for *The Godfather*, needed a leading lady to play opposite McQueen in *The Getaway* (1972) based on Jim Thompson's nihilistic noir novel. Peckinpah was in the land he loved, El Paso, Texas, and was also doing what he loved, drinking and movie-making. This was a cowboy's world, Steve McQueen country. Still, Ali MacGraw coming off *Love Story* was about as hot as McQueen was super-cool. Her life with Evans was turbulent and punctuated with work-enforced separations. She'd met McQueen and felt sparks. She didn't want to light the fire and go off to El Paso to work with him, but her husband insisted – many believe he wanted out of the marriage. In the absurdity of this world, Henry Kissinger, busily trying to conclude the Vietnam War, offered to go to Texas as a marriage counsellor. Evans demurred, but Korshak played the role at meetings in the south of France. Mr Silk Stockings made momentary repairs to the marriage. Next, Evans told him he wanted McQueen murdered.

It was an 'only in Hollywood' moment.

It was debated at Kurt Niklas's Bistro in Beverly Hills. In his autobiography *The Corner Table: From Cabbages to Caviar, Sixty Years in the Celebrity Restaurant Trade*, published in 2000, the astute Niklas, who died age 83 in 2009, says Sidney Korshak and Evans met in the upstairs private room. He overheard the murder request and Korshak's 'Calm down, Bobby.' Evans left.

Just ten minutes later, McQueen arrived, asking for Korshak. Back to the private room, with every waiter and Niklas straining to hear from the upstairs corridor. In his book, Niklas quotes what he could hear of the conversation:

'Mr Korshak, please. I don't want any trouble, but he's threatening to kill me.'

'Nobody's gonna get killed unless things keep going sour.'

'But I'm talking about my life!'

'Just shut up and listen to me . . .'

Niklas lost the conversation there and picked it up again, with Korshak speaking louder: 'You do as I say and nobody's gonna get hurt.'

McQueen – looking 'sheepish', according to Niklas – left, but the affair with MacGraw went on and they married in 1973. On screen, Steve McQueen was then among the most macho men on earth (in 2012, his image is still selling luxury, from sunglasses to racing cars). Cool was everything. He'd hang out at a bar up near Paradise Cove on the Pacific with Peckinpah and bikers and film crew guys. They had seatbelts on the barstools and you could strap in for the evening. They were happy to talk, as long as you kept the talk to beer (Mexican Dos Equis) and any sort of vehicle, in which they included women.

Clean-cut with cropped hair and startling blue eyes, McQueen was an original. He was *The Cincinnati Kid*, seducing Tuesday Weld and Ann-Margret with that big grin; the motorbike ace outwitting the Nazis in *The Great Escape*. He was the detective Jackie Bisset couldn't resist in *Bullitt* and the actor who put sex into chess, outmanoeuvring Faye Dunaway in *The Thomas Crown Affair*.

He was the Magnificent One. Even after his cruel death from cancer, age 50, in 1980, a horror he suffered with dignity, he was voted No. 1 in the world's women's all-time Top 100 Favourite Fantasies. But there was no question he was reclusive. And he was difficult.

For years, stories were told of his repressed homosexuality. And it just made him more of a man's man. In reply, he became a compulsive womaniser, losing his first wife, dancer Neile McQueen, because of it. She says he slept with all but two of his female co-stars.

McQueen's great friend in Hollywood was Elmer Valentine, who owned nightclubs on Sunset Boulevard, including the Roxy: 'I treated him nice, gave him the best booth, introduced him to all the girls. Steve liked me for three reasons: he never had to pick up a check [bill], I was a bachelor and was available to him any time and put no pressure on him. I was kinda like his old lady, except I didn't bug him and he wasn't screwing me.'

Valentine was much more than a nightclub host for McQueen. He had the keys to the bedroom. When the married actor met a girl, he would take her off to Valentine's home.

'I'd give him the keys to the burglar alarm, but somehow the dumb bastard always managed to set it off. One night we picked up two girls who had just arrived in Los Angeles from some hick town. It's their first day here and already they're screwing Steve McQueen. They were thrilled. He comes out of the bedroom with his arms around them and says: "Well, girls . . . this is Hollywood."' Such antics make McQueen's next face-off with his wife's ex-husband somewhat ironic.

Evans had agreed for Ali MacGraw and McQueen to have legal custody of his son, Josh. They then told Evans they were changing his son's name to Josh McQueen. He thought not. McQueen then lambasted Evans on the phone about his fast-lane lifestyle: 'It's not the environment that's right for Joshua.' McQueen concluded the call by saying his lawyers were preparing the legal paperwork. Evans says he replied: 'Good. Take your best shot, motherfucker. One of us, pal, only one of us, is going to come out of this in one piece.'

Enter, again, Sidney Korshak.

Korshak instructed Evans to hire a specific lawyer to investigate McQueen. Within two weeks, the dossier was twelve inches thick. Korshak had it shown to McQueen and his legal team, who backed off instantly. A legal agreement was drawn up by Korshak. From then on, if McQueen needed to speak with Evans about Joshua Evans or anything else, he must call him 'Mister Evans'.

Today, Evans is walking around his 16-room home, reflecting: 'I was an idiot to lose Ali. All my priorities were screwed up. I was so absorbed in *The Godfather* I didn't even know she was there or that she was involved with someone else. A woman rarely leaves a man until she has someone else to go to. But once she's decided to go, that's it. You could threaten to kill yourself and the woman wouldn't care at all.

'I'll never forget something Ava Gardner told me when we were on location for *The Sun Also Rises* [1957]. She was madly in love with Frank Sinatra, but his career was in a bad way. His voice seemed to have gone and he was drinking heavily. She said they'd had a huge fight one night and she told him she was leaving because he was a no-good washed-up drunk. He begged her not to leave and took out a gun. He threatened to kill himself. She said: "Do it" and walked out to the elevator. Suddenly there was the sound of a gun going off in the apartment. But Ava didn't even turn around.

'I wasn't faithful to Ali and behaved the way I did because I wanted to get rid of her. I wanted freedom, so I pushed her out to work with Steve McQueen. I would have gone back with her, but she didn't want to go back with me. It was a mistake.'

His error in 1980 was not to call *Mister* Korshak. He'd become hooked on cocaine. ('I had a bad back . . . the drugs really didn't help my back, but they gave me this false energy. I was working 18-hour days. It was addictive.') That year, along with his brother Charles and his brother-in-law Michael Shure, he pleaded guilty to cocaine possession. He maintains it was his stupidest move not to reach out to the man he called his consigliere.

Charlie Bluhdorn disowned him, as did much of Hollywood. Korshak was angry that he hadn't asked for his help; it made him look ineffectual that Evans was found guilty. 'I went from royalty to infamy in one day,' says Evans.

It was the 'Cotton Club Murders' that made him a pariah. When hired killers pumped a dozen .22-calibre slugs into the hard head of aspiring movie big-shot Ray Radin in the environmentally protected seclusion of California's Caswell Canyon on the warm evening of Friday, 13 May 1983, it was an early, violent scene in another Hollywood saga. This was a hit that was going to run and run. It still is, still haunting. Which is much more than the movie, which conspired in the unlikeable movieland interloper's demise, ever managed to do.

Radin's killers had stolen his gold Rolex watch, but otherwise the corpse was still dressed for dinner in a tailored three-piece suit from the specialist store Big and Tall on Canon Drive, Beverly Hills. Radin's crime was to be a nuisance; this was death by conspiracy, involving the usual suspects: greed, drugs, sex, power, politics, money and manipulation, and a cast, other than the obese victim, of connected and beautiful people, none more pretty – in his youth – than Robert Evans, who began this particular misbegotten chapter of his Hollywood life by setting out to make a huge budget 'film noir with music' based on Prohibition mobsters bootlegging booze. He was snared into the ferociously malevolent world of the modern Mafia and the masters of the worldwide drug trade. Ugly as the Mafia of old had been, this was a more cut-throat and fast-moving environment.

You'd think Evans, after all that had gone before, would have known better. Yet he went for the offer that resulted in his being associated with a Mob murder and, in 1989 – six long deal-making years later – the resulting murder-for-hire court case, which paraded his personal peccadilloes alongside Hollywood's perennial partnership with organised crime, the ongoing masters of the box office. It advertised that Hollywood – and America itself, at all levels of society – is more about the Mafia and secret control than Mom, Pop and apple pie.

Evans had his status and a constant cocaine supply to feed. Yes, the drugs made him paranoid, but he lacked what many in Hollywood lack: humility. This is a man who could sell you a good time while you were asleep. No matter how many people help them to success, the Hollywood successful always believe they've done it alone, a solo performance, standing ovation please.

Evans had been the *wunderkind* producer for a time, but he found himself riding the snake not the rainbow as he planned to make the Jazz Age-era film *The Cotton Club*. For Evans no longer had his consigliere onside. Sidney Korshak had disassociated himself from Evans after his friend's very public arrest for cocaine possession in 1980. Evans only just escaped a narcotics trafficking conviction. The headline boy was writing the wrong headlines. The Mafia machine hates attention – and they were getting it with Evans and the drugs – the Mob in 2012 move around $1 billion of drugs through the West Coast of America every two months.

Suddenly, his movie cash supply closed down. *The Cotton Club* was to be Evans's return to the top table ('I'll be toasting everyone') and he was desperate to fund it; around $35 million would have got the cameras rolling.

He believed he'd persuaded arms dealer Adnan Khashoggi, then billed as 'the richest man in the world', to invest $12 million in the production. But everyone's a movie critic. Khashoggi didn't like the script adapted by Mario Puzo from his novel, which had done so much for Evans and the world's understanding of Mafia-speak (*Keep your friends close but your enemies closer*) and walked away from the deal. Evans thought he had an arrangement with a Texas billionaire, but then that tycoon died – of natural causes.

Finally, he did a deal with Las Vegas businessmen brothers Ed and Fred Doumani, who ran the El Morocco Casino. He rented a townhouse on East 61st Street in New York for pre-production work and started creating a $1 million Cotton Club movie set. He was running $140,000 a week in pocket expenses – at that point they hadn't even budgeted for the cocaine in the production costs.

But Ed and Fred Doumani turned out to be critics, too. They didn't like the script, reworked by Francis Ford Coppola. Evans was distraught.

He'd been trying to make the deal for two years when a dancer called Gary Keys, moonlighting as a driver for STAR limousines, collected him from Paramount Pictures, over by Formosa Avenue out in West Hollywood. On the drive back through the low hills and over Sunset Boulevard to Evans's home, the young Keys said he knew Ali MacGraw. She'd told him to ask Evans about a role in *The Cotton Club*. Evans displayed a sparkle of a smile you could only get in a dental clinic around the corner from Neiman Marcus on Wilshire Boulevard: 'You find me some investors and I'll set you up in the film.'

Kismet! Keys knew Lanie Jacobs, who was out of Miami. She had looks and style – like Evans's many girlfriends and former wives (Camilla Sparv, Phyllis George, Sharon Hugueny and, of course, Ali MacGraw). Soon she and Evans were sharing a bed and the cocaine she carried in her zirconium-studded make-up compact.

'Lanie Jacobs' was as sparkly and fake as the zirconium 'diamonds'. She was Karen DeLayne Goodman, from Birmingham, Alabama, and a super-agent for a drug-distribution outfit with a central supply coming through Fort Lauderdale in Florida and run by Cuban-connected Milan Bellechesses; the drug connections were global, with supply coming from places as far distant as Milan and Caracas.

Evans had no interest in the geography. He was willing, it was claimed in court, to use narcotics money to finance *The Cotton Club*, starring Richard Gere and Nicolas Cage. He also wanted other investors. Lanie Jacobs brought him together with Ray Radin. The big man had made his money running vaudeville theatrical shows with yesterday's stars, such as Milton Berle and Johnnie Ray. He had money and a cocaine habit to share with Evans. He, in turn, brought in a Puerto Rican banker and before long it wasn't just the one movie but others, including *The Two Jakes*, a follow-up to *Chinatown* and also starring Jack Nicholson. They were all going to make movies and millions together.

But then Radin decided to cut out Lanie Jacobs. Possibly as a result of the narcotic haze, the New York producer, who was 33, didn't compute just who her connections were. Her cocaine supply was ultimately Mafia run and anyone messing with her was interfering with the money-making machinery of the Mob.

Jacobs was angry with Radin, who she believed had stolen a quarter of a million dollars and ten kilos of cocaine from her apartment. Now she wasn't going to be in the movies or get a producer credit on *The Cotton Club*. She called up Radin's assassination.

But first, the Mob tried their old friend: persuasion.

CALL ME *MISTER* EVANS

Radin was offered $3 million to walk away, leave Hollywood. He wouldn't be persuaded. He kept talking to the wrong people about the wrong things. He got another phone call. The message was not as sophisticated, although the caller was. He was told: walk away or be dead. Radin stayed in town.

On the pleasant evening in which he died, Radin was tempted from his Hollywood Regency Hotel suite – a set-up not as grand as it sounds – with an invitation from Lanie Jacobs to a 'making the peace' dinner at La Scala, the Italian restaurant of choice in Beverly Hills. She'd pick Radin up in the foyer. And she did. She appeared in a figure-hugging gold lamé dress and walked Radin the few steps to a waiting black limousine.

Radin, a New Yorker, didn't realise his problem as the limo pulled off Hollywood Boulevard and took Santa Monica Boulevard east not west, but he did when it stopped and the driver, a hit man and former bodyguard of porn magazine publisher Larry Flynt, opened the door and two other men, built like the bodyguards, came in. Before they got comfortable, Lanie Jacobs shuffled from the limousine to keep a proper dinner appointment.

The new arrivals held Radin at gunpoint as the third hit man squeezed through the bumper-to-bumper Friday night Los Angeles traffic along Sunset Strip before getting to the Holiday Inn exit and taking San Diego Freeway north up to Interstate 5 and into the high desert; the car pulled off the road near Gorman, the Hungry Valley exit. The driver took the limousine as far as it would go into the US Forest Service land; it was a bumpy last ride for Radin along the dirt road, with only rabbits and sagebrush in the headlights.

When he was pulled out of the car and into the off-road brush, up in the clear sky were the only true stars he ever saw. Six weeks later, a beekeeper found Radin's tailored, decayed corpse.

When detail of the 'Cotton Club Murder' came tumbling out, the still defiant Evans found that, though Sidney Korshak was angry with him, America's most influential lawyer and the Mob had not abandoned him. It was Korshak who engaged

Robert Shapiro to keep Evans clear of any indictments. He did. Under his lawyer's guidance, Evans took the Fifth Amendment. It was Lanie Jacobs and the hit team who were finally convicted and jailed in 1991 for the murder of Ray Radin, who became another slice of collateral damage in the Mafia's Hollywood.

Evans had broken off his friendship with Henry Kissinger after the 1980 guilty plea for cocaine possession. They didn't speak for a decade. He survived with support from Warren Beatty and Jack Nicholson: 'Jack got my house back for me when I was nearly bankrupt, but I've done things for him as well. He's a strange cat, but when it comes to loyalty there's few like him. I've been friends with Warren for even longer. Warren, Jack and me are very close.

'Henry Kissinger told me the simplest thing. He said that whether you're Prince Charles or a doorman, everyone has three circles of people in their life. At the centre is the rock, your blood relatives. The first circle consists of the most important people in your life. The people you're closest to. If you have six, you're lucky. It's with these people that you share your ups and downs, your knocks, your highs. You must give 1,000 per cent to these people and they must do the same for you. The second circle is normally made up of 30 or so acquaintances. You like them and enjoy spending time with them, but it stops there. The third circle is the outside world. Henry said that it's possible to bring someone from the outside world into your circle of acquaintances, but if you take them into that inner circle you must let someone out because it cannot expand.'

Robert Evans was protected, as were the studios and the executives. The Mob looked after their interests, just like they had from the beginning, when Chicago first moved in and Mickey Cohen was waving a customised .38 revolver around like a forgotten cigarette. And just like they had since Jules Stein and Lew Wasserman laid the Mafia's deep foundations in Hollywood and Las Vegas. As always, they cover up their cover-ups. It was about public relations for their multi-billion-dollar drug-trafficking empire. Radin wasn't killed because he wanted to be a star. He was murdered because he was a sap. He'd walked into the wrong story and never ever caught on.

Sidney Korshak knew the story right from its beginnings. He died from heart failure, aged 88, on 29 January 1996 at his home in Beverly Hills. He had never been indicted for any criminal activity yet the FBI called him 'an enigmatic player behind countless twentieth-century mergers, political deals and organised-crime chicaneries. He was the primary link between the underworld and the corporate overworld.'

Of course, Korshak was the one protecting himself, so he knew how to cover himself. A contemporary and pupil of Meyer Lansky, he rose out of the Chicago Jewish neighbourhoods with the help of the Capone mob. Korshak's law practice brought him into contact with many infamous characters and racketeering businessmen.

He met Robert Evans at the Racquet Club in Palm Springs in 1955. Forty-one years later Evans gave the eulogy at his mentor's funeral. He didn't hold back: 'From the '40s through the '70s, organised crime was controlled by one person, and no one knew it. He was totally legitimate and he was not Mafia. The Mafia went to him. He could press a button and close down Las Vegas. The country was Sidney's and I was his godson.'

BOOK FOUR

DEAD MAN'S GULCH

'John Wayne dead? The hell I am!'
   – Graffito on Sunset Boulevard, Los Angeles, 1979

13

THE INCONVENIENT WOMAN

'Men take one look at you and all of a sudden their wives don't understand them.'
— Connie Emerson (Audrey Meadows) to Cathy Timberlake (Doris Day), *That Touch of Mink*, 1962

'HE LIKED TO FUCK IN HER FUR,' SAID MARVIN MITCHELSON as another point of fact before ordering the Caesar's salad with extra anchovies. 'Yeah, he bought her this mink coat to fuck in. She thought it might spoil the coat. She was a little difficult about it, so he bought another mink *not* to fuck in. She keeps that locked up at Saks.' The participants in this particular activity were multimillionaire Alfred Bloomingdale, friend and financial supporter of President Ronald Reagan, and Vicki Morgan, the daughter of a GI bride from Norfolk, England.

Marvin Mitchelson knew these sorts of things. He was the love lawyer. For half a century, he heard more pillow talk, dirty dialogue, than any man in the world. He listened to the intimate secrets of powerful people, about the White House, the bedrooms of Hollywood stars, European royalty, Arabian palaces and the Mafia. His work, unashamedly, revolved around sex and every interpretation, deviation, indulgence, delight, peccadillo and perversion. It was also about the power of sex. And the power of discretion, of silence.

Marvin Mitchelson knew too much, and finally all the secrets almost destroyed him. But he fought back. In the months before he died in September 2004, he was pursuing the biggest cash divorce settlement in the world – worth $216 million – and helping his friend, the rock producer Phil Spector, who was facing a murder charge (of which he would be convicted). Typically Marvin, he told me: 'Murder? It was suicide. She shot herself.'

'Twice in the head?' I ask.

'That's what our evidence says.'

Marvin Mitchelson was a minx, but he knew how sex, or certainly the possibility of it, drove some of the most famous names in the world to folly, madness and much worse. And by the time Vicki Morgan needed legal help, he was by far the most famous divorce/palimony lawyer in the world. He operated in an industry town with its own peculiar codes. He upset many powerful people and that made for powerful enemies. As it played out, Vicki Morgan's were more dangerous.

Alfred Bloomingdale was a stage door Johnny. He hung around Broadway shows in New York and married a showgirl in 1941. He produced several plays that were no great hits. Success arrived with the song-and-dance show *High Kickers* and a 1943 revival of the *Ziegfeld Follies* – which was good, because he had investors, including some not-too-angelic members of the Mob. It also gave him the incentive to move West to put his show-business talents into film. The grandson of a founder of the great department store, he had the cash to indulge himself.

He became a Hollywood player when he married Betty Lee Newling, a Californian socialite. With Betsy 'Good Queen Betts' Bloomingdale, who was 90 in 2012, the couple formed a close friendship with Ronald and Nancy Reagan. The two women were credited as the originators of 'You can never be too rich or too thin.' Despite this motto, they were regular patrons of the Bistro and other ladies-who-lunch spots throughout the golden triangle centred on Beverly Hills. With his wife a devoted Catholic, the newly married Bloomingdale became a Roman Catholic himself. They bought an estate in Holmby Hills from where the truly rich look down on Beverly Hills – if they ever glance in that direction.

Alfred Bloomingdale was lunching on the open terrace of mock health-food café the Olde World restaurant on Sunset Boulevard (weirdly only five blocks west from Marvin Mitchelson's home, 'The Castle', overlooking Sunset) when he first saw Vicki Morgan. She was 18 years old and made Alfred, 52, extremely hot and bothered. She knew it – men of all ages had been panting after her for years. He rather made it more obvious than most. He slipped her a cheque for $8,000, 'a gift for a lovely girl who has brightened my day'. He got a phone number in return – a 'Hooray for Hollywood!' moment.

Vicki's father, Delbert Morgan, an American Air Force sergeant, had met and married Connie Reid while he was posted in England during the war. Their daughter Barbara was born in 1946 and Vicki followed in the August six years later. Her father left before she could talk. Vicki grew up tall and shapely and was told all the time she could be a model or a movie star, but becoming pregnant at 16 interrupted that. Her mother raised her son Todd; she repeated to me many times during long conversations that 'Vicki was just unlucky – like me, she picked the wrong men.'

But Vicki was street-wise. Like many of the young girls around 1970s Hollywood, she made herself a 'party girl'. It didn't always instantly involve sex – she would be invited to parties to provide glamour – but that skipped easily into a far more excessive world, awash with relatively cheap drugs (less expensive, sometimes, than jugs of Gallo wine) being used to open up the market from farms around Ensenada in Baja California.

Sex sells. It's also for sale. It is the ultimate guilty pleasure for men who have everything – sex with the women they couldn't have if they couldn't afford it. And if they desire different dreams or kinks every night or day or lunchtime or teatime, any time, players can have whatever style of women or sex they want. In 2012, it's all computerised. They pick their lusts from the pages of glossy magazines or the latest television shows or cinema sensations. Women will literally walk off the pages of the glossy fashion magazines or entertainment screens into bed with those willing to pay a lavish price.

In Hollywood, there is a price for everything. And, seemingly, everyone. Hollywood sells sex. But it also buys it. Lots of it. Every second of the day. And the men buying are rich and famous, powerful and celebrated. If you pay for everything else, from Lear jets to dog psychologists, what's different? There was a time when you could walk into the bar of the Beverly Hilton Hotel and see strings of girls who worked for the convicted madam Heidi Fleiss waiting their turn with actor Charlie Sheen. Or maybe someone else, if Charlie was having an afternoon off. The stories of the game are fascinating and intriguing, it's difficult not to be interested: the customer who runs up an annual $1 million 'tab' for girls; the cross-dressing; the erectile problems of famous names – name drooping, really; the OPEC minister who had a 'regular' – a six-foot-tall former ballet dancer; the sexaholic producer who never sees a girl twice; the CPA who loves sex and wants to work as a hooker to make money and 'meet interesting people' – she was flown first class from Los Angeles to spend time at New York's Carlyle Hotel with a film financier.

The author William Stadiem wrote a book about it titled *Madam 90210* based on the exploits of Madam Alex Adams, an early mentor of Heidi Fleiss. It is a tale of stars and sex and, appropriately, vice versa. He was researching a business book about a Hollywood studio takeover but found most people were reluctant to talk about dirty money. Dirty secrets were an altogether different matter. He says of his book: 'It's about sex and power in Hollywood told from the point of view of Madam Alex Adams, who was the madam to the stars. She's retired now, but through her I was able to interview about a hundred of the most beautiful call girls in the world and many of their clients.

'In Hollywood, it's a status symbol to even have been on Alex's list of customers. It was a very exclusive list, you had to have really, really arrived. It was the equivalent of a good table at Spago: to be at Alex's, you knew you were a player, one of the big players. The men were very proud that they could have – and talk about – all the now famous women or cover girls they had had. It was great fun. They talked to me about it. They weren't ashamed. Alex was just another way for these powerful and rich men to meet the women they wanted. They liked to challenge themselves and put their egos on the line. They didn't mind paying a few thousand dollars to meet the woman for the first time. Then the challenge was: can I get this girl to sleep with me for free the next time? It was a game.'

And an expensive game for one Beverly Hills billionaire: 'One of the former call girls married this incredibly wealthy man, but even after they were married she demanded $2 million for 50 acts of sex. It was very much a quota system – she still wanted to get paid for her services. He paid her. It was so good he couldn't resist it. It's the sheer excitement of being in bed with these women.

'These are women that you would see in magazines like *Vogue* or on TV. Men would often call Alex and say: "I saw this girl – can you get me her?" And she could do it. She had an amazing network and for "X" thousands of dollars you could have an affair with this girl. Alex's price started at $1,000 for an hour of pleasure and then $2,000 for an extended afternoon. For a whole night, it could be $5,000. And if they went on trips, then the cost was more.

'The first class sections of British Air and Air France were frequently populated with a number of Alex's creatures. If they were starlets or models and someone spotted them, they would say they were going on a photo shoot in Milan, but it was something else in London or Milan or wherever.

'A lot of the men pay by cash. It's a cash business. Although some of the clients of Alex and her successors run up huge tabs – it's not surprising for people to have six-digit tabs. They run up bills just the way they would at Armani. It's very conventional sex – very normal, nothing particularly kinky. It's not so much the idea that you want to tie the girl up or degrade her or something like that; it's the idea of having her, having someone you never thought you could have. That's the excitement. It's fucking the unfuckable.

'That's one of the reasons a rich man, a handsome man, a movie star, a man who theoretically could have anybody in the world, would pay for sex. He goes to a madam and says: "Find me this incredible creature. I want to have sex with her." This is a town where time is money. People don't want to waste a lot of time in courtship, in pursuing women that basically all they really want to do is have sex with and probably never see them again. I think a lot of men would like to think that perhaps everybody has her price at some point. I'd say that a lot of young and ambitious women, women under 25, could use extra money. Unless they had made it in the movies by that age, they, you know, could always use more money.

'These men can meet the most beautiful women in the world and have sex with them, any kind of sex they want, within reason, and pay a lot of money. But they've got a lot of money. I met clients – so-called "power johns" – who spent more than $1 million a year on call girls. There are no bargains in sex. They are not wanted. The more they pay, the better they feel. It's like going to an elite French restaurant. They feel that it's safer, it's more glamorous, it's a higher tone experience. They want to pay as much as they possibly can because they feel that if they pay more they're getting more.

'Brad Pitt and Angelina Jolie or Leonardo DiCaprio get millions a picture and because of that people think they are seeing a bigger picture and a bigger star. It's the same thing when the same people who are making these big movies want to hire call girls. They want to pay more. They feel more secure that they're really getting quality.'

Providing 'entertainment' for stars and executives in Hollywood has long been accepted. Stadiem, who talked while driving through Beverly Hills, acknowledges the long-time 'perk' of Hollywood success. 'This is the golden triangle of sex in America, the most expensive neighbourhood in the world.' And he's correct.

Up Rodeo Drive and into the Hollywood Hills, the ranch-style home of Heidi Fleiss is not much compared with others in Benedict Canyon. But it's not drab for a high school dropout who moved in on Madam Alex's territory – and was later arrested and convicted on prostitution charges – when the former queen of the game was busted and placed on probation. 'Heidiwood' was the Hollywood scandal of the summer of 1993. It may have scandalised the rest of the world but having a 27-year-old woman supplying movie stars, male and female, film studio executives and captains of industry with the most stunning women you will ever see is still shrugged off in the town where it happens.

'Alex was a florist in town and in the course of that business she met her predecessor, an Englishwoman who decided to get out of sex and become a dog breeder. She told Alex she wanted to sell her her black book. Alex hesitated and the Englishwoman told her: "You were in flowers; now you can be in deflowers."

'Alex became probably the world's most important madam, with movie stars and major politicians and statesmen and some of the biggest moguls in the world, from America and Europe. She's had them all – it's one of the great luxury items. If anybody has the money, they kind of want to try it out of curiosity.

'It's very, very civilised. It's like a dating service. These girls are charming. They're from all over the world. I've met lawyers, accountants, development girls from the studios, and they find it an amazing way to make a lot of money in a very short time. When you walk around Beverly Hills, you see beautiful women in the street who look very Grace Kelly and refined, but these people know what the world is about. And to spend a hour or several hours with a man and make thousands of dollars for that can buy a lot of nice clothes and a lot of apartments in Beverly Hills, which is the most materialistic place on earth: it's hard to resist the need, the desire to have as much money as you possibly can.

'Some of the girls have married very well and become Hollywood Wives. Others have become Hollywood producers or executives. A large number have become actresses, starlets, models. And a lot of the models, when their modelling careers are over and they are too wooden to act, manage to marry very rich and prominent men.

'In Beverly Hills and Hollywood, superficial is fine. If a woman is beautiful, that's enough, yet that's why you see so many ugly divorces here. After a while a lot of these women let their mercenary roots show and the men who marry them are not cured of their sexaholism by marrying perfect call girl types. They find themselves calling the madams again. It's a hard habit to break. They're often busted by becoming patrons of younger call girls and their ex-call girl wives catch them. Nobody can smell a call girl like a former call girl – there's not a better sleuth to sniffing out a husband's commercial indiscretions.'

Stadiem talks of another starlet who is now a famous name who cost a Hollywood producer tens of thousands of dollars. 'She's a huge star now, one of the biggest. It [is] a brief window of opportunity in their path. One didn't have to be a call girl for a long time to make wonderful contacts. They become trophy girlfriends, trophy call girls, trophy wives. When a woman marries a famous man in Hollywood, she is immediately accepted in Beverly Hills. Money talks. Power talks. This is a town where knowledge is knowledge and power is power. Power really derives from money here and if a call girl marries a rich and powerful man her past is accepted and forgiven. It has a market status because it meant you were one of the most beautiful and one of the best. Blue stockings may sneer at it. But this is not a town of blue stockings, is it? This is a town of meshed stockings.'

It was against this background that Vicki Morgan emerged. She'd witnessed and participated in many a sex game by the time Alfred Bloomingdale wanted her to fulfil his sexual fantasies – and become an even greater problem for the FBI.

They had investigated Bloomingdale's dealings with Moe Dalitz in Las Vegas. Bloomingdale had also been involved through Jimmy Blue Eyes in Meyer Lansky's plans to take Mafia gambling into London. Alfred Bloomingdale was seen as a front man for a hotel-casino operation at the Dorchester. The deal went sour, in part because of the millionaire's penchant for beating up prostitutes and talking too much. 'Bloomingdale looked the part, but couldn't play it,' a gambler involved in that particular adventure told me in Las Vegas in 2011. Which was the opposite of Vicki. She could turn a 'trick' to everything, from faux lesbian shows to indulging in what her lover Alfred Bloomingdale's psychiatrist called his 'Marquis de Sade Syndrome'.

Bloomingdale didn't beat around the bush, as it were: on his first 'date' with Vicki Morgan, they met again at the Olde World. Another girl called Samantha joined them and the trio drove to a house down from the Sunset Plaza Hotel, a few minutes away. Samantha told Vicki: 'He won't hurt you much.' Mistress Kay, the black-leather-clad dominatrix who welcomed them, looked as though she could. Immediately, Alfred Bloomingdale conducted the sadomasochistic sex follies, wild indulgences that were arranged for three times a week. Mistress Kay was indeed a little rough for Vicki, and so the millionaire lovers readjusted the stars of their shows. For Bloomingdale's 54th birthday, she hired 15 girls at $2,500 a time. There was no mention of a cake. There were, however, candles. It was all part of the times: free love and California life liberalism.

But after Bloomingdale had been unshackled, he was going off to dinner with Ronald Reagan, the Governor of California and an already talked-up presidential candidate. Bloomingdale was a prominent member of his 'Kitchen Cabinet'. He had public-relations problems with his sex games and his Mafia connections. And an FBI file, some of which remains off limits in 2012.

The authorities may have been unhappy, but the lovers were not. For 12 years, Vicki was the lavishly kept mistress of Alfred Bloomingdale. She received cars and clothes and 'things with diamonds on' and between $10,000 and $18,000 a month in expenses. She was usually paid by cheque through one of his companies, in return for her companionship and 'therapy'. She travelled with him on many overseas trips, often following him in secret when Betsy Bloomingdale accompanied him.

Like Judith Exner before her, she became part of the circle.

She lived at Grayhall (once home to Douglas Fairbanks) on the high-hedge-guarded and twisting Carolyn Way. Grayhall was the disgraced 'international financier' Bernie Cornfeld's sybaritic mansion, sitting conveniently next door to Hugh Hefner's 'Playboy' estate in Beverly Hills. The Turkish-born, charming and amorous crook Bernie Cornfeld operated Investors Overseas Service, Ltd. (IOS), a mutual fund enterprise with the catchline: *Do you sincerely want to be rich?* He had built up IOS holdings to more than $1.5 billion but attracted the attention of the Securities Exchange Commission (SEC). When Vicki Morgan found him in 1974, he was not long free from spending 11 months in a Swiss prison. There were many girls at Grayhall by then, around the swimming pool, in the billiard room or making toast and tea – at 2 p.m. – in the kitchen. When you waited for Cornfeld, you could count a dozen or maybe 18 girls just sunbathing in the garden, including a couple who would become famous faces. Some became stars, others notorious, like Heidi Fleiss. Cornfeld, who never lost his pale look from prison, was short and tubby, a most unlikely Lothario. He gave Vicki her own bedroom, linked to his by one of the rambling house's hidden corridors. But Vicki was a restless sort. And she preferred individual luxury.

She'd lived in the Sierra Towers, an imposing skyscraper of upmarket condominiums in West Hollywood, next door to Beverly Hills on Doheny Drive. She liked it around there, saying hello in the elevator to Harry Belafonte or Joan Collins or, for a short time, Peter Lawford, who also owned apartments in the landmark building.

Marvin Mitchelson said that she had affairs with several Middle East dignitaries. She herself claimed an affair with the King of Morocco. But what was all important to the American authorities was what she was learning in pillow talk from Bloomingdale. The First Friend.

He became besotted with Vicki – there's no other word. And because of his influence with the Reagan support teams – echoes of the JFK election campaign – his girl was indulged. She was in the car when Reagan's presidential running mate, President George Bush, was taken on a tour of Los Angeles. She worked on the Reagan election campaign.

When he took office in 1981, President Reagan appointed Bloomingdale to his Foreign Intelligence Advisory Board, an outfit overseeing CIA undercover operations of every kind, one of the most sensitive intelligence apparatuses of the US government. A little later, Bloomingdale was made a member of the United States Advisory Commission on Public Diplomacy.

Was it an in-joke? *Public Diplomacy?* Bloomingdale had wanted to be named US Ambassador to France; he'd told his lover she could work at the US Embassy in Paris. His Mafia connections in Las Vegas and Vicki being in his life stopped that.

Yet Vicki Morgan talked freely about her unique view of the Reagan White House. Marvin Mitchelson said she told him she 'knew political and sexual secrets about this administration that would make Watergate look like a playschool'. She most certainly was one to know. She had a good connection: the Bloomingdales stayed regularly at the White House during Reagan's first months in office. In July 1981, they accompanied Nancy Reagan to London for the wedding of Prince Charles and Princess Diana. It was only a couple of weeks later that Alfred Bloomingdale's nagging sore throat was diagnosed as cancer and his prognosis poor.

Vicki visited him in hospital. On 12 February 1982, he dictated two letters, revealing his intentions toward her: 'Her name should be included in all contracts so that this cannot be taken away from her in the event of my incapacitation or absence.' They specified she should receive 50 per cent in a Showbiz Pizza franchise he owned and monthly payments of $10,000 for two years. Betsy Bloomingdale went ape. In June 1982, she stopped the Showbiz Pizza arrangement and

THE INCONVENIENT WOMAN

cancelled the monthly cheques. It was at this point Vicki went
to see Marvin Mitchelson.

As I've said, Mitchelson was born for Hollywood. A
flamboyant egotist, he gloried in the spotlight. The answering
machine at his house – and his office – greeted callers with the
first bars of the Righteous Brothers' 'You've Lost that Lovin'
Feeling'. For years, he reigned supreme from his palatial
baroque office in Century City, his surroundings opulent, his
chair a throne upholstered in red velvet that had once belonged
to Rudolph Valentino. From there, on offer was a spectacular
view, taking in a panorama from the Hollywood Hills to the
Pacific Ocean. Directly above his desk the ceiling contained a
backlit stained-glass reproduction of Botticelli's *Birth of Venus*.

His legacy to the affairs of men and women is that he
changed family and marriage law forever with 'palimony': that
live-in lovers can enjoy the same legal rights as married
couples. His legacy to his wife Marcella, to whom he was
married for 45 years, were memories of his Hollywood
infidelities and, at times, outrageous fast living. And his abuse
of cocaine and booze. And his cases.

He acted for the wives and lovers of men as diverse as James
Mason, Groucho Marx, Mickey Rooney, Mel Torme, Neil
Young, Marlon Brando, David Bowie, Bob Dylan, Mick Jagger
and Rod Stewart. He acted for nightclub singer Helena
Lisandrello in a case bidding to make Robert De Niro pay
child support for her ten-year-old daughter. And there was
Marsha Hunt against Mick Jagger.

Joan Collins, Zsa Zsa Gabor, Bianca Jagger and Soraya
Khashoggi all went to him when the marital bell hit a discord.
Marvin attracted all sorts of women in trouble, and often those
who *were* trouble. All over California, women especially
benefited from his courtroom successes.

There was the white Rolls-Royce regularly seen driving
down Rodeo Drive in Beverly Hills with the number plate
ALIMONY. Or the Mercedes sports coupé with EX-WIFE.
Playboy model Carrie Leigh hired him to take millionaire
publisher Hugh Hefner to court in a $20 million palimony

279

claim, following the end of her five-year affair with the bunny empire boss. Mitchelson performed a remarkable coup for Leicester-born Soraya Khashoggi, at one time Jonathan Aitken's mistress. She had remarried after her divorce from arms dealer Adnan Khashoggi, but belatedly believed the divorce to be invalid and went back to court to demand a further $2.5 billion. Marvin, and against the odds, succeeded in getting her an out-of-court settlement of $100 million.

I first met Mitchelson in the early 1970s, when, over several dinners with Michelle Triola, the ex-girlfriend of the actor Lee Marvin, I heard of Mitchelson's exploits, of his then fledgling legend. Triola had lived with Marvin for almost seven years before he kicked her out of his Malibu beach house so he could marry his childhood sweetheart. She had turned to Mitchelson, who had promptly filed a suit for $1.3 million – half the assets acquired by the movie star while the couple had lived together. It was an audacious move. The idea that former partners might enjoy legal rights as a result of a non-marital relationship was completely unknown. Yet he had persuaded the California State Supreme Court to accept his argument that unmarried couples base their relationships on unwritten contracts. He was the one man in Hollywood I had to meet. He was more important than famous actors and film studio bosses. He'd become his own celebrity – when it was still something of an achievement. We kept in regular touch for the next three decades and he pointed material – usually front-page stories – my way.

The son of Russian–Jewish immigrants, Mitchelson's family moved to Los Angeles, where his father gave up painting houses and became a successful property developer. He paid for his courses at Southwestern University School of Law by working part-time as a process server: he once broke into the MGM lot to serve papers on Joan Collins, who would later become a client; he gatecrashed a charity function to serve a writ on legendary studio boss Louis B. Mayer.

His career began properly in the Hollywood of 1957. He acted for B-movie starlets, petty criminals and negligence victims. He built his business by strategically feeding stories to reporters at the local courthouse. Marvin first gained attention in America in 1963, when he won a Supreme Court ruling that guaranteed free legal representation for defendants who could not otherwise afford it. His big reputation began the following year, when he acted for Pamela Mason, the wife of the hugely popular, suave British film star James Mason. His client was suing her husband for divorce on the grounds of his adultery and said she wanted $1 million alimony, a first at the time – and a staggering amount all those decades ago.

Displaying the bluster and bravado that would become his trademark, Marvin subpoenaed 43 witnesses and warned Mason's lawyers that he was prepared to reveal in open court various embarrassing sexual secrets. The actor chose to settle out of court for $2 million, famously declaring the money: 'Nothing but a flea bite.'

Many more unhappy wives soon appeared at Marvin's door. In addition to handling two of Zsa Zsa Gabor's seven divorces, he acted for Connie Stevens in her break-up with Eddie Fisher – after his break-up with Debbie Reynolds and Elizabeth Taylor. He represented the third Mrs Groucho Marx and the fourth and seventh Mrs Alan Jay Lerners. He also stepped into one of Hollywood's longest-running and most bitter custody battles – between Marlon Brando and Anna Kashfi over their son Christian, who has his own tragic tale. Mitchelson won visiting rights for Kashfi after arguing that Brando's performance in *Last Tango in Paris*, in which he played a 'sexually maladjusted and perverted person', made him unfit to retain exclusive custody of his son.

His success travelled well. He was instructed by *Hair* star and singer Marsha Hunt when she filed a paternity suit in London against Mick Jagger and by Angie Bowie to negotiate a divorce settlement in Switzerland with rock star husband David. Mitchelson wowed Angie Bowie when he struck a deal within 24 hours. She declared: 'Marvin is like a superhero out of a comic book.'

He squeezed $13 million out of Bob Dylan for his wife,

Sara. 'I had never listened to much of Bob Dylan when she hired me, but, $13 million later, I knew every song.' Vicki Morgan had some incentive to call upon the services of Marvin Mitchelson.

Together they filed in Los Angeles Superior Court on 8 July 1982 a $5 million breach-of-contract lawsuit. The story went around the world. The headlines all had sex and White House and Reagan and Bloomingdale in some arrangement. In Mitchelson's office that evening, the phone never stopped. He smiled a lot and offered Havana cigars. He sprayed Aramis around the room. Vicki Morgan had told him Bloomingdale liked the cologne. Vicki Morgan's long days of depositions – the final document ran to 234 pages – was a riveting read.

When Alfred Bloomingdale died, aged 66, on 23 August that year, the whole world knew of his sexual games and preferences. Betsy Bloomingdale admitted the affair but said Morgan was a well-compensated prostitute who was due no future support. But Vicki knew what others didn't. She said under oath: 'Alfred told me about his judgments concerning Reagan's appointments, the President's Cabinet and his role in the "Kitchen Cabinet". Alfred continuously confided in me by telling his private opinions about influential and important people with whom he was intimately involved, such as Ronald and Nancy Reagan. He told me about his involvement in secret and delicate matters.'

The FBI knew some of the facts, but it only became more widely known that Bloomingdale had other affiliations as their investigations intensified. He belonged to the Knights of Malta, as did Sam Giancana, Johnny Rosselli and William Casey, the director of the CIA until his death in 1987. Other members close to Bloomingdale were President Reagan's brother Neil and William Clark, the one-time US Secretary of the Interior.

What was not known was that Bloomingdale was one of the American Mafia's connections into the Vatican. On many of his trips there, he had met with Michele Sindona and 'God's Banker' Roberto Calvi, the chairman of Italy's second-largest private bank, Banco Ambrosiano, which collapsed in 1982 with $1.5 billion of debt. Calvi was hanged from Blackfriars Bridge in London before he could link heroin and the Holy See.

For many people, Vicki Morgan was inconvenient. She had knowledge: the deals, the control, the philandering. The corruption. Some weeks after Bloomingdale's death, Judge Christian E. Markey ruled that Morgan's relationship with Alfred Bloomingdale was 'no more than that of a wealthy older man, a married paramour and a young, well-paid mistress'. Morgan had been paid by the trick; any agreement between them was invalid because it involved sex for hire.

She moved across town to Apartment D, 4171 Colfax Avenue in Studio City near the Black Tower headquarters of MCA-Universal. Her room-mate was Marvin Pancoast, 32, a homosexual and Hollywood showbiz drifter who wanted to be noticed. They liked each other and could share the bills. But, as always, Morgan wanted more money. It got around Hollywood that she was writing a tell-all book – describing the sex games and naming the wealthy and powerful politicians and businessmen involved. There was also gossip of lurid videotapes of Vicki in perverted sex games with members of the Reagan administration. It only stopped at any suggestion that Reagan himself was into more than jelly beans. It caused media hysteria.

On 7 July 1983, three weeks after she'd gone 'over the hill' from Beverly Hills to live in Studio City in the San Fernando Valley, she was clubbed to death in her bed with a baseball bat. Her murder became official at 3.20 a.m. that morning, when Pancoast appeared at North Hollywood police station and said: 'I just killed someone. I left the door open but look out for the Dobermann.'

In the days that followed, just about everybody was seeking the mysterious videotapes. Pancoast recanted his confession, that he'd killed Vicki. His lawyer Arthur Barens said 'persons unknown' had killed her to suppress the videotapes of her having sex with government officials. Barens issued subpoenas to the FBI, the CIA and the LAPD for any videotapes and documents pertaining to Vicki Morgan's Washington liaisons. No names were listed in the court documents, but Barens insisted: 'We have information that the videotapes exist and that the government has them.'

At this point, Robert Steinberg, a Beverly Hills lawyer, appeared. He told a tale of yet another *blonde* woman carrying a Gucci bag who'd handed him three of the videotapes. When asked for proof, he said the tapes had been stolen from his office. Mitchelson, however, was adamant that a White House aide had confirmed to him that there were such tapes. (He was close to actor James Mason's son, Morgan Mason, whom his own son was named after. Mason was Special Assistant to President Reagan and America's Acting Chief of Protocol during the Reagan administration.)

The case against Pancoast, other than his repudiated confession, was thin. The police inquiry was, being kind, poor. The Colfax apartment was never sealed off, no fingerprints were taken from the bloodied baseball bat. The District Attorney's office did not interview probable key witnesses. Deputy District Attorney Stanley Weisberg lamely offered: 'We had other cases more important.'

Yet probably not murders with a White House connection.

Pancoast was convicted in 1983. He was being treated for an AIDS-related illness when he died in prison hospital in Chino, California, in 1991. For television news, he made a deathbed 'confession' – he again recanted his statement that he'd killed Vicki Morgan. The TV station KNBC would not report all his remarks or reveal what they were, other than saying the material was 'too explosive' to broadcast. Arthur Barens remained convinced of his client's innocence; he saw Pancoast as another sad sap in the Hollywood game, a fantasist who had once tried to confess to the Manson murders. He wasn't alone.

The late Dominick Dunne, brother-in-law of Joan Didion, party photographer of Sidney Korshak and author of a *roman-à-clef* of the Bloomingdale affair, quoted a film star whom he did not name at the time (it was Elizabeth Taylor) telling him after Pancoast's conviction: 'Oh no, darling! Marvin [Pancoast]'s not guilty. We knew Marvin. He worked for my ex-husband. Nutty as a fruitcake: yes. A murderer: no. You check his mother's bank account after this and you'll see she's been taken care of for life. They'll just put Marvin in the nuthouse for a few years. It's Marilyn all over again! Did you ever know that the CIA were sent to Marilyn's house afterwards and cleaned out everything? I bet they did that at Vicki's place too. That's where those tapes went . . .'

14

SEX, LIES AND AUDIOTAPE

'Hey, look at that. It's going to be the longest
suspension bridge in the world. And the graft will
probably set a world record, too.'
— Dashiell Hammett (Frederic Forrest), gazing at the
Golden Gate Bridge (the longest, 1937–64),
San Francisco, *Hammett*, 1982

THE HOLLYWOOD OF SEX AND DRUGS AND FAR TOO MUCH
attention irritated the Mafia overlords and their icy heirs, the
lawyers and accountants moving into the leadership and being
groomed to legitimise what was becoming the most profitable
business organisation ever. Meyer Lansky had boasted in the
1960s that the Mob would be 'bigger than US Steel', but he'd
underestimated the market for drugs and degeneracy.

Across the ocean, in 2012, the Mafia *was* Italy's biggest
business, making a profit of €100 billion, roughly equivalent to
7 per cent of the country's GDP. The trade association
Confesercenti had named the Mafia as 'Italy's number one
bank'.

Italy's Mafia groups – the Cosa Nostra in Sicily, the Camorra
in Campania and Naples, and the 'Ndrangheta in Calabria –
had an annual turnover of €140 billion. People couldn't get
cash anywhere else, so they went to their godfathers for help.

The American authorities say it is impossible to be even
close when pinpointing Mob profits in the US, as so much of
the money is laundered through a sophisticated network of

clever if malicious schemes that do somersaults through the accounting system. Pick a number in the billions. And across America it wasn't just *money* the Mob were continuing to clean up.

The ultimate business plan, which reaches from Hollywood to Vladivostok via street corners across the world, needed more progressive blood. Some personnel had to go, in a strange manifestation of a stockholder rebellion, to make way for the new. And to settle scores. The organisation didn't concern itself with a human resources department.

The new breed began to take over during the Hollywood years in Washington: the Reagan administration. They worked alongside their brotherhood members in Italy and across the Continent, especially in West Berlin, where sex clubs profited alongside heavy drug trafficking and gambling – and worked as a conduit to the Soviet Union. Increasingly, film piracy was the most cost-effective 'legitimate' game.

By then, many who knew secrets had taken their leave; others would have to follow. Virginia Hill had, not surprisingly, separated from Hans Hauser after they'd moved to Koppl, near Salzburg, to escape an IRS indictment. She lived with her son, Peter, in Austria but died aged 49 on 24 March 1966. It was a strange business.

Two days earlier she'd met up again with her lover Joe Adonis, the power of the Genovese Family. After their meeting, two of his bodyguards escorted her home. In Las Vegas, they said she'd been putting pressure on Adonis for money, using as blackmail her inside track on the drug cartels and trafficking routes. Two walkers found her body by a stream in a lonely woodland area. The Austrian authorities ruled suicide; the ebullient Virginia Hill had taken cyanide.

Her one-time lover Johnny Rosselli – the man with the business card reading 'strategist' – got a Mafia farewell in the hot July of 1975, when he was still in charge of the Chicago Mob's gambling interests in Las Vegas. He was living quietly with his sister, Mrs Joseph Daigle, in Plantation, Florida, a little to the west of Fort Lauderdale. He was, his neighbours said, a nice silver-haired gentleman who liked to walk his poodle and talk about such local environmental concerns as the caterpillars munching the foliage. Although he had arthritis of the spine, he played golf regularly. Earlier in the year a local wiseguy had been assassinated on the golf course, so Rosselli never played the same course twice in a row. Still, he rejected his lawyer's advice to hire a bodyguard.

Rosselli was choked to death, his legs sawn off and his body sealed in an empty 55-gallon oil drum. Heavy chains were coiled around this 'casket' and holes punched in the sides to make it stay underwater when it was dumped in the ocean off the Florida Gold Coast. But Rosselli rose from the depths: the gases from his decomposing body forced the oil drum to float to the surface. Three fishermen found it in Dumfoundling Bay near North Miami Beach. Police ran the victim's fingerprints with the FBI and up came the ID: John Rosselli, 71, emphysema sufferer and a Mafia executive who'd been involved in landmark capers and made the error of talking about them.

In June 1975, Rosselli had testified before a special Senate Intelligence Committee (SIC) investigating the excesses of the CIA. At this point he should have counted up to five and pleaded the Amendment, but not only did Rosselli talk, he also provided the details of how he and Sam Giancana had been recruited by the CIA to assassinate Fidel Castro.

Five days before Rosselli sang, his Chicago boss Sam Giancana had been murdered in the kitchen of his heavily protected home in Oak Park, Illinois. He was shot in the back of the head as he was frying sausage and peppers. After he had collapsed to the floor, the killer (who I was told in Las Vegas was Tony Spilotro) flipped the body over and blasted the man who'd shared JFK's lover six more times in the face and neck. Giancana, who knew more secrets than most, was scheduled to testify, like Rosselli, before the SIC about the CIA's collusion with the Mafia to kill President Kennedy.

By the mid-'70s, the Cal Neva Lodge, where Marilyn Monroe had spent her last weekend alive and in which Sinatra had invested, was under new ownership. It couldn't trouble

Giancana, but in February 1981 the problems that had cost Sinatra his gaming licence still managed to haunt him there. It was an extraordinary event to witness, Sinatra being quizzed about his Mafia ties by the Nevada Gaming Board of Control over his application to renew his casino licence (he'd lost it in 1963 because of Sam Giancana's presence at the Cal Neva).

US Senator Harry Reid, who was chairman of the Nevada Gaming Commission at the time, didn't believe Sinatra would get his way when he applied for a licence that would allow him to own a share of Caesars Palace Las Vegas Hotel-Casino in exchange for performing at the hotel.

But he did.

I sat a few feet from him for two hearings in which he gave one word answers – often 'Negative' – or pointed his thumb behind at lawyer Milton Rudin with a gruff: 'Ask him!' What was most on display, other than Sinatra's arrogance, was Hollywood power.

The big names of entertainment testified on his behalf – including President Ronald Reagan, inaugurated just the previous month. Gregory Peck said: 'He is one of the most noble, trustworthy and truthful men I have ever known.' As for those alleged friends in the Mafia: 'I have been with him on hundreds of occasions and I have never met or heard discussed any of these characters he has been alleged to be associated with.' He compared Sinatra to Laurence Olivier, as 'one of the great performers of the century'.

Kirk Douglas described Sinatra as 'colourful, impulsive and extraordinarily talented'. He said he had known him for 40 years and said he knew of no association between the singer and organised crime. In a sworn affidavit, Bob Hope said: 'It's not fair to assume because Sinatra was photographed with Mafia figures that he was in business with them.'

Just as clear as the testimonials was the link between Sinatra and mobsters, admitted and alleged, but the connections weren't always solid. Under questioning, Sinatra denied any involvement with organised crime.

Two damaging questions were raised during this Damon Runyon episode.

The first involved Sinatra's ties to Giancana. For two hours, he fielded questions about his Mafia links with a steady stream of denials. It was the first time in 40 years that he had answered publicly such speculation. Asked about horse's head-type rumours, that his career blossomed thanks to organised crime, he said sharply: 'Simply, it's ridiculous.' At that point, he looked over at his fourth wife, Barbara, who sat with his bodyguard, Jilly Rizzo.

The second was Mafia killer-turned-FBI informant Jimmy 'the Weasel' Fratianno's evidence that Sinatra had offered to help break the legs of a troublesome bodyguard. Sinatra, wearing someone else's hair and a grey worsted suit, denied the claims and insisted he was clean. In one angry outburst, he stated: 'For the record, I wish that we didn't have to discuss Mr Fratianno because he is a confessed murderer, a perjurer . . . He's a fink. I don't know what he is doing in my life!'

On illegal payments involving a theatre in New York where he had performed, he said: 'I've never in my life received any illegal money. I have had to work very hard for my money.'

On Giancana at the Cal Neva, he said Giancana did not go to the hotel at his invitation and was not given any red carpet treatment. He said he did not even see the crime boss, who was in a bungalow on the property with singer Phyllis McGuire. He denied any financial dealings with Giancana and said there were no hidden interests in the hotel and that he was not acting as a 'front' for anyone. He said he voluntarily gave up his gambling licence at the request of Jack Warner, the head of the film studio. Sinatra said he was involved in a deal with Warner, who insisted that he got out of Las Vegas. He played down social ties with Giancana but admitted he had played golf with him in Palm Springs. Asked if he had ever tried to help underworld figures with Robert Kennedy, he replied: 'Negative.' Asked the same question about former Vice President Spiro Agnew and other government agencies, he made the same reply.

He was questioned about taking $2 million in an attaché case to Havana when he met Lucky Luciano. He admitted being introduced to Luciano but testified: 'If you could find $2 million in an attaché case, I will give it to you.'

He defended a row with a casino manager at Caesars Palace, saying it happened because a man stuck a gun in his ribs: 'I slapped his hand and took the gun from him. I shook myself to death two minutes later when I realised what had happened. When reports about the incident came out, I was the one with the gun.'

More difficult, it seemed to be for him, was to explain the 1976 photograph showing him smiling arm-in-arm with a bunch of Mafia hierarchy. It was pointed out to Sinatra that he was with a 'who's who of what's what in the area of organised crime'. He was adamant: 'Shaking hands and knowing are two different situations. I didn't even know their names. How could I know their background?'

There was a nervousness in that answer, in the belligerence in which it was delivered. Smiling in the photograph are Carlo Gambino, Fratianno, Paul Castellano, Joseph Gambino and others, all gathered round a grinning Sinatra. Fratianno said Sinatra insisted on the photo because 'he loves the wiseguys and always had'. Sinatra remembered it differently: 'Mr Gambino had arrived with his little granddaughter at the theatre. I was asked to have my photograph taken with the little girl. Before I realised what was happening there were eight or nine men standing around me. That's when the snapshots were made.'

He insisted throughout the questioning that he had no links with crime figures, rather that they were 'good customers' at the hotels and concert circuits in which he and other entertainers played.

Sinatra seemed most upset that he was still dodging questions going back to when Giancana was found staying at Cal Neva Lodge. Many before and after the hearings said he would never have lost it in the first place if he'd kept his temper. 'You know, it was Frank's own fault, because he called the gaming man names,' was how Phyllis McGuire recalled it.

Sinatra admitted that he lost his cool. He'd been angered not just by the decision to revoke his gaming licence but also that the Cal Neva had been closed down during the big holiday weekend of 1963: 'When he decided that we should shut down for Labour Day weekend, it absolutely burned me to a crust. I thought this was the most unfair thing to do.'

It all seems such a gaudy, ominous and often desperate world. And it was one that the Mafia used to hide – or at least disguise. The Sinatras of this world were just the *donnée* on which to string peccadilloes rather than criminal takeover. Leverage of headline people is bankable.

So, following the clean-up, the Mafia, and Hollywood with it, aimed towards the millennium, shrugging off a past where virtue and honour were made much of. The height of personal courage was never questioned or the brain power of the Hollywood stars who were idolised. The Mafia were cruel and greedy, and so were the moguls. Now they had different faces.

Sinatra's photographic partner, godfather Carlo Gambino, whose mild manners and often decrepit appearance were deceiving, and generally deadly, was arguably one of the most important dons of the twentieth century. He never raised his voice, but in 1976, when he died from a heart attack, his softly spoken words were Mafia law in America. His son, Joseph Gambino, had superb connections in the international rackets, including a drug trail from Turkey that was used as an exclusive 'feed' for the burgeoning Hollywood market. The rising star of the Gambino organisation was John Gotti, the 'Dapper Don', who favoured handmade suits, fine wine and told anyone he suspected of disloyalty: 'I'll blow your house up.'

Gotti had learned the Carlo Gambino tactic of 'taking off the velvet glove' at what he believed were important corporate moments. Gambino had rewarded Gotti, elevating him to the level of *capo* for 'good works'.

Those 'good works' had involved the execution of James McBratney, who, with a group of other mobsters, had kidnapped the don's nephew Emmanuel 'Manny' Gambino. A ransom said to have been around half a million dollars was demanded, but Gambino claimed he could only 'find' $50,000. After that instalment had been handed over, Manny's rigid corpse was discovered dumped in New Jersey. McBratney was the only one to escape the cops and Gambino ordered him dead. He was shot point-blank three times at Snoope's Bar & Grill on Staten Island on 22 May 1973. Gotti was convicted of the killing, but when he got out of Green Haven maximum security in Stormville, New York, he was rewarded with his promotion.

Nerves were stretched in the Gambino Family after the long-time don died. The *capo-regime* was Paul 'Big Paulie' Castellano, whom the FBI wiretapped talking to John Gotti at the Ravenite Social Club on Mulberry Street in Little Italy. There was much behind-the-scenes Gambino politics going on, but personalities only played a part if they got in the way of business. Paul Castellano had, as far as John Gotti was concerned. Gotti ordered the murder of Castellano and his Mafia companion and bodyguard Thomas Bilotti.

Castellano, although a wily businessman, owed his status more to being the brother-in-law of Carlo Gambino and forgot that the Mafia don't change the chairman of the board by proxy vote. He and Bilotti turned up unarmed at Spark's Steak House at 210 East 46th Street in Midtown Manhattan. They had no back-up protection car. The hit was on 16 December 1985. Gotti's team thought that on a late afternoon in the middle of Manhattan only days before Christmas there would be thousands of shoppers on the streets; a quick assassination and escape in the confusion of a very public underworld killing was the plan. The four shooters did their duty in front of Spark's and walked off into the crowds. The gunmen all wore long beige trenchcoats and coal-black fur hats, Cossack-style affairs. When witnesses were quizzed, they recalled the dramatic outfits, not the faces of the killers. It was a classic hit, with a twist. And no innocent bystanders were hurt. In 2012, they still hadn't been able to clean away all the bloodstains outside Spark's. Likewise, the consequences of the assassinations continue to haunt twenty-first-century Hollywood.

With the Spark's killings, John Gotti became the Gambino Family boss. It was a cut-and-thrust election process. He appointed Salvatore 'Sammy the Bull' Gravano as *capo-regime*. Gotti became the 'Teflon Don' after escaping three separate indictments, but he flourished his image – he was a television mobster. The other Families disapproved, but 'Teflon' won again when the car bomb meant for him blew someone else far away.

In the end, it was the FBI that got him. That wiretap at the Ravenite Social Club paid off and, on 2 April 1992, Gotti and his consigliere, Frank LoCascio, were sentenced to life without parole. (Gotti died from throat cancer in 2002 at a federal prison hospital.)

So began a series of events that marched into the next century. The FBI in New York indicted 'Red' Scollo, the President of Local 1814 of the Longshoremen's Union, along with John Gotti's brother Peter, Anthony Ciccone and 13 other Gambino Family members on racketeering, extortion, illegal gambling operations and money-laundering charges. The indictment charged they were all committed as part of the Mafia's corrupt influence over Local 1814 and Local 1 of the International Longshoremen's Union. The indictment mentioned the extortion of 'an individual in the film industry'. Enter martial-arts screen superhero Steven Seagal.

And, a little later, the dead fish.

And the rose in the fish's mouth.

And the safe packed with $240,000 in cash. And jewellery and gold bullion.

And C-4 plastic explosives.

And two hand grenades.

The wiretapping equipment could fill a room. The cast could fill cinemas worldwide. The Gambino Family affair was the catalyst for the revelations of decades of Hollywood and Mafia-entwined skulduggery, which brought in a galaxy of names. But the leading man has not changed: Anthony Pellicano.

*

What can you say about Anthony Pellicano? He doesn't really fit into Chandlertown, where the private eye business had some dignity. Pellicano is no Philip Marlowe. He might even be a grave robber. But we can't be too sure of that. Yet.

On 6 February 2006, Pellicano (aged 67 in 2012) was served with a 110-charge indictment for his activities as a Sunset Strip private eye. It was a long read, accusing Pellicano of destroying evidence, witness tampering, identity theft and illegal wiretapping of movie stars and others. The clincher in the case was that the indictment was brought under the umbrella of a 'racketeering enterprise'. The Racketeer Influenced and Corrupt Organizations Act (the RICO Act) is used to bring charges against Mafia organisations but rarely in other legal actions.

It began with a tin-foil baking tray pinned to what was left of the shattered windscreen of *Los Angeles Times* reporter Anita Busch's silver Audi convertible. She was involved in reporting the dispute between Steven Seagal and his former producer-partner Jules Nasso. Nasso was said by the FBI to have connections with the Gambino Family. In turn, the Family had been 'shaking down' Seagal for $150,000 for every film he made – and the actor, under threats, had paid over $800,000 in a lump sum. On 20 June 2002, Anita Busch was on her way downtown to work on that story when she found the tin-foil baking tray and its attached message, which in red capitals said: STOP.

By the time she stopped shuddering, the LAPD bomb squad, detectives and uniforms had arrived. They love to put on a show. They found the long-stemmed rose and the dead fish in the tin-foil tray. The bomb squad left. Her car was now 'evidence' and a truck arrived to take it off to Parker Center headquarters. The remaining cops were too frightened to move the car. It might have been wired up to explosives. The writer David Robb – a journalist who had investigated and confronted Sidney Korshak – took Busch's keys and drove the car onto the truck. There was no bang, but the paranoia in Hollywood wasn't just within the police force.

No one knew what was under their hoods. Over the next

few months the reporter told the LAPD her parents felt threatened, her phone was tapped, her computer was hacked into and someone had tried to run her down. FBI agents told her they believed she was being shadowed and tormented by Anthony Pellicano, who had *The Godfather* theme on his telephone and of whom his fourth (of five) wife Kate said: 'He started to think he was Don Corleone.'

When investigators searched his office they had discovered a cache of plastic explosives, home-made grenades and revolvers. That led to court and jail. And just as he was about to be freed on the weapons convictions he was indicted for wiretapping – hundreds of hours taped out of a small, secure room he called 'the Bat Cave' – and denied bail. Pellicano entered a plea bargain in 2003 and was given a 30-month sentence in the Taft Correctional Institution, north of Los Angeles, while the FBI investigation went on. His jail term over in February 2006, he was indicted again, this time with two former cops and two former employees of the Pacific Bell telephone company.

Pellicano was a plausible private detective. The FBI had hired his high-tech talents to analyse and improve the quality of taped recordings. He had enhanced an aged recording on which a Ku Klux Klansman incriminated himself in the bombing of an Alabama church that killed four girls.

He grew up in Al Capone's neighbourhood – Cicero, Illinois – and worked as a bill collector before becoming a private investigator in Chicago. He went bankrupt in 1974. One of his creditors, whom you can see on the bankruptcy paperwork, was Paul DeLucia Junior, son of Paul 'the Waiter' Ricca – born Felice DeLucia in Naples – the mentor of Sam Giancana and guiding light of Johnny Rosselli.

Business picked up three years later when he cracked a big case – maybe literally. The remains of movie producer Mike '*Around the World in 80 Days*' Todd, the third husband of Elizabeth Taylor, had been robbed from his coffin in a Chicago cemetery. It had been well publicised that Taylor had buried him with his favourite diamond ring after he'd died in a plane crash in 1958. Pellicano involved himself in the search for Todd's remains, which he found in an area 70 yards from the grave, where the cops had already searched – but 'obviously must have missed' the ring. Taylor was grateful; Pellicano had a major Hollywood connection.

By the 1980s, Pellicano was working Hollywood and improving his skills in audio technology, which found him recruited by feisty lawyer Howard Weitzman, who was defending carsmaker John DeLorean on cocaine trafficking charges. The 1983 trial of DeLorean looked a slam-dunk for the prosecution – the silver-haired tycoon had been filmed by the FBI doing the drug deal – but Pellicano gave evidence that put doubt on the authenticity of the tapes. DeLorean walked free. It was (and remains to all those who sat through the evidence) an incredible jury verdict. Pellicano wandered around the courtroom corridors like Marlon Brando. He knew he was the 'Godfather', but for many of us he was simply a dubious 'expert' witness who got DeLorean off. When the carmaker's wife Cristina, who had attended every day of the trial, filed for divorce the day after the not guilty verdict, you felt something more was going on.

But for DeLorean and anyone else in trouble, the big sunglasses-wearing private eye appeared like a saviour. Pellicano, a big brute of a man, who is not as nice as he looks, became the Chiclets-chewing 'Detective to the Stars' in the newspapers and his own hero.

The question was: how far would he go to enhance his reputation as 'the Neutraliser'? There was always a baseball bat, a Louisville Slugger, in his car, and the computerised phone-hacking system in his Sunset Boulevard office was running 24/7. His soundbites include: 'I always start out by being a gentleman. I use intimidation only when I have to. I can shred your face with a knife.'

In 1991, a woman alleged that William Kennedy Smith had raped her at his family's home in Palm Beach. Against all the rules, the claimant's name and negative details about her were published. Smith was controversially acquitted of the charges.

Pellicano was named as the private investigator for the Kennedy family, who provided the information. Several journalists made legal complaints about Pellicano's intimidation and there were other reports of nasty incidents involving those who had come up against him or his clients' interests.

It was extensively reported that Pellicano was asked to investigate on behalf of President Bill Clinton when he faced impeachment in 1998 over his alleged sexual encounters with Monica Lewinsky. It was suggested in Las Vegas that Clinton was helped out by Pellicano – but not to find compromising background on the White House intern.

He worked with Roseanne Barr to help find her own daughter, whom she had put up for adoption. Pellicano was credited with being behind the disappearance of videotape evidence in 1998 that linked a TV star to a sex scandal. He helped Farrah Fawcett deal with a difficult boyfriend. Pellicano went after his clients' enemies and helped make problems go away. He worked for Warren Beatty, Sylvester Stallone and Gary Shandling; Tom Cruise, Arnold Schwarzenegger, Madonna, Chris Rock, Kevin Costner, Yoko Ono, Dustin Hoffman, Keith Carradine, Nicole Kidman and John Travolta.

As the Anita Busch investigation continued, Hollywood's stellar lawyer Bert Fields and other film industry lawyers, agents and managers became embroiled because of either who they were or whom they worked for or with. Other major industry names brought into the case were Brad Grey, the head of Paramount Studios – and executive producer of *The Sopranos* – and Ron Meyer, the president of Universal Studios, who both held their posts in 2012.

In 1993, Bert Fields had hired Pellicano to work on a case brought by the parents of Jordy Chandler, 13, who claimed Michael Jackson had molested him. He went after the teenager's father, dentist Dr Evan Chandler, who, he said, had tried to negotiate a multimillion-dollar deal with Jackson in return for remaining quiet about allegations concerning his son. Members of the Chandler family accused Pellicano of acting like a Mafia mobster. It didn't work. Jackson paid out $20 million in an out-of-court settlement.

Bert Fields is a most careful man. The most prominent of lawyers – he sued Germany over their attitude to Scientology on behalf of Tom Cruise – he told *The New Yorker* magazine, in the issue of 24 July 2006: '[Pellicano] came up with stuff that other people didn't. He did that over and over again. He was just better.' He was also quoted as saying: 'I never knew him as a thug. I never saw an instance of Anthony hurting anybody or really threatening anybody.' Fields (who charged upwards of $900 an hour just to enter his Century City offices) has always denied any knowledge of the detective's illegal electronic methods.

It is evident why Hollywood remains obsessed with the wiretapping, Pellicano and the contemporary Mafia connections to movie-making. It seems so rough and tumble, something from the 1940s. Fields's involvement is also fascinating. His offices are in a tower block that sits, appropriately, on Avenue of the Stars, just off Santa Monica Boulevard, and is one of the skyscraper symbols of Century City, of Los Angeles and Hollywood. The serried ranks of buildings are populated, one overlooking the other, by those who got there by crime and those who stopped them being jailed or prosecuted for their misdeeds. It's a strange place, where there are no wrongs, only problems to be solved.

Anthony Pellicano was a useful weapon in Hollywood. The federal indictment against him explained he was hired to illegally tap conversations to provide 'a tactical advantage in litigation by learning their opponents' plans, strategies, perceived strengths and weaknesses, settlement positions and other confidential information'. Those who bought his services also got 'personal information of a confidential, embarrassing, or incriminating nature regarding other individuals'.

Pellicano was brought into Fields's circle in 1989 through the producer Don Simpson, one of Hollywood's more maverick characters. He was a super-producer – with his partner Jerry Bruckheimer, they were responsible for films like *Top Gun*, *Flashdance* and *Beverly Hills Cop*. Simpson's drugs bill was

$60,000 a month and he was dedicated to sadomasochistic sex, multiple prostitutes and plastic surgery – the overindulgence saw his heart give out in 1996. The autopsy report said the heart failure was brought on by 'combined drug intoxication'. Simpson was facing a sexual harassment lawsuit from a former assistant. With information provided by Pellicano, the woman's credibility was put in doubt and the case dismissed.

Pellicano was retained to work for Tom Cruise to suppress possible unpleasant stories during his divorce from Nicole Kidman; for the comedian Chris Rock in a paternity lawsuit against a Hungarian model; for Mike 'Austin Powers' Myers against Universal Studios; and for Michael Jackson.

A decade before his death in 2001, the former Beatle George Harrison began receiving death threats. They were written from the American East Coast. Fields put Pellicano on the case and in two days he had solved it. 'I thought it was extraordinary. It was one of the reasons I used him after that,' Fields told *The New Yorker* in 2006.

The continuing intrigue in Hollywood was what Pellicano could reveal. Or who might be indicted. His client Terry Christensen, a prominent legal figure in Hollywood, was. He had worked for 35 years for the billionaire Kirk Kerkorian, former owner of MGM and in 2012 the largest shareholder in General Motors. The charges involved work he did on Kerkorian's behalf over child support. The indictment alleged that Christensen had paid Pellicano $100,000 to bug the telephone (for 28 days) of the former wife of Kerkorian. It quoted from what appeared to be taped conversations between Christensen and Pellicano, during which Pellicano cautioned: 'Be very careful about this because there is only one way for me to know this.'

The next Hollywood name charged was John McTiernan, a director of films including Bruce Willis's *Die Hard* (1988) and the Sean Connery–Alec Baldwin thriller *The Hunt for Red October* (1990). McTiernan pleaded guilty to lying to the FBI when asked if he knew that Pellicano had wiretapped a producer.

But if Pellicano had taped one conversation, it certainly follows that, given his technical expertise at phone hacking, he taped them all – he recorded every star and lawyer and producer. He's often said he is no rat, no stool pigeon; his loyalty is unquestionable, he lives by *omertà*, the Sicilian vow of silence.

That he knew more secrets became even clearer in 2011, when Christine Pelisek, a staff reporter for the Daily Beast internet service, talked to Prisoner No. 21568-112 on a hot August day at Big Spring Federal Correctional Institution in Texas.

Even there, Pellicano couldn't quite escape Hollywood. Big Spring has little going for it – bust businesses, a couple of other 'correctional facilities' and a dust-blown bar where you wouldn't idle over a drink even on the hottest of days – but the town had a role in *Midnight Cowboy* (1969), a film that won a Best Picture Oscar, as the home the film's star Jon Voight leaves to start life as a gigolo-hustler on the streets of New York.

His *omertà* didn't stop him generalising: 'If you saw the stuff I found in celebrity homes: cocaine, heroin, Ecstasy, vials of narcotics. There was a doctor shooting up celebrities with morphine for $350.'

He maintained his clients became his family: 'That was the attitude I kept. I wasn't really a PI. I was a problem solver. People came to me because they had a problem. The government wanted me to turn on them.'

Christine Pelisek said that he told her he'd discovered material about Arnold Schwarzenegger that would have stopped him becoming Governor of California in 2003 (his second term ended in 2011). In the run-up to his first election, Schwarzenegger faced several accusations of sexual misconduct. His marriage to JFK's niece, Maria Shriver, was disrupted in 2011 when she discovered he had a child with their maid. Pellicano would not say if that was the information he had, only: 'I have personal stuff on Arnold . . . If they found that stuff, he never would have been governor.'

During Pelisek's interview, the disgraced private eye talked stories but not names. He said he had 'killed' a news story about a male superstar who liked to play with a female sex toy. He said that when he worked for Michael Jackson he warned the entertainer that he'd better not be guilty. 'I said: "You don't have to worry about cops or lawyers. If I find out anything, I will fuck you over."' He said he accepted the case but resigned: 'I quit because I found out some truths . . . He did something far worse to young boys than molest them.'

It was a strange encounter and one in which Pellicano retained his leverage in Hollywood. If you listen closely, you can hear the skeletons rattling.

15

HOLLYWOOD NOIR

'Made it, Ma! Top of the world!'
  – Cody Jarrett (James Cagney), *White Heat*, 1949

THE MAFIA NEVER GAMBLES UNLESS THE GAME IS RIGGED. Hollywood has been an odds-on winner for them for more than a century, the closest they've ever got to a sure thing. Hollywood provides a universal product. It is the brand that dominates.

In 1950, California produced films with all-American stars that amounted to 30 per cent of the European box office. In 1990, it was 80 per cent. A decade later, it reached more than 90 per cent. Hollywood is the same sort of powerhouse throughout South America and India, and in the increasing Asian markets. A hit 'European' movie like *The Girl with the Dragon Tattoo* or a BBC TV series like *State of Play* has to be remade with the Hollywood treatment to be allowed mass distribution in America. It makes no difference if they are comedies (*3 Hommes et un Couffin*) or thrillers (*La Femme Nikita*), they have to talk and walk and act the American way, as *Three Men and a Baby* and *Point of No Return*.

Watch the evening news and on the red carpet in Paris or London or Berlin or Madrid there are Hollywood stars in a parade of self-acclaim, with their new films. The Hollywood marketing millions make it impossible not to be aware of their product: the big studio movies and television can be watched anywhere and everywhere; the demographics bridge culture and language. People *crave* to be entertained. There is a passionate public demand. As there was for booze during Prohibition – and is every twenty-first-century day for drugs of all chemical confection.

With the demand comes profit for the suppliers. *Cool* is everything: on the streets, kids are killed for brand-name sneakers, mugged for status mobile phones. That is the everyday crime of need and desperation, greed and social malfeasance. The Mafia control the nickel-and-dime end, too, but those making the fortunes operate high above the streets. For street crime reflects a society where forever is not so long any more.

In our high-tech times, you never know when you're being stuck-up: they pick your pockets by rota, not happenstance. Sometimes you don't even know you're dying. The Chicago way is long gone: no longer do gangsters get shot halfway through a short back and sides or while spooning spaghetti alla puttanesca at their favourite Italian. Pivotal witnesses, stock market traders, Russian oligarchs, Vatican bankers, and Hollywood producers and financiers succumb to viruses that are never identified. Judges have a change of heart, or a heart attack. Potential witnesses are lost at sea or in a plane crash 'on location'. They might choke on a piece of steak. Businessmen involved in multimillion-dollar scandals or wayward politicians find life too hard to take and kill themselves. Once suicide was simple: you jumped off the Hollywood sign because you hadn't become a star. Now it can be part of the business package. A career move.

Film financing can be the most complex and stressful of endeavours. Hollywood is renowned for 'creative accounting' after the fact: often blockbusters never make any money, the profits vanish into mythical costs and offshore accounts. Yet it is in pre-production that lies the mystery that will never die. There always seems to be that financing available: extra cash can be moved from one profit into the financing – usually co-financing – of another movie or the more and more expensive cable television series. When you hear 'You can see all the money on the screen', it's usually the cue that you can't. And if you can, there's another set of books.

Of every three movies you see, one at least has been created through Mafia money. How better to launder 200 million warm dollars than through a special-effects extravaganza? Only half of that cash will cover the marketing budget. Trusts and shelters and islands faraway, the fondly known sunny places for shady people, hide and store the cash. Investing in haphazard Hollywood, banking with the *artistes*, not only washes the cash but also it makes it work: a carousel of always spinning and increasing profits. It's especially helpful if you make a movie with freshly laundered money. 'New' money.

The $94 million budget for the Angelina Jolie display *Lara Croft: Tomb Raider* (2001) involved remarkable arithmetic. It only cost Paramount Studios $7 million, but they had that covered, too. They used a tax shelter in Germany and a tax break in the UK as part of the $87 million they had to hand before Lara Croft began her exceptionally profitable franchise adventures. The studio paid legal costs, which are tax deductible in America (federal) and California (state).

In Germany, investors in 'German-owned' film projects can take an immediate tax deduction on their investments, even if the film has not gone into production. And it's not a rule that films are made in Germany or have German actors; the law requires that the film is produced by a German company that owns its copyright and shares in its future profits. The Hollywood studios sell the film's copyright to a German company. There is a *production service agreement* and a *distribution service agreement* with the studio that limits their responsibility to temporary ownership: as part of this token ownership, the Germans pay the studio around 10 per cent more than their return in lease and option payments. They immediately lease it back with an option to repurchase it, but a German company appears to own the movie.

With *Lara Croft: Tomb Raider*, Paramount sold the copyright for $94 million to a group chaired by German mogul Herbert Kloiber and bought it back for $83.8 million in lease and option payments. The studio's $10.2 million 'extra' cash paid for Angelina Jolie ($7.5 million) and some other cast costs. To qualify for Section 48 tax relief in the UK, the movie had to include some scenes filmed in England and employ a couple of British actors. Paramount entered into a complex sale–lease-back transaction with Lombard Bank, which produced another $12 million, which paid for the director and the script. And here came the cross-culture, cross-media leap. *Tomb Raider* was a video-game winner and the movie with Lara Croft a dream date for teenage boys. Paramount pre-sold distribution rights in Japan, Britain, France, Germany, Italy and Spain for $65 million. Altogether a total of $87.2 million. The remaining $7 million was met by licensing the film's American pay-television rights to Showtime, the cable network owned by Paramount's corporate parent, Viacom.

It is an effective – and legal – way of lowering the risk in a high-risk business. Every studio takes what 'break' they can. The Oscar-winning *Lord of the Rings* trilogy was hedged by New Line Studios using German tax shelters, New Zealand subsidies and pre-sales.

In the 1970s and 1980s, when cocaine and heroin shipments were shipped by the Mafia via the Mexico–California 'Happy Trail' set up by Virginia Hill, and written into the budgets of serious-minded and financed films, including Oscar winners, it was, like the film fashion of the time, *high concept*. The drugs were moved and sold, and the movies were bankrolled. An effective, if despicable, business plan. The Colombian cartels never got a screen credit. And neither do the behind-the-camera moguls of the present. The clean and the dirty money are now so entwined that it counts up as grey money. And always another *opportoonity*.

When they buried Sidney Korshak on a warm January afternoon in 1996, in a private service at the Hillside Memorial Park in Culver City in the heart of the city (Hollywood people checked several times that he was in the ground), many secrets were interred with him. But not the Mafia masterplan: the *legitimacy* of the project that Korshak and his masters and minions had plotted for much of their century.

They had founded an empire on that most dangerous of beings – the honest crook. He is a difficult enemy to detect and deter. Corrupt cops and politicians, swindling businessmen and fraudulent industrialists all fail and fall somewhere in their greedy ambition, but a business built on 'crooked' control, with lethal consequences for mistakes, is all but fail-proof.

It's influence that trumps terror in modern Hollywood.

It's not on the film sets either, but in the offices and restaurants of Beverly Hills and Century City, where today's Sidney Korshaks roam and rule. Some don't even know the reality of their roles: they deal in numbers (which must always be going up) and those oh-so-neatly packaged deals. The Mafia are now so entrenched in the official world of business and government there is no need for them to lurk in the underworld.

Fed up getting nowhere against, arguably, the world's most sophisticated Mafia operation, the Attorney General's office in California seems a dispirited place. Investigator Connie Carlson left her job and Los Angeles. She said Sidney Korshak was created by the Mob, but what was most interesting was her analysis: 'Where you see the Mob influence isn't in LA, it's in the Beverly Hills crowd, the movie people and the lawyers.'

Which is indeed the domain of the power-players and the power-seekers: it's always a scramble to be top of the table, like Cagney's Cody Jarrett, at the top of the world. Many people, not only figuratively, are buried in the past.

For actors, the movies are all about becoming anyone the studios want them to be. California has always been the place for that off-screen. It's where Archie Leach from Bristol, England, became Cary Grant. It was where Norma Jean Baker metamorphosed into Marilyn Monroe. It transformed B-movie actor Ronald Reagan into one of the most popular American presidents ever. The Mafia simply began trading under different names.

Hollywood is a place where you can rub out your past and

your past problems, physically in some cases. It's run by a crowd who pee iced water and for whom lifting an eyebrow is a display of high emotion. There's no room for Disney in this world. It is, as Mickey Cohen said, all about the money.

The Mafia's Hollywood network is worldwide, dominating a global business of which just one branch – DVD piracy – is valued by government agencies at between $300 billion and $350 billion a year. That's the sort of turnover that can turn anyone who edges out off-line into a suicidal depression.

It seems obvious for *organised* crime to be running the racket; they have the experience and the routes for moving people and drugs and money; a 'cheap DVD' is often brushed off as victimless crime, but those fighting against the rackets repeat again and again that it returns massive profit margins against low risk.

The Mafia never do anything in a straight line. The prime ability is handling the curves. Which encircle the globe. With movies a worldwide commodity, it all begins where it starts – in Hollywood.

It is here that the major big budget movies are not only made but also processed. There are editing rooms, colour labs, transportation – to a cinema (films are still moved physically, not digitally, in many areas) or a pay-per-view outlet (to be turned into viewing cartridges for hotels, airlines, etc.) – and the 'ripping' of legitimate DVDs and peeling away their encryption. That's for starters.

For every protective innovation, the counterfeiters learn another couple of clever steps to dance around it. A highly anticipated film is often 'edited' as it is being filmed. Specialists placed on the production staff lift the 'dailies' of film, then legitimate film editors make extra cash working their magic. The pirate version can be on sale before the original. It's become known as a 'buzz screening' on the black market circuit.

'They'll be having premieres and their own Academy Awards for the pictures before long' was the view in 2012 of one unofficial film editor about the distributors of his product.

However the original is stolen, it can be replicated in any required form: compressed and digitalised for online distribution or stamped out in copies for street sales. Often a pirate DVD will be available on the same counter as the real product – they look as good and play as well. The movies are also posted on 'top sites' that are privately controlled, high-powered servers available to (paying) members. The LAPD told me the majority of DVDs sold on the street worldwide have laser-printed covers and come in 5 mm cases, not the standard 10 mm.

Of course, there is a hierarchy, but, all through the chain, money is being made from the production and distribution of the films. It has to be fast: overnight blockbusters can soon be ballbusters for the sales teams, who often comprise the victims of human smuggling and trafficking.

Nothing has highlighted high-concept Hollywood crime quite so tragically as the deaths on 5 February 2004 of 23 illegal Chinese immigrant cockle pickers drowned in the rising tide of Morecambe Bay. The young men and women had been willingly smuggled from the poverty of Fujian on the South China Sea through Russia and into England by the Snakehead trafficking organisation. These Chinese gangsters will move anything – people, movies, guns – anywhere.

Their prime routes go into Western Europe and the East and West Coast cities of America: it's a links-chain of evil endeavour. There are management offices in Milan, Madrid, London, Tokyo, Beijing, New York and Los Angeles. The Mafia don't call themselves olive oil import-export merchants any more.

Human smuggling is profitable: there is money upfront, upwards of $30,000 per person. It seems to work like that – $30,000 *per person*. The people are bought and owned until the money is paid off. The cockle pickers who perished in the sea arrived in the UK with false or no documents. They were herded into minivans and buses in Liverpool and driven to Morecambe Bay, where they worked long and eventually lethal hours. They did so to free themselves from what was slavery – to pay off the Snakeheads. It was only after the deaths of so many that another 'shadow' industry was revealed: the Chinese immigrants were the sales force for illegal DVDs.

The network stretched both north and south of Liverpool, with other 'hubs' in Blackpool and Newcastle. Police discovered tens of thousands of counterfeit DVDs, disk copiers and high-end printers when they turned over the homes of the gangmasters. An international think-tank investigation into Hollywood piracy and human and drug trafficking reported that movie copying was the most profitable and least risky of all of them: 'Protected spaces for piracy are created when governments are too stretched, too complacent or too corrupt to take serious action against it.'

And governments can help the Mafia cause. China restricts the number of foreign films to only twenty per year, in a country of one billion people: it is an invitation for pirated merchandise. In a shrinking world, consumers know what is available and want it *now*.

Even where a legitimate product is freely available, however, everyone wants a bargain. Low-priced pirate DVDs are attractive, as they are often only viewed once. And they're not going to kill you, as fake medicine could. The worst-case scenario is that the movie doesn't play and that's not fatal. Then there is the ever-present peer pressure to be on trend, to be up to that important *moment*, to be a signed-in member of the global community.

The marketing of the Mafia's Hollywood product is little different from the mainstream and that's because they steal most of it. Or they get artwork for upcoming DVD titles that are still in cinemas free on websites. They piggyback on the worldwide advertising campaigns and use their own distribution networks to make it known they have the movie that matters. At a cut price.

Hollywood's 'China connection' operates in the suburbs of Los Angeles, where raw material – the movies – is gathered and then moved in computer-camera warehouse vans north to the geographical homes of Apple and Facebook and all manner of New World technology. Silicon Valley on the San Francisco Peninsula, bunched between Sunnyvale and San Mateo, is geek paradise. Although few have the billions of Mark Zuckerberg – one of the richest people on earth following Facebook's flotation in May 2012 – they have skills to feed another billion-dollar industry. These clever 'freelance' technicians can turn a 20-cent blank optical disk into a money-making movie as quick as a smile. Getting high volumes of the illicit material created is cheap and safe. Likewise moving this cash-and-carry product around the world. The Mafia control many shipping routes and have 'treaties' with pirates for safe passage. The movies also fly freight to distribution centres, which can be anywhere.

The beauty, and also the difficulty, of such a lucrative enterprise is that it's a cash business, which means it's the perfect partner for the most profitable criminal enterprise of the day – corporate crime – and for that the money has to be 'honest'.

It goes in tiers: vast amounts of cash are invested in a series of businesses (high street property, like hairdressing salons) and those profits are invested into the next, more ambitious level (shipping and shopping malls). The higher it goes (oil pipelines and depots), the bigger the cash flow and the cleaner the investment. Capital that began as funds from drugs, prostitution, extortion or fraud becomes corporate dollars – in time. This was – and is – the advantage of the movies. They require urgent investment and provide a swift kickback.

And now the Mafia are by proxy 'insured' for failure. With staggering premiums giving them the incentive, global insurance companies are insuring against box-office flops. If a movie does not return the amounts needed to repay loans and investors, the costs are met by insurance. And those companies have also hedged off their risk to other companies. So by the time the music stops, the 'grey' money is sitting pretty in its Sunday best. All neat and clean.

It initially amounts to many millions but soon becomes

billions – ready to be used to build cities or develop countries, or to spread influence. And money, of course, makes much more money.

It's argued that much of Hollywood is owned by corporations with shareholders, that there are many regulations and governance guidelines. But who owns the corporation? Who owns the shareholders? Who'd have thought the Vatican Bank would have been in the money-laundering business? Sicilian banker Michele Sindona got his own Hollywood company, Marathon Pictures.

Law-enforcement agencies in California like to play down the Mafia in Hollywood, but it's a different Mob. There may be no need for the Gangster Squad, but the vacuum created by its abandonment has been filled by the awkwardly abbreviated 'FinCen', the US Treasury Department's Financial Crimes Enforcement Network. It works on a daily basis with its counterparts in London, France, Milan and Madrid, and Interpol and other government agencies are briefed.

Money can be supplied to terrorists, too. Organised crime has no notion of political boundaries: it operates across them and jurisdictions to wrong-foot authority. And of all the rackets, from which the profits only become greater, much of the 'seed' money is from user-friendly film piracy.

The cultural crossover is astonishing; for example, on 2 June 2008 Spanish police raided an organised-crime piracy ring run by Chinese nationals in ten different cities, arresting thirty-two people. They collected 162,000 recorded DVD-Rs and 506 burners, nearly 500,000 unrecorded disks, and printing and packaging equipment; with the materials, you could have produced up to 150,000 films per day. Police said that courier shipments to cities outside Madrid weighed more than three tons in April and May that year. The couriers and workers were all Chinese illegals smuggled into Spain by the Snakeheads.

The Spanish–Chinese connection was linked to Italy's Camorra, which, of all the homeland Mafia groups, has the most influence and the highest number of partners in New York, Chicago and Los Angeles.

The Camorra, whose headquarters are in Naples, is a little old-fashioned – its methods contribute to Campania having the highest murder rate in Europe. Its specialities are the disposal of toxic waste, construction, and the fashion industry and its companion drug trade. This international Mafia operation, involving more than 20 separate 'Families', is known as 'the System'. And you don't play it. The Camorra runs thousands of factories in China contracted to manufacture high-street fashion and backstreet drugs. The goods are shipped to Naples, then quickly distributed worldwide. Its drug-money profits are estimated by Milan prosecutors to be around $33 billion a year.

Financing the narcotics trafficking since 1986 has been film piracy, in an arrangement with the Mafia in Chicago and Los Angeles. The Camorra bosses made a deliberate decision to get into what was the video cassette- and CD-counterfeiting racket. The move, according to a court witness, was for the Mafia group to 'expand [its] business portfolio'. The Frattasio Family, which remains active in the Hollywood piracy enterprise, partnered, said the witness, 'other organised crime groups'. That the Camorra required partners reflects the enormity of the operation; it has 8,000 wiseguys itself, belonging to more than 100 Families, and more than 120,000 footsoldiers.

Anti-Mafia magistrates such as Armando Spataro confiscated an estimated $780 million worth of counterfeit DVDs and goods following raids that led to arrests in Spain, France, Canada, New York and Los Angeles. The magistrates' report said the DVD piracy was 'an attempt by the Camorra to reinvent itself as less evil and more a provider of coveted goods and services, one with a lower profile for law enforcement'. It continued:

> An important aspect of the Camorra's new 'business model', with regard to counterfeiting in particular, has been increased cooperation with the Taiwanese and Chinese triads. The triads moved easily into piracy from

running powerful extortion rackets in the Hong Kong film industry since the early 1980s.

And the movies provided another link for all manner of arrangements with their Mafia counterparts. Hong Kong's strongest triad societies, the Wo Shing Wo (WSW) and the Sun Yee On, are run by hugely intelligent white-collar criminals with allegiances to street gangs. They indulge in all the usual suspects: narcotics, protection rackets, gambling, loan-sharking, prostitution, people trafficking and smuggling. The WSW triad is the most powerful on and off the streets and created that dominance using film piracy cash to fund narcotics and prostitution rackets. The movie money bought the best drugs and the best girls and brought the best profit margins.

And, it would seem, things can only get better. The Hong Kong Organised Crime and Serious Crime Ordinance (OSCO) reported: 'The digital revolution swelled into a perfect storm for pirate activity as the Asia economic turmoil pushed cash-strapped consumers to turn more readily to cheap counterfeits.'

It echoes Al Capone's words, when he paid his first visit to Hollywood in 1927 and was overwhelmed: 'I never saw them make movies before. That's a grand racket.'

16

THE JACKPOT

'So there's this guy Walsh, do you understand? He's tired of screwin' his wife ... So his friend says to him, "Hey, why don't you do it like the Chinese do?" So he says, "How do the Chinese do it?" And the guy says, "Well, the Chinese, first they screw a little bit, then they stop, then they go and read a little Confucius, come back, screw a little bit more, then they stop again, go, and they read a little bit ... then they go back and they screw a little bit more and then they go out and they contemplate the moon or something like that. Makes it more exciting." So now the guy goes home and he starts screwin' his own wife, see. So he screws her for a little bit and then he stops, and he goes out of the room and reads *Life* magazine. Then he goes back in, he starts screwin' again. He says, "Excuse me for a minute, honey." He goes out and he smokes a cigarette. Now his wife is gettin' sore as hell. He comes back in the room, he starts screwin' again. He gets up to start to leave again to go look at the moon. She looks at him and says, "Hey, what's the matter with ya. You're screwin' just like a Chinaman!"'

– J. J. Gittes (Jack Nicholson), *Chinatown*, 1974

MACAO *IS* A GRAND RACKET. IT IS ALSO WHAT THE GUIDEBOOKS say it is: a former Portuguese colony, and a tropical peninsula, with a couple of islands (Coloane and Taipa), on the western side of the Pearl River Delta across from Hong Kong. The

South China Sea surrounds it to the east and south. Now, like Hong Kong, it is one of the special administrative regions of the People's Republic of China. It's also the Mafia's stepping stone to the future.

Macao is 11 square miles of gambling territory. It is the only part of China where gambling is legal; you can't even pursue a gambling debt on the mainland. It is overpopulated and over-used. In the past, players would stand at the casino tables for days and never eat, just play, play, play. Some died as they rolled the dice.

It's difficult to say whether Dutch writer Hendrik de Leeuw was a fan or not after his visit in 1933, while researching for his book *Cities of Sin*. He made it sound intriguing: 'It is home to all the riffraff of the world, the drunken shipmasters; the flotsam of the sea, the derelicts, and more shameless, beautiful, savage women than any port in the world. It is a Hell.'

Some decades later, it's an *opportoonity*.

With zillion-dollar investments, the biggest players from Las Vegas are in the highest stakes game ever: for control of the Chinese gambling market. The Chinese government has watched Macao be transformed by the New Age gaming industry into something sleek and clean, paying dividends in investment and taxes on revenues expected to exceed $100 billion. The gamble for the investors – and it's not seen as a great risk – is that before 2020 China will open for play. That will require astronomical arithmetic and a new vocabulary to describe it.

With the truly legitimate gambling tycoons already posted, the Mafia on the West Coast of America – flights out of Los Angeles or San Francisco are the simplest way to chase the rainbow to the potential pots of gold – are establishing a geographical set-up that will bring all new consignments of Hollywood entertainment – drugs, sex and rock 'n' roll – to the 1.5 billion population of China. Of whom a high percentage like a punt.

Baccarat, which is extravagant in its madness, is the favourite card game of the Chinese gambler. You use the same skills to play as you do to guess which bus will come around the corner next. The house advantage is 1.15 per cent and the bet's over as soon as the cards are dealt. The cultural draw and the saving of 'face' is you are casting your lot with fortune and, no matter what it brings, you meet it with dignity.

To exploit this Zen-led market – sitting ducks, maybe, to Confucius – meetings in Milan and Geneva in 2011, and one in Moscow in February 2012, were held with representatives of Mafia organisations. A summit is planned for Las Vegas in 2013. Another in Hong Kong.

The Mob read the financial pages. As some of the world's most successful business people – two women now hold senior financial positions within the organisation – they need to be involved in such a growth area.

By 3 January 2012, the gaming market in Macao had grown at a rate that 'defied even the most bullish expectations [in 2011] to become five times bigger than Las Vegas, powered by the eagerness of China's nouveau riche to gamble', according to Aaron Fischer, Asia head of consumer and gaming research at CLSA. The gaming revenue for December 2011 rose 25 per cent from the previous year, taking the total to $33.5 billion – up 42.2 per cent.

Asian gaming expert Aaron Fischer explained the phenomenon of the world's biggest gambling centre: 'Following the 57 per cent growth in Macao's gaming revenue in 2010, nobody expected the market to grow at the rate that we have seen. It's true that Americans are still a lot wealthier on average than people in mainland China, but I would guess that a Chinese gambler would bet up to ten times more than his foreign counterpart.'

But much of the money circumvents the law by arriving as illegal money transfers from mainland China. Mafia banks use 'mules' to take in cash (not drugs) and valuable items that can be pawned for cash. Gamblers are allowed to take the equivalent of $3,170 from the mainland into Macao. But they have debit cards and get money for money, for a payment. One pawnbroker near the historic and now grandly revamped

Grand Lisboa Casino said: 'There is no risk. We pretend to sell the customer an expensive watch or a piece of jewellery, charge the amount in renminbi [Chinese currency] to the debit card and then give him the equivalent amount in Macao patacas or Hong Kong dollars, as if the customer had decided to return the object for an immediate cash refund.'

Fraud detectives and gaming analysts estimate that up to 30 per cent of Macao's gaming revenue comes through illegal channels. VIPs gamble on credit provided by junket operators who receive commissions from the casinos or get a share of the profits. They, or their agents, use underground banks to return the money they have collected as debt on the mainland to Macao. The lenders use gangsters from next door Fujian and Guangdong provinces, who pay the 'mules' as little as $5 – compared with Guangdong's average daily wage of $7 – to smuggle cash across the border to this anomaly on the rocky coastline.

It is a perfect place for the Mafia to launder their illicit takings. How appropriate that a 'skim' from elsewhere should tumble over the gaming tables and be all washed out. The American Congressional-Executive Commission on China issued a report in 2011, stating: 'The growth of gambling in Macao, fuelled by money from mainland Chinese gamblers and the growth of US-owned casinos, has been accompanied by widespread corruption, organised crime and money laundering.' In US government memos, it's shorthanded as the 'Macao Laundry Service'. Senior investigators described it as a financial crime 'cesspool'; the State Department's David Asher said: 'It's gone from being out of a James Bond movie to being out of *The Bourne Identity*. Naturally, the Mafia men believe the authorities are suffering from *optical rectosis*, a shitty outlook.'

The Mediterranean Macao, with its landscape of Catholic buildings, now operates more like the United Arab Emirates. Government tax revenue is often more than double the budget and residents are rewarded through the 'wealth partaking scheme'. (In 2011, it was $875 per person.) Unemployment is below 3 per cent. There's plenty of paper money, but Macao nearly ran out of coins. It does not have enough houses or roads or proper medical services and facilities. For a decent dentist, you go to Thailand.

Gambling flourished in China until 1949, when Chairman Mao banned the capitalistic vice. But Macao was only an hour on the ferry and entrepreneur Stanley Ho had the monopoly on what truly was a pirates' den of prostitution, violence and ever-present triads. Over the decades, it has always been claimed that Chinese Mafia men ran the place. It was seedy. In 1999, shortly after the city – Portuguese for 500 years – became part of China, Stanley Ho's total control ended.

From then on, a limited number of new gaming licences would be issued. One went to Sheldon Adelson, who, in June 2012, was the third-richest person in America, but might be the second or the first as you read this. Or have dropped down the top ten a little. He owns two Las Vegas casino resorts, the Venetian and the Palazzo. He also owns a great deal of Macao. With $12 billion in four casino projects there, he's the largest foreign investor in China ever. It adds up to 57 million square feet of resort space, which, to give it a perspective, someone added up to 21 Empire State buildings. He has influence in Israel and the White House, and clearly in China.

In July 2001, Adelson met with Vice-Premier Qian Qichen. He was accompanied by Bill Weidner, the president of his company, Las Vegas Sands, and Richard Suen, a Hong Kong businessman who had helped arrange the meeting. The businessmen had been briefed not to talk about gambling and so Adelson concentrated on his experience in the hotel and convention business.

In 1979, he launched a computer trade show, Comdex (Computer Dealers Exposition), and over the next decade it became one of the largest in the world. In 1989, he bought Las Vegas's Sands Hotel and built the biggest privately owned convention centre in the country. In 1996, Adelson demolished the old Sands complex – in which Frank Sinatra had his percentage and Teddy Kennedy tried to have his way with

Judith Exner – and began building the Venetian. Instead of boxes of accommodation with no amenities and all-you-can-eat buffets, it provided 4,000 big rooms with minibars, fax machines and telephones equipped for conference calls. It offered world-class restaurants, a shopping mall with luxury boutiques and the world's largest casino (which he didn't mention).

Qian told Adelson that he wanted to do much the same in Macao and introduced the subject of casinos. He asked how many hotel rooms Adelson might build; he replied it would be dependent on how many people from the mainland could visit – the Chinese need a permit. Qian asked: 'How many do you want?' It was the jackpot. How many gamblers do you want? *Eureka!* didn't cover it.

In May 2004, the first gamblers entered the $265 million Sands Macao – an investment Adelson recouped within a year. That December, Adelson made the Las Vegas Sands public (*Forbes* magazine reported he owns 69 per cent of the stock) and became a multi-billionaire overnight.

The following year, with fewer travel restrictions, Macao had 10.5 million mainland Chinese visitors – 147 per cent higher than three years earlier. By the end of 2006, Macao revenues were more than $6.9 billion, a quarter of a billion dollars more than those on the Las Vegas Strip. In 2007, revenues climbed to $10.3 billion.

In 2007, Adelson opened the $2.4 billion Venetian Macao – with canals and stripe-shirted gondoliers, as well as an extensive shopping mall and a 546,000 square foot casino, the largest in the world, a huge cavalcade of acclaim and replica of the Las Vegas Venetian.

The *New York Times* reported that since the Sands Macao opened, Adelson's personal wealth has multiplied fourteen times and in the two years after his company went public he earned $1 million an hour.

He literally landmarked 'the Las Vegas Strip of Asia' on what is the Cotai Strip (for Coloane and Taipa), an area of reclaimed land between the two small islands, connected by bridges to Macao's peninsula. Adelson's construction company created what wasn't there with a landfill of three million cubic metres of sand – spending an additional $10 billion on new hotels and casinos. The crown there is the Venetian Macao.

In April 2012, he opened the Sands Cotai Central, with 6,000 rooms and cascading waterfalls – and another giant casino. The feisty businessman, who was 78 in 2012, suffers from peripheral neuropathy, which makes it difficult for him to walk. It in no way hampers his business pace. He is a buccaneer, one of the forgotten old-school stylists: when he wants something, he goes for it – and usually gets it.

Much the same can also be said of Steve Wynn, 70 in 2012, the man who rebranded Las Vegas, changing it from sordid to sexy, classless to classy. Close friends with Frank Sinatra, the singer having appeared for him at his early downtown Vegas casino, the Golden Nugget, Wynn opened the first 3,000-room hotel in Las Vegas, the Mirage.

Together, Wynn and Adelson led the Asian expansion by Las Vegas groups. They were once aggressive rivals, with Wynn, who brought Picasso and Van Gogh to the Nevada desert, accusing Adelson of running a 'Walmart-style operation'. They are now on much better terms.

Wynn built on his early success and fame and his Bellagio became a must-see attraction for its art and dancing fountains, which shoot jets of water into the air in time to classical music and favourite pop songs. He put a Ferrari showroom in the Wynn Hotel: it sells more Ferraris than anywhere on the planet.

Wynn was the only other American casino magnate to win a licence in Macao, which he did in early 2002. Now much of the half-million population of Macao know his name as well as the residents of Vegas. He makes more than two-thirds of his global profits in Macao. He is learning to speak Mandarin. He has spent, to any curator's envy, multimillions on Chinese classical art: he paid $10 million for a 650-year-old red vase from the Hongwu period, which he gifted to Macao's official cultural affairs bureau. Four Qing Dynasty vases, which Wynn bought for $12.7 million in London in October 2011, arrived at the Wynn Macao in March 2012 to go on display. His company donated $135 million to the University of Macao in 2011. At the same time, of course, he is enhancing the Chinese heritage of gaming, which has been a passion since the Xia Dynasty.

In his hotel complex is a Louis Vuitton shop that makes more money than any other Louis Vuitton outlet worldwide. There is a Michelin-star restaurant, with an in-house poet with a VIP verse for all who matter. White leather stools are provided for handbags.

Every hour on the hour in the lobby, as if by magic, the floor opens and a giant animatronic dragon climbs out, coiling into the air, red eyes blazing, smoke pouring from its nostrils.

There is every attraction possible.

And a true *opportoonity*.

17

THE DRAGON'S DEN

'You're going to have to get used to me dripping wet
from the shower.'
— Nick Cochran (Robert Mitchum) to Julie Benson
(Jane Russell), *Macao*, 1952

'WE ALL WENT TO DIP OUR BEAKS OUT THERE IN CHINA-LAND.
It's raining dollars over there' was the considered view of one
of the more maverick of gambling entrepreneurs who once ran
casinos and the stars who went with them. He pointed out the
difficulties for legitimate gaming developers such as Sheldon
Adelson and Steve Wynn – mainly that they were going about
their business legally. 'Out there you need cash to get things
done. Bribery is the way of life.'

The American Department of Justice and the Securities
Exchange Commission is ever watchful. The catch-22 is: if
companies follow the law, they can lose out. Others, showing
their generosity, shall we say, prosper.

The cultural gap is that in Asia the bribery of officials and
regulators is socially accepted. 'Companies from the US and
UK, which have rigid bribery laws, risk being locked out of
deals in Asia,' Warwick Bartlett, chief executive of Global
Gaming and Betting Consultants, an Isle of Man-based adviser
on the industry, told the *Financial Times* in 2012.

The regulators' chief concern is a repeat of Las Vegas from
the early days of Benny Siegel and then Meyer Lansky's
gambling campaigns through the Caribbean and Europe. It

was only time that stopped them getting further east than Moscow. For all involved, there is significant risk, but it was Lansky who said there is always risk in business.

Yet, for underworld business people the threat of retribution has diminished. In our high-tech corporate world, there are so many ways to move and hide cash; as the world's police discover one scam, another is already operating. It's the same game: different weapons, different rules, but sometimes there are double-barrelled blasts from the past.

Stanley Ho is the past for Macao. A renowned tango dancer, he was 90 in 2012. In Hong Kong, you could often see him drive around in his Rolls-Royce, with the vanity plate HK-1. He is an intriguing man, with four wives, sixteen children and unlimited grandchildren. In 2006, his favourite gelding, Viva Pataca – named after the Macao currency – was winner of the Hong Kong Derby.

Ho took over the Macao casinos in 1962 and was ambivalent about how his partners made their fortunes. He ran horse racing for the Shah of Iran, gambling with Ferdinand Marcos and an island casino under Kim Jong-il. Ho was himself an attraction to the cops and legislators because of his supposed close connections with the Chinese triads and, through them, with the European, Russian and American mafias. He had regulatory problems in Australia and America because he and his daughter, Pansy, came into the 'notorious or unsavoury persons' category because of their alleged association with the Chinese Mafia.

Nothing points into the twenty-first-century future of gaming more than a decision by the MGM conglomerate: they were told to cut off the Ho family by the New Jersey Gaming Commission and they could go ahead with their participation in the richest casino in Atlantic City. MGM said it would rather be in Macao. In 2012, it was selling its stake in the New Jersey Boardwalk.

The majority of the revenue in Macao is from bets made in the 24/7 VIP private rooms. Casinos operate through junket-group operators to recruit rich customers from across China, issue them credit and then handle the complicated collections. It helps the punters get huge quantities of cash out of China. Cash on one side, casino chips on the other, which can be played or cashed for clean foreign currency. It's no wonder they're getting excited in certain circles.

The prospect of such a Chinese bonanza, a true takeaway, has helped smooth the rough edges of the more brutal partners in the illicit exploitation of tomorrow's world. Extreme violence was an instrument of the triads in their sex trade and money-lending, but as money laundering, financial fraud and gambling have become the chief trio of their profits, they are now what the authorities call 'grey entrepreneurs' – it's hard to tell if the triads are acting like businesses, or vice versa.

But gangsters are the same all over. Even though so few Western movies are officially allowed into China in any year, across Asia there are always copies of *The Godfather*, giving the younger thugs their 'bad guy' vocabulary and methods. Traditionally, the 'Dragon Heads' are the board members and the 'Red Poles' do the business. Macao seems to specialise in corruption and minting millionaires.

Between 2005 and 2011, the FBI, the Secret Service and the IRS between them cracked several gangland schemes. One involved $33 million worth of cigarettes, methamphetamines and high-quality fake currency – the North Korean-made 'supernotes' of myth, in that they can't be detected from the real thing – imported in boxes and boxes of toys. One undercover FBI agent posed as a Colombian guerrilla and was given a catalogue from which to choose weapons; he ordered anti-tank missiles, grenade launchers, submachine guns and AK-47s. No item was a problem. The mobsters did everything but ask *which colour?*

In 2012, a high-speed train line was being built by the Chinese government to link Beijing and other far-off cities to Macao. The world's longest sea bridge, connecting Macao to Hong Kong, is planned to open in 2016.

And soon there will be more choice. The Cambodian government has sold off more than 130 square miles of a national park to a Chinese developer, Tianjin Union Development Group, which promised 'extravagant feasting and revelry'. It has made a 40-mile road through the forest home of endangered tigers and elephants to bring in the baccarat tables. Planned is a city-size $3.8 billion complex, with a casino with its own dock for cruiseships and an international airport. It's a quid pro quo: the Chinese are being generous to Cambodia and in return, during the ten years to 2011, Chinese businesses have invested in mining and hydropower on what was public land. Casinos are a new goal for Chinese developers; the largest in Cambodia is controlled by one.

The Mafia is in the global market just as Meyer Lansky had planned it to be. He could never have envisaged the route. The Families still work the same way – they're just bigger.

A 2011 United Nations report suggested: 'The traditional Mafia-type organisation – which is linked to its territory and which exercises pressing control by means of intimidation and extortion tactics – has gradually expanded to include new opportunities deriving from the globalisation of markets and the widespread distribution of technologies. Trade in narcotics and contraband products required a move toward alliances with other groups across the globe. Crime became *transnational*.

'With the coming of the digital age, information technology allows operations to shrink the "minimum sustainable scale of operations". That is true for commerce, especially the huge "virtual" market of the internet.

'It is also true for illicit commerce, especially for crimes where the barriers to entry are relatively low. Small groups can make major money – and cause major mayhem.'

'*Transnational!* What the hell is that?' asked my man in Las Vegas. 'All the boys are doing is following the money. Always have. Always will.'

And it seemed to be heading east. Yet, given what we know of 'the boys', it will probably venture west and north and south, too.

At Easter time in 2012, one enterprising financial writer

caught up with Sheldon Adelson, who rarely says much. It appeared then there would be more opportunities arising from gambling expansions in Spain and other areas of Europe. The billionaire was asked about the economic mess building like a turbulent swarm over Europe, but he responded with a gusto that would have impressed even the early Las Vegas pioneers: 'It will take us four or five years. By then, everything will be solved. There are tens of billions to be made.'

Place your bets.

POSTSCRIPT

HOORAY FOR HOLLYWOOD

'Mother of mercy, is this the end of Rico?'
– Caesar Enrico 'Rico' Bandello (Edward G. Robinson),
Little Caesar, 1931

CITY A.M.
Monday, 13 February 2012, 4.09 a.m.
BANKING
PETER EDWARDS

A SERIES of City bankers have been arrested in a probe into tax evasion related to film financing.

Four current and one former member of staff at the investment banking arm of Royal Bank of Scotland, as well as three London workers from US bank Jefferies and one from commodities broker Marex Spectron, are believed to have been held.

Officials from HM Revenue & Customs (HMRC) carried out several raids last week after looking into allegations that bankers had used film finance schemes to avoid paying taxes. Around 16 people are thought to have been arrested.

APPENDICES

THE HOLLYWOOD DOSSIER

'This paperwork is like Bob's wife here – thick, ugly,
got Danson's fingerprints all over it! No offence, Bob.'
'Dahh, it's all right.'
     – Police Captain Gene Mauch (Michael Keaton) to
     Bob Littleford (Michael Delaney), *The Other Guys*,
     2010

POLITICS HAS OFTEN BEEN DESCRIBED AS GOSSIP WITH consequences, and from the off it was FBI director J. Edgar Hoover's mission to know everything about everybody, especially his enemies. Some information was acted upon, while some was used as leverage to get more information or compromise opponents. Much was tittle-tattle, but it all became a historical record of what the authorities knew about organised crime in Hollywood and across America.

Many of the characters who appear in *The Dark Heart of Hollywood* also made star and cameo appearances in FBI files. What follows is but a sample offering of the mass of important documents stored along claustrophobic corridors and behind anonymous doorways in Washington DC. Because of the Freedom of Information Act in the USA much of the material is available both as hard copy and electronically. But there are just as many files that are not.

The CIA was more reluctant than any other US Government department, intelligence or otherwise, to release material that had been classified – the 'for your eyes only' dossiers – simply because so much of the information revealed activities that were at best inappropriate, at worst illegal. Often dubbed the *Criminal* Intelligence Agency, the dirty tricks brigade was pressurised into allowing the skeletons out of its closet on 25 June 2007. The reports, dubbed 'The Family Jewels', linked the spooks to mobsters such as Sam Giancana and Johnny Rosselli, as well as to the Bay of Pigs and assassination plots against foreign leaders.

The 702-page dossier that spans American master spooking from the early 1950s to the mid-1970s was commissioned in 1973 by James R. Schlesinger, the then CIA director. Schlesinger, who had organised a previous study into America's Intelligence Community (IC) two years earlier, when he was a budget bean-counter for President Richard Nixon's administration, took over at CIA Headquarters in Langley, Virginia, from super-spook Richard Helms, who was dismissed for not stopping the investigation into Watergate. Schlesinger spent only six months in the job, but was so hated at Langley that he had to have protection – from his own CIA agents. As such, he was rather more relaxed than others may have been in releasing the Family Jewels dossier.

It details some distasteful aspects of the CIA's history, many of them in violation of the 1947 National Security Act which established the organisation. Much is redacted in the dossier and we can *presume* – how can we not? – that beneath the blackout lines lie even more sordid secrets.

The documents do not answer the questions that remain; yet, whatever the withholdings, the FBI and CIA files do complement years of journalistic and historical studies and revelations. It's for us to extract the facts while making a choice whether or not to disturb the myths.

LV 92-126

It is noted that the Bureau has several pending cases involving the Riviera Hotel and its operation including the following:

"THE RIVIERA HOTEL, Las Vegas, Nevada, AR" (Las Vegas file 92-705);

"RIVIERA HOTEL, Las Vegas, Nevada, JAMES R. HOFFA, ET AL, AR", (Las Vegas file 92-768);

b7C

(Las Vegas file 92-779, ▮▮▮▮▮▮▮▮▮▮▮▮▮▮▮ AR",

"JAMES R. HOFFA, California Life Insurance Company, ET AL, ACCOUNTING AND FRAUD , (Las Vegas file 62-213).

It is noted that all of these cases are associated and connected with Riviera Hotel investigation in the Las Vegas, Nevada area.

Information developed by previously identified Las Vegas sources shows an important involvement in these operations by KORSHAK. KORSHAK has continuously been identified as an attorney representing the hoodlum element in the Los Angeles, California, and Chicago, Illinois areas.

The Los Angeles Office, in referenced airtel, advised that KORSHAK is not subject of an active investigation under the Criminal Intelligence Program, and that due to his position as a prominent attorney, and because of the Bureau's previous instructions that any KORSHAK investigation be handled in a circumspect manner, they do not desire to write a report or make KORSHAK a subject of an active investigation under the Criminal Intelligence Program.

It is noted, however, that the Las Vegas Office has no current report on KORSHAK, no background information, and no current photograph, and often learns of KORSHAK's presence in Las Vegas either after he has departed or is about to leave the Las Vegas, Nevada area. This situation severely hampers any adequate investigation of KORSHAK and his activities in the Riviera Hotel operation.

LV 92-126

92-461-683. [redacted] advised SA [redacted] on 1/17/62 that on 1/10/62 MORRIS B. DALITZ called SIDNEY KORSHAK at Granite 6-1937 and also attempted to contact him in Palm Springs, California.

92-461-699. [redacted] advised SA [redacted] on 1/22/62 that on 1/19/62 SIDNEY KORSHAK called from Los Angeles telephone number Granite 6-2231 and asked to speak to either MORRIS DALITZ or [redacted]

92-423-115. Information re KORSHAK furnished Los Angeles via Chicago airtel to the Bureau dated 12/8/63, entitled, "Activities of Top Hoodlums, Chicago area." Copy of information furnished to Los Angeles file 92-642 and information on page 20.

b2/b7D/b7C

92-423-135. Information concerning KORSHAK furnished Los Angeles via Chicago airtel to the Bureau dated 2/27/62, entitled as entry above.

92-423-99. Information concerning KORSHAK furnished Los Angeles via Chicago airtel to the Bureau dated 6/27/61, entitled as above two entries. (Pages 2, 3, and 6).

92-423-38, pages 5 and 27. Information re KORSHAK furnished the Los Angeles Office in Chicago airtel to the Bureau dated 10/25/60 entitled as above communication and designated for Los Angeles Office file 92-789.

92-308-355, page 18. [redacted] Information re KORSHAK furnished Los Angeles in report of SA [redacted] dated 12/22/62 in Chicago entitled, "SAMUEL M. GIANCANA, aka." (Los Angeles file 92-135).

92-308-53, page 1J. Information contained in administrative pages 1G through J of report of SA [redacted] dated 12/1/60 at Chicago, entitled, "SAMUEL M. GIANCANA, aka." No copy for Los Angeles. Information was furnished by [redacted] on 10/24/60 reflecting that during discussion between [redacted] and MURRAY HUMPREYS, SIDNEY KORSHAK, the attorney, was mentioned. The financing of the Fremont Hotel.

- 13 -

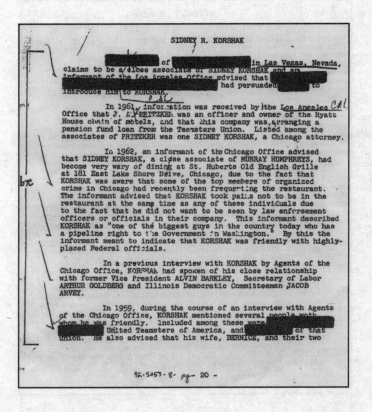

SIDNEY R. KORSHAK

███████ of ███████████ in Las Vegas, Nevada, claims to be a close associate of SIDNEY KORSHAK and an informant of the Los Angeles Office advised that ████████ had persuaded ███████ to introduce him to KORSHAK.

In 1961, information was received by the Los Angeles Office that J. A. PRITZKER was an officer and owner of the Hyatt House chain of motels, and that this company was arranging a pension fund loan from the Teamsters Union. Listed among the associates of PRITZKER was one SIDNEY KORSHAK, a Chicago attorney.

In 1962, an informant of the Chicago Office advised that SIDNEY KORSHAK, a close associate of MURRAY HUMPHREYS, had become very wary of dining at St. Huberts Old English Grille at 181 East Lake Shore Drive, Chicago, due to the fact that KORSHAK was aware that some of the top members of organized crime in Chicago had recently been frequenting the restaurant. The informant advised that KORSHAK took pains not to be in the restaurant at the same time as any of these individuals due to the fact that he did not want to be seen by law enforcement officers or officials in their company. This informant described KORSHAK as "one of the biggest guys in the country today who has a pipeline right to the Government in Washington." By this the informant meant to indicate that KORSHAK was friendly with highly-placed Federal officials.

In a previous interview with KORSHAK by Agents of the Chicago Office, KORSHAK had spoken of his close relationship with former Vice President ALVIN BARKLEY, Secretary of Labor ARTHUR GOLDBERG and Illinois Democratic Committeeman JACOB ARVEY.

In 1959, during the course of an interview with Agents of the Chicago Office, KORSHAK mentioned several people with whom he was friendly. Included among these were ███████ ███████ United Teamsters of America, and ███████ of that union. He also advised that his wife, BERNICE, and their two

92-5053-8- pg- 20 -

SIDNEY R. KORSHAK

introduced KORSHAK to WILLIE BIOFF, pander and labor racketeer, this way: 'I want you to pay attention to KORSHAK. When he tells you something, he knows what he is talking about. Any message he may deliver to you is a message from us.'" VELIE showed that BIOFF so testified in the million-dollar movie shakedown trial of 1943, "which sent seven CAPONE mobsters to jail." (One who went to jail is the afore-mentioned JOHN ROSELLI).

Continuing, VELIE wrote that KORSHAK had gone on to have powerful friends in Illinois and West Coast politics, in the underworld and in racketeer-tainted unions. He added "he is close to JIMMY HOFFA, the Mid-west Teamster boss now under indictment on charges of bribing a Senate investigator."

VELIE went on that although KORSHAK is a lawyer who rarely puts his name in a legal document and has seldom appeared in court on labor matters, "SHEFFERMAN finds his services valuable. As SHEFFERMAN's own records show, the two confer frequently...It is not surprising, then, that KORSHAK played a role in the events that led to a substandard contract for the employees in the Indiana plant of The Englander company."

The rest of the VELIE article is devoted to additional illustrations showing the relationship then extant between HOFFA and KORSHAK, and between other Teamster leaders with SHEFFERMAN.

VELIE's story about the introduction of WILLIE BIOFF and KORSHAK is supplemented in other news media to show that the meeting took place in 1940 at the Bismark Hotel in Chicago and was attended not only by "CHERRY NOSE" GIOE, but by other CAPONE mobsters such as FRANK NITTI, PAUL RICCA and LOUIS CAMPAGNA.

Testifying before the Kefauver Committee in 1950, CHARLES "CHERRY NOSE" GIOE himself admitted frequent meetings with Attorney SIDNEY KORSHAK, his neighbor, at the Seneca Hotel

- 22 -

LA 165-223

Federal Grand Jury regarding any bets or telephone contacts regarding bets that they might have had with ███████ The investigation has also determined that seven of the nine witnesses were ████████████ at Los Angeles, California, and also ████ ██████ ████ receiving the sum of $25,000 per annum from ██████████████ of Chicago, Illinois, in connection with an ███████ ██████████ ██ possessed for ████████████████ It was also ███████████ ████ a non-resident membership in the ████████████ membership had been sponsored by SIDNEY KORSHAK, ████████████ of ████████████████ and ████████, Las Vegas, Nevada.

The USA's Office in the person of ████████████████ Chief of the Criminal Division, has made an informal request for any information available concerning SIDNEY KORSHAK, whom he plans to subpoena before the Federal Grand Jury within the next few weeks regarding ████ and also for any information available regarding the activities of ████

For the information of the Bureau, in connection with witnesses appearing regarding ████████████ the witnesses were to make their appearance and testify on 5/21/63. The witnesses did appear and the information they furnished was not of such a nature that would really have occasioned them to take the Fifth Amendment in the first place, according to the USA's Office. However, in the early morning hours of 5/21/63, the residence of ████████, one of the witnesses, was visited by an unknown person or persons and five .25 caliber bullets were fired through the front window. The only damage was to a chandelier and to the window itself. ████████ has advised the USA's Office that he is positive that the gun shots had nothing to do with his testimony and the US 's Office, who has taken testimony from ████ agrees that ████ testimony was of such an innocuous nature that no violence could have possibly stemmed from it, and in the opinion of the USA's Office there would be no Federal violation involved in the shooting.

It is to be noted, however, that the IRS has been receiving information from a volunteer informant by the name of ████████████████████ in Los Angeles. ████████ has been known to the Los Angeles and New York Divisions and information concerning him has previously been furnished to the Bureau reflecting his complete emotional instability.

- 2 -

MORI DocID: 1451843

SECRET

EYES ONLY

16 May 1973

MEMORANDUM FOR: Executive Secretary,
                        CIA Management Committee

SUBJECT   :   "Family Jewels"

    1. The purpose of this memorandum is to forward for your personal review summaries of activities conducted either by or under the sponsorship of the Office of Security in the past which in my opinion conflict with the provisions of the National Security Act of 1947.

    2. These activities cover the period from March 1959 to date and represent as accurate a record as is available in our files. Those activities which took place prior to the date of my appointment as Director of Security on 1 July 1964 have been developed to a certain extent through the recollection of the senior people in this Office who were involved or who had knowledge of the activities at the time they occurred.

    3. I have gone back to March 1959 because I believe that the activities occurring since that time still have a viable "flap potential" in that many of the people involved, both Agency and non-Agency are still alive and through their knowledge of the activity represent a possible potential threat or embarrassment to the Agency. I would be glad to provide clarification or an explanation of any of these activities if desired. You have my assurance that unless otherwise stated each of these activities was approved by higher authority--the

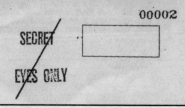

00002

SECRET

EYES ONLY

MORI DocID: 1451843

SECRET
EYES ONLY

SUBJECT: Johnny Roselli

1. In August 1960, Mr. Richard M. Bissell
approached Colonel Sheffield Edwards to determine if
the Office of Security had assets that may assist in a
sensitive mission requiring gangster-type action. The
mission target was Fidel Castro.

2. Because of its extreme sensitivity, only a
small group was made privy to the project. The DCI was
briefed and gave his approval. Colonel J. C. King,
Chief, WH Division, was briefed, but all details were
deliberately concealed from any of the JMWAVE officials.
Certain TSD and Communications personnel participated
in the initial planning stages, but were not witting of
the purpose of the mission.

3. Robert A. Maheu, a cleared source of the
Office of Security, was contacted, briefed generally on
the project, and requested to ascertain if he could
develop an entree into the gangster elements as the first
step toward accomplishing the desired goal.

4. Mr. Maheu advised that he had met one Johnny
Roselli on several occasions while visiting Las Vegas.
He only knew him casually through clients, but was given
to understand that he was a high-ranking member of the
"syndicate" and controlled all of the ice-making machines
on the Strip. Maheu reasoned that, if Roselli was in
fact a member of the clan, he undoubtedly had connections
leading into the Cuban gambling interests.

5. Maheu was asked to approach Roselli, who knew
Maheu as a personal relations executive handling domestic
and foreign accounts, and tell him that he had recently
been retained by a client who represented several international business firms which were suffering heavy financial
losses in Cuba as a result of Castro's action. They were
convinced that Castro's removal was the answer to their

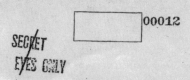

00012

SECRET
EYES ONLY

MORI DocID: 1451843

SECRET
EYES ONLY

problem and were willing to pay a price of $150,000 for its successful accomplishment. It was to be made clear to Roselli that the United States Government was not, and should not, become aware of this operation.

6. The pitch was made to Roselli on 14 September 1960 at the Hilton Plaza Hotel, New York City. Mr. James O'Connell, Office of Security, was present during this meeting and was identified to Roselli as an employee of Maheu. O'Connell actively served as Roselli's contact until May 1962 at which time he phased out due to an overseas assignment. His initial reaction was to avoid getting involved, but through Maheu's persuasion, he agreed to introduce him to a friend, Sam Gold, who knew the "Cuban crowd." Roselli made it clear he did not want any money for his part and believed Sam would feel the same way. Neither of these individuals were ever paid out of Agency funds.

7. During the week of 25 September, Maheu was introduced to Sam who was staying at the Fontainebleau Hotel, Miami Beach. It was several weeks after his meeting with Sam and Joe, who was identified to him as a courier operating between Havana and Miami, that he saw photographs of both of these individuals in the Sunday supplemental "Parade." They were identified as Momo Salvatore Giancana and Santos Trafficant, respectively. Both were on the list of the Attorney General's ten most-wanted men. The former was described as the Chicago chieftain of the Cosa Nostra and successor to Al Capone, and the latter, the Cosa Nostra boss of Cuban operations. Maheu called this office immediately upon ascertaining this information.

8. In discussing the possible methods of accomplishing this mission, Sam suggested that they not resort to firearms but, if he could be furnished some type of potent pill, that could be placed in Castro's food or drink, it would be a much more effective operation. Sam indicated that he had a prospective nominee in the person of Juan Orta, a Cuban official who had been receiving kick-back payments from the gambling interests, who still had access to Castro, and was in a financial bind.

00013

2

SECRET
EYES ONLY

MORI DocID: 1451843

10. TSD was requested to produce six pills of high lethal content.

11. Joe delivered the pills to Orta. After several weeks of reported attempts, Orta apparently got cold feet and asked out of the assignment. He suggested another candidate who made several attempts without success.

12. Joe then indicated that Dr. Anthony Verona, one of the principal officers in the Cuban Exile Junta, had become disaffected with the apparent ineffectual progress of the Junta and was willing to handle the mission through his own resources.

13. He asked, as a prerequisite to the deal, that he be given $10,000 for organizational expenses and requested $1,000 worth of communications equipment.

14. Dr. Verona's potential was never fully exploited, as the project was canceled shortly after the Bay of Pigs episode. Verona was advised that the offer was withdrawn, and the pills were retrieved.

15. Of significant interest was an incident which involved a request levied by Sam upon Maheu.

> At the height of the project negotiations, Sam expressed concern about his girlfriend, Phyllis McGuire, who he learned was getting much attention from Dan Rowan while both were booked at a Las Vegas night club. Sam asked Maheu to put a bug in Rowan's room to determine the extent of his intimacy with Miss McGuire. The technician involved in the assignment was discovered in the process, arrested, and taken to the Sheriff's office for questioning. He called Maheu and informed him that he had been detained by the police. This call was made in the presence of the Sheriff's personnel.

> Subsequently, the Department of Justice announced its intention to prosecute Maheu along with the technician. On 7 February 1962, the Director of

3

00046

MORI DocID: 1451843

Security briefed the Attorney General, Robert Kennedy, on the circumstances leading up to Maheu's involvement in the wiretap. At our request, prosecution was dropped.

16. In May 1962, Mr. William Harvey took over as Case Officer, and it is not known by this Office whether Roselli was used operationally from that point on.

17. It was subsequently learned from the FBI that Roselli had been convicted on six counts involving illegal entry into the United States. Our records do not reflect the date of conviction, but it is believed to have been sometime during November 1967.

18. On 2 December 1968, Roselli, along with four other individuals, was convicted of conspiracy to cheat members of the Friars Club of $400,000 in a rigged gin gummy game.

19. Mr. Harvey reported to the Office of Security of his contacts with Roselli during November and December 1967 and January 1968. It was his belief that Johnny would not seek out the Agency for assistance in the deportation proceedings unless he actually faced deportation. Roselli expressed confidence that he would win an appeal.

20. On 17 November 1970, Maheu called James O'Connell, Roselli's first Case Officer, to advise that Maheu's attorney, Ed Morgan, had received a call from a Thomas Waddin, Roselli's lawyer, who stated that all avenues of appeal had been exhausted, and his client now faces deportation. Waddin indicated that, if someone did not intercede on Roselli's behalf, he would make a complete expose of his activities with the Agency.

21. On 18 November 1970, you were briefed on the latest development in this case, and it was decided that the Agency would not in any way assist Roselli. Maheu was so advised of the Agency's position, and he was in complete agreement with our stand. He further advised that he was not concerned about

4

00047

BIBLIOGRAPHY

'I see a man in your life.'
'What, only one?'
– Rajah 'the Fortune Teller' (Nigel De Brulier) to Tira
(Mae West), *I'm No Angel*, 1933

Andrew, Christopher *The Defence of the Realm: The Authorised History of MI5* (Allen Lane, 2009)

Atherton, Mike *Gambling: A Story of Triumph & Disaster* (Hodder and Stoughton, 2006)

Baker, Carlos *Ernest Hemingway* (Scribner, 1969)

Bartlett, Donald L., and James B. Steele *Empire: The Life, Legend and Madness of Howard Hughes* (Norton, 1979)

Beauchamp, Cari *Joseph P. Kennedy's Hollywood Years* (Faber and Faber, 2009)

Biskind, Peter *Easy Riders, Raging Bulls* (Bloomsbury, 1998)

Blakey, G. Robert, and Richard N. Billings *The Plot to Kill the President: Organised Crime Killed JFK* (Times Books, 1981)

Bloch, Michael *The Duke of Windsor's War* (Weidenfeld and Nicolson, 1982)

Block, Alan A. *Masters of Paradise, Organised Crime and the Internal Revenue Service in the Bahamas* (Transaction, 1991)

Blond, Anthony, *Jew Made in England* (Timewell Press, 2004)

Brenner, Teddy, as told to Barney Nagler *Only the Ring Was Square* (Prentice-Hall, 1981)

Breslin, Jimmy *Damon Runyon: A Life* (Ticknor and Fields, 1991)

— *The Good Rat* (Mainstream, 2008)

Cagney, James *Cagney By Cagney* (New English Library, 1976)

Cantor, Bert *The Bernie Cornfeld Story* (Lyle Stuart, 1970)

Catterall, Peter *The Macmillan Diaries: The Cabinet Years 1950–1957* (Macmillan, 2003)

— *The Macmillan Diaries Vol II: Prime Minister and After: 1957–1963* (Macmillan, 2011)

Chepesiuk, Ron *The Trafficantes: Godfathers from Tampa, Florida: The Mafia, the CIA and the JFK Assassination* (Strategic Media Books, 2010)

Cirules, Enrique *The Mafia in Havana: A Caribbean Mob Story* (Ocean Press, 2004)

Cockburn, Alexander, and Jeffrey St Clair *Whiteout: The CIA, Drugs and the Press* (Verso, 1998)

Cohen, Mickey, as told to John Peer Nugent *In My Own Words* (Prentice-Hall, 1975)

Conrad, Harold *Dear Muffo: 35 Years in the Fast Lane* (Stein and Day, 1982)

Crane, Cheryl, with Cliff Jahr *Detour: A Hollywood Story* (Arbor House, 1988)

Dale Scott, Peter *Crime and Cover-Up: The CIA, the Mafia, and the Dallas-Watergate Connection* (Open Archive Press, 1977)

— *Deep Politics and the Death of JFK* (University of California Press, 1996)

Dallek, Robert *Nixon and Kissinger: Partners in Power* (Harper Collins, 2007)

Davis, John H. *Mafia Kingfish: Carlos Marcello and the Assassination of John F. Kennedy* (Signet, 1992)

— *The Kennedy Clan: Dynasty and Disaster, 1848–1984* (Sidgwick and Jackson, 1995)

Deitche, Scott M. *The Silent Don: The Criminal Underworld of Santo Trafficante Jr* (Barricade Books, 2007)

Denker, Henry *The Kingmaker* (Mayflower, 1974)

Didion, Joan *The White Album* (Simon and Schuster, 1979)

Eisenberg, Dennis, Dan Uri and Eli Landau *Meyer Lansky: Mogul of the Mob* (Paddington Press, 1979)

English, T.J. *The Havana Mob: Gangsters, Gamblers, Showgirls and Revolutionaries in 1950s Cuba* (Mainstream, 2007)

Exner, Judith Campbell, with Ovid Demaris *My Story* (Grove Press, 1977)

Farrell, Nicholas *Mussolini: A New Life* (Weidenfeld and Nicolson, 2003)

Fitzgerald, F. Scott *The Great Gatsby* (Charles Scribner's Sons, 1925)

Fleming, Ian *Casino Royale* (Jonathan Cape, 1953)

Fraser-Cavassoni, Natasha *Sam Spiegel: The Biography of a Hollywood Legend* (Little, Brown, 2003)

Gates, Daryl F., with Diane K. Shah *Chief: My Life in the LAPD* (Bantam, 1992)

Goldsmith, Lady Annabel *Annabel: An Unconventional Life* (Weidenfeld and Nicolson, 2004)

Goodwin, Betty *Hollywood du Jour: Lost Recipes of Legendary Hollywood Haunts* (Angel City Press, 1993)

Heller, Peter *Bad Intentions: The Mike Tyson Story* (Da Capo Press, 1995)

Hennessy, Peter *Having It So Good: Britain in the Fifties* (Penguin/Allen Lane, 2006)

Hersh, Seymour *The Price of Power: Kissinger in the Nixon White House* (Summit Books, 1983)

Hill, Billy *Boss of Britain's Underworld* (The Naldrett Press, 1955)

Kahn, Roger *A Flame of Pure Fire: Jack Dempsey and the Roaring '20s* (Harcourt Brace, 1999)

Keeler, Christine, with Douglas Thompson *The Truth at Last: My Story* (Sidgwick and Jackson, 2001)

Kelley, Kitty *His Way: The Unauthorised Biography of Frank Sinatra* (Bantam Books, 1986)

Kessler, Ronald *The Richest Man in the World: The Story of Adnan Khashoggi* (Warner Books, 1986)

Lacey, Robert *Little Man: Lansky and the Gangster Life* (Little, Brown, 1991)

Leasor, James *Who Killed Sir Harry Oakes?* (Heinemann, 1983)

Lewis, Norman *The Honoured Society: The Sicilian Mafia Observed* (Eland Books, 1984)

Mailer, Norman *Oswald's Tale: An American Mystery* (Random House, 1995)

Manchester, William *The Death of a President* (Michael Joseph, 1967)

Mass, Peter *The Valachi Papers* (Putnam's, 1968)

McClintick, David *Indecent Exposure: A True Story of Hollywood and Wall Street* (William Morrow, 1982)

McDougal, Dennis *The Last Mogul: Lew Wasserman, MCA, and the Hidden History of Hollywood* (Crown, 1998)

Messick, Hank *Lansky* (Putnam's, 1971)

Moldea, Dan E.W. *The Hoffa Wars: Teamsters, Rebels, Politicians and the Mob* (Paddington Press, 1978)

— *Dark Victory: Ronald Reagan, MCA, and the Mob* (Viking Penguin, 1986)

Noguchi, Thomas T. *Coroner* (Simon and Schuster, 1983)

Norwich, John Julius *The Duff Cooper Diaries* (Weidenfeld and Nicholson, 2005)

Oglesby, Carl *The JFK Assassination: The Facts and the Theories* (Signet Books, 1992)

Owen, Frank *The Eddie Chapman Story* (Allan Wingate Ltd, 1953)

Owen, James *A Serpent in Eden: The Greatest Murder Mystery of All Time* (Abacus, 2005)

Piaf, Edith, and Marcel Cerdan *Moi pour toi: Lettres d'amour* (Ud-Union Distribution, 2004)

Pileggi, Nicholas *Wiseguy* (Pocket Books, 1985)

Plimpton, George *Shadow Box* (Lyons Press, 2010)

Raab, Selwyn *Five Families: America's Most Powerful Mafia Empires* (Thomas Dunne Books, St Martin's Press, 2006)

Ragano, Frank and Selwyn Raab *Mob Lawyer* (Charles Scribner's Sons, 1994)

Reid, Ed, and Ovid Demaris *The Green Felt Jungle* (Trident Press, 1963)

Reynolds, Bruce *Autobiography of a Thief: The Man Behind The Great Train Robbery* (Bantam Press, 1995)

Richardson, Charlie, with Bob Long *My Manor: An Autobiography* (Sidgwick and Jackson, 1991)

Robert, Randy *Jack Dempsey: The Manassa Mauler* (University of Illinois Press, 2003)

Runyon, Damon *Guys and Dolls* (Penguin Books, 1992)

Sandbrook, Dominic *Never Had It So Good: A History of Britain from Suez to the Beatles* (Little, Brown, 2005)

— *White Heat: A History of Britain in the Swinging Sixties, 1964 to 1970* (Little, Brown, 2006)

Scheim, David E. *Contract on America: The Mafia Murder of President John F. Kennedy* (SPI Books, 1981)

Schulberg, Budd *The Harder They Fall* (Random House, 1947)

Sheehan, Jack E. *The Players: The Men Who Made Las Vegas* (University of Nevada Press, 1997)

Sinkow, Barry *The Count in Monte Carlo* (AuthorHouse, 2008)

Speriglio, Milo *The Marilyn Conspiracy* (Pocket Books, 1986)

Spiegel, Penina *Steve McQueen: The Untold Story of a Bad Boy in Hollywood* (Fontana Books, 1987)

Summers, Anthony *The Kennedy Conspiracy* (Warner Books, 1992)

— *The Arrogance of Power: The Secret World of Richard Nixon* (Phoenix Press, 2001)

— and Robbyn Swan *Sinatra: The Life* (Corgi, 2006)

Talese, Gay *Honor Thy Father* (Souvenir Press, 1971)

Tate, Barbara *West End Girls* (Orion Books, 2010)

Teresa, Vincent, with Thomas C. Renner *My Life in the Mafia* (Doubleday, 1973)

Thomas, Donald *Villains' Paradise: Britain's Underworld from the Spivs to the Krays* (John Murray, 2005)

Thompson, Douglas *The Hustlers: Gambling, Greed and the Perfect Con* (Sidgwick and Jackson, 2007)

— *Shadowland* (Mainstream, 2011)

Tosches, Nick *Dino: Living High in the Dirty Business of Dreams* (Doubleday, 1992)

— *The Devil and Sonny Liston* (Little, Brown, 2000)

Turkus, Burton B., and Sid Feder *Murder Inc.: The Story of the Syndicate* (Da Capo Press, 1992 reproduction of 1951 edition)

United States Treasury Department, *Mafia: The Government's Secret File on Organised Crime* (2007)

Unsworth, Cathi *Bad Penny Blues* (Serpent's Tail, 2009)

Vaill, Amanda *Everybody Was So Young* (Little, Brown, 1998)

Von Tunzelmann, Alex *Red Heat: Conspiracy, Murder and the*

Cold War in the Caribbean (Simon and Schuster, 2011)

Waldron, Lamar, with Thom Hartmann *Ultimate Sacrifice: John and Robert Kennedy, The Plan for a Coup in Cuba, and the Murder of JFK* (Constable, 2005)

— *Legacy and Secrecy: The Long Shadow of the JFK Assassination* (Counterpoint, 2008)

Wilkerson, Tichi, and Marcia Borie *The Hollywood Reporter: The Golden Years* (Coward-McCann, 1984)

Wilson, Earl *Sinatra* (Signet, 1976)

Yablonsky, Lewis *George Raft* (Mercury House, San Francisco)

Ziegler, Philip *King Edward VIII* (Collins, 1990)

INDEX

INDEX

Moceri, Leo 'Lips' 76–7, 103
Monroe, Marilyn 19, 104, 105, 109, 176–8
  death of 178, 182–3, 185, 285
  exploitation of 124, 141, 181–5
  and Kennedys 175, 176, 181, 182, 185
Montana, Lenny 236–7
Montgomery, Robert 59, 82
Morgan, Vicki 268, 269, 270, 275–9, 282–4
Moss, E. Kipper 173
Muir, Florabel 114, 115, 116

Ness, Eliot 54–5
Nicholson, Jack 208, 262, 264
Nielsen, Brigitte 251
Niklas, Kurt 124, 256–7
Nitti, Frank 'the Enforcer' 53–7, 82–5, 87, 90
Nixon, Richard 203
Novak, Kim 139–40
Nugent, John Peer 68–71, 73, 81, 148

Olson, Ed 188–9, 190
O'Mara, 'Mad' Jack 110–13, 115–16
Oswald, Lee Harvey 196–7, 198–201

Pacino, Al 231–3, 245–6, 251–3
Page, Milton B. 'Farmer' 28, 29–30
Pancoast, Marvin 283, 285
Paramount Studios 40–2, 58, 83, 225, 242, 298
  The Godfather 224, 226–40, 243–6, 250, 252
  Lara Croft: Tomb Raider 305–6
  see also Bluhdorn, Charlie; Evans, Robert
Parrot, Kent Kane 28, 30, 34
Parsons, Louella 43
Peckinpah, Sam 227–8, 256, 257
Pelisek, Christine 301, 302
Pellicano, Anthony 294–5, 296–302
people smuggling 309–10
Peyton Place 144, 145–6, 152
Polanski, Roman 213–20, 222
prostitution 27, 28, 37, 53, 55, 66–7, 75–6, 81, 92, 250–1
  Hollywood call girls 270–5
  Mann Act 126

Prowse, Juliet 134, 156, 159, 183
The Public Enemy 35–6
Puzo, Mario 224, 226–9, 239–40, 243, 261

Radin, Ray 259–60, 262–4, 265
Raft, George 21, 65–6, 77, 97, 114
Ragen, James 89–90
Rappe, Virginia 40–1
Reagan, Ronald 105, 205–6, 213, 243, 268, 283, 289
  and Bloomingdale 269, 276, 278, 282
Reed, Donna 133, 137, 138
Reid, Wallace 39–40
Reles, Abe 'Kid Twist' 52, 58, 79–81
Ricca, Paul 'the Waiter' 31, 54, 56, 83–5, 87, 90–1, 296
Rosen, Millicent 68
Rosenthal, Frank 246
Rosselli, Johnny 'Handsome' 29, 30–2, 36, 47–9, 66, 83, 91, 106–8, 175
  and CIA 168, 288
  and Cohen 74–5, 144–5, 149
  death of 287–8
  and Dragna 33–4, 74
  and Exner 155, 156, 171
  film production 108–9
  gambling 37, 45, 68, 76–7, 133–7, 195
  Hollywood 36, 52, 59, 67–8, 107–9
  Kennedy assassination 201–2
  racketeering trial 84–5
  and Sinatra 95, 138, 195
Rothstein, Arnold 'the Brain' 45, 50–1
Rubens, Alma 39
Ruby, Jack 179, 196, 198, 199, 200–2
Ruddy, Al 227, 229, 233, 234, 235, 236, 238, 239

St John, Jill 237
Schenck, Joe 45, 59, 82, 109
Schneiderman, Davy 'Little Dave' 74
Schwarzenegger, Arnold 301–2
Scorsese, Martin 246, 248, 249
Screen Actors' Guild (SAG) 59, 105
Seagal, Steven 294, 295
Sebring, Jay 183, 217, 218, 255